Functions
of
Victorian Culture
at the
Present Time

Functions
of
Victorian Culture
at the
Present Time

edited by

CHRISTINE L. KRUEGER

OHIO UNIVERSITY PRESS · ATHENS

Ohio University Press, Athens, Ohio 45701
© 2002 by Christine L. Krueger
Printed in the United States of America
All rights reserved

Ohio University Press books are printed on acid-free paper ⊗™
10 09 08 07 06 05 04 03 02   5 4 3 2 1

Material from Ronald R. Thomas,
"The Home of Time: Plotting the Prime Meridian,
the Dome of the Millennium,
and Post-National Space," in *Nineteenth-Century Geographies:
The Transformation of Space from the Victorian Age
to the American Century*, edited by Ronald R. Thomas and Helena Michie,
forthcoming, © 2002 by Ronald R. Thomas.
Reprinted by permission of Rutgers University Press.

Cataloging-in-Publication Data

Functions of Victorian culture at the present time / edited by Christine L. Krueger
    p. cm.
    Includes bibliographical references and index.
    ISBN 0-8214-1460-7 (alk. paper) — ISBN 0-8214-1461-5 (pbk. : alk. paper)
    1. Great Britain—Civilization—19th century. 2. United States—Civilization—
British influences. 3. English literature—Appreciation—United States. 4. Great
Britain—History—Victoria, 1837–1901. 5. United States—Relations—Great
Britain. 6. Great Britain—Relations—United States. I. Krueger, Christine L.

DA533 .F86 2002
306'.0973—dc21
                                                                    2002030736

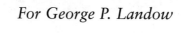

For George P. Landow

Contents

Part 4
Law and Order, Victorian Style

Part 5
Future Reading: Recovery, Dissemination, Pedagogy

Acknowledgments

It is easy to make fun of MLA conventions, perhaps too easy, as the annual *New York Times* convention pieces might suggest. I would like to believe that this volume is one of the good things to come out of my profession's annual gathering. It arose out of the sessions organized by the Division for the Victorian Period in 2000. As program chair, I wanted to know how Victorianists were responding to the centenary of Queen Victoria's death as we stood at the "coppice gate" of the new millennium. Happily, the other members of the committee were similarly interested, and so my first thanks goes to them: Hilary Schor, Herbert Tucker, and Elizabeth Langland. I would like to thank everyone who responded to our call for papers, offering many more fascinating ideas than could be accommodated by either our MLA sessions or this volume.

Editing this volume has been a remarkably pleasant experience, facilitated by the contributors' care and promptness and the expert labors of my research assistant at Marquette University, Jessica Demovsky. David Sanders, director of Ohio University Press, has been a wonderfully enthusiastic, wisely critical, and amazingly efficient editor. Copyeditor Tammy Rastoder and manuscript editor Nancy Basmajian have been enormously helpful, heroically shielding me from the consequences of diverse technologies and assuring consistency. My thanks, too, to the anonymous readers for Ohio University Press. Together with David Sanders they have helped to ensure that this volume would appear in a timely manner. I am also grateful to the staff of the Huntington Library and the Marquette University English department for their help.

Finally, in gratitude to George Landow, who has done more than anyone to guarantee the future of Victorian studies in the new millennium, I dedicate this volume to him.

Introduction

CHRISTINE L. KRUEGER

A century has passed since the death of Queen Victoria, and though her empire is no more and her own nation is radically transformed, yet the culture of the period that bears her name remains vital, not only in Britain but around the world. No matter how vociferously we protest our postmodern condition, we are in many respects post-Victorians, with a complex relationship to the ethics, politics, psychology, and art of our eminent—and obscure—Victorian precursors. The essays in this volume were written in the months before attacks on the World Trade Center and the Pentagon inspired pundits to declare that nothing would ever be the same. Yet, once again, news of a radical rupture in history was grossly exaggerated, for the events of September 11, 2001, brought into popular consciousness the long—and largely Victorian—history of the "great game" of empire played across Afghanistan and did more than any cultural critic could have to impress upon us the urgent need to address our role as heirs of continuous historical processes.

Even without these traumatic reminders of the legacy of Victorian empire, fascination with Victorian culture could certainly have been noted as a sign of our times. In our very efforts at "revival" and "restoration," we extend the Victorians' own practices and manifest a markedly Victorian self-consciousness about our own place in time, as at once belated and a culmination, as agents of change and effects of infinitely complex processes. The contributors to this volume take the occasion of the centenary of Queen Victoria's death to reflect upon the enduring functions of Victorian culture with the "double vision" Elizabeth Barrett Browning's Aurora Leigh urged poets to exert on past and present, viewing the Victorian legacy both as an intimate part of who we are and an alien other against which our own peculiar needs are thrown into relief and from which we still may have much to learn.

Borrowing our title from Matthew Arnold's germinal work of cultural theory, *The Function of Criticism at the Present Time* (1865), we acknowledge the profound influence of the Victorians on the continuing project of developing cultural values in conditions Arnold could never have imagined. Perhaps Arnold's most enduring contribution to criticism has been his function as a worthy opponent, a productive antagonist. In 1932, T. S. Eliot referred to him as "rather a friend than a leader," and a half-century ago Walter Jackson Bate valued him less for the content of his arguments than for "his constant support of the dignity of critical thinking." Like the "persistently self-renewing nature of the capitalist economy" Gary Day identifies as one source of the longevity of Victorian culture,[1] Arnold's critical method has similarly proven resilient insofar as it has driven the dialectics of cultural criticism itself, in the work of scholars of the nineteenth century from Raymond Williams and E. P. Thompson to Frederic Jameson, Catherine Gallagher, and Terry Eagleton. Even in our most anxious, ambivalent, or hostile responses to Victorian culture, we often find ourselves contributing to a critique—of capitalism, nationalism, gender roles, for example—that had its counterpart, if not origins, in Victorian cultural criticism. Rather than imagine ourselves as reaching across a postmodern historical rupture when we construct a functional Victorian past, we may instead begin to suspect how far we haven't come in one hundred years, that we appeal to Victorian culture in order to think about problems and needs that are not wholly unprecedented.

Arnold's own preservation project in *Function of Criticism at the Present Time* and in *Culture and Anarchy* (1867–68) was forward-looking. We too look back in order to articulate hopes for the future. In Arnold's view, public intellectuals had an obligation to the future "to learn and promulgate the best that is known and thought in the world" in order to bring about a new age of social cohesion and artistic creation. Ours is hardly the future that Arnold wished for and he would doubtless have been dismayed to learn that it is not the culture of Hellenism but the culture of his own age, one which he found to be disturbingly fragmented, narcissistic, jingoistic, instrumentalist, and vulgar, that has so captured our imaginations and tastes. Nor is our interest mainly in the high culture that Arnold valued but in popular culture, his bête noire, and in material culture as well. We embrace different hierarchies of value and entertain diverse functions of culture rather than a unitary one. Nevertheless, we bring to our subject both critical and aspirational arguments, as Arnold did. The astonishing proliferation of Victorian ideas, texts, and artifacts in contemporary media, political discourses, psychology, and material culture necessarily shapes the efforts of scholars who seek to understand and teach Victorian culture in the early twenty-first century and enjoins upon us the task of addressing the relationship between our work as public intellectuals and the constituencies we hope to serve. So, despite the transformations that have occurred in our definitions of culture and the eschewal of many of Arnold's values, ours remains an Arnoldian project in its understanding of the broad relevance of Victorian culture to contemporary practices and values.

Not only is the centenary of Queen Victoria's death an opportune time to assess the functions of Victorian culture, then, but the diverse qualities and sites of those functions put us in places—as students, teachers, and critics of Victorian literature and culture—where we can engage with audiences beyond the confines of our discipline and, moreover, beyond the boundaries of academic culture, much as our Victorian precursors did. For whereas (as Sue Lonoff notes in her contribution to this volume) the field of Victorian literature appears to be threatened within departments of English, in our society at large Victorian culture has probably never been more popular and influential. Happily, we may no longer feel compelled to exorcise the ghost of Victorianism as modernists tried to do, nor should we dismiss the popularity of things Victorian as bad faith or rank nostalgia. Instead, the diversity of viewpoints on the various current-day uses of Victorian culture represented in this volume reflect not a desire to police or censure nonscholarly appropriations but to offer a critical understanding of the needs they serve and to open our own professional endeavors as Victorianists to the concerns we share in common with people who read, consume, view, imitate, and deploy Victorian culture for reasons we must engage. At the present time, then, Victorian culture is a key site at which academics and nonacademics can enter into dialogue, and this collection is intended to forward that discussion. Practically speaking, we address ourselves not only to other Victorianists and Victorianists-in-training, that is, graduate students, but also to undergraduates encountering the academic study of Victorian culture for the first time in the hope that they will recognize the familiar in our subject matter and to a wider audience who we trust will appreciate more deeply what their encounters with Victorian culture entail and who can respond to us from their own expertise as collectors, readers, viewers, and citizens of societies in which "Victorian values" still have a significant purchase.

Finally, though my contributors would be too modest to claim a place in history for themselves, I would like to think that the authors of these essays address themselves to the future, not with an Arnoldian teleology, perhaps, but with the belief that we, like the Victorians themselves, will become the objects of future historical scrutiny. It is well, therefore, to leave these records of the functions of Victorian culture at the outset of the twenty-first century. While we attend to the place of Victorianism in a postmodern historical crisis, cogently analyzed by John Kucich and Dianne F. Sadoff in *Victorian Afterlife: Postmodern Culture Rewrites the Nineteenth Century,* many essays in this volume are also concerned to create "a fresh current of ideas" regarding Victorian culture, in order to render its uses not only more accurate but more just.[2] Of course, ours are necessarily limited and provisional perspectives on the functions of Victorian culture at the present time. We are all academics, though we range from graduate students to senior professors. And while we are eleven Americans and one Briton, we are all affiliated with American institutions, and all work in the field of literature, broadly defined. Still, by recognizing and pointing beyond these boundaries, we can hope, too, that the discussion to which we contribute will encourage new revisions of Victorian culture that will keep it alive as a source of pleasure, object of inquiry, and spur to critique.

The eleven essays in this volume are arranged under five headings: "On Victorian Time: Historiographies of Culture," "Victorian Commodities for Postmodern Consumers," "The Ways Victorians Live Now," "Law and Order, Victorian Style," and "Future Reading: Recovery, Dissemination, Pedagogy." Necessarily, many of the essays connect with one another across these headings. To a significant degree they all address the issue of historiographic inheritance in that each author reflects on his or her own historical position vis-à-vis the Victorian past and raises questions about the constructed qualities of that past, problems of dissemination and mediation, and our investments in historical narratives.

For the contributors to part 1—"On Victorian Time: Historiographies of Culture"—the intersections between temporality and culture are the primary focus. In "The Victorians in the Rearview Mirror," Simon Joyce sets out the historiographic problematics of our relation to Victorian culture, in general, and the particular difficulties deployments of Victorian culture, such as those by Margaret Thatcher and Gertrude Himmelfarb, pose for progressive cultural critics. Insisting on the mediated nature of our view of the past, rendering "the Victorians" both distorted and "closer than they appear"—like the image in a rearview mirror—Joyce argues that both the key modernist and postmodernist responses to the Victorian period exhibit a dominant binary opposition, what he aptly describes as Thatcherite versus Kinnockian views of Victorian values. To oppose either view of the Victorians may simply entail an inversion that leaves the binary intact. In order to suggest a more productive critical historiography, Joyce returns us to the spectrum of reactions by Victorian journalists to the death of Queen Victoria herself for the earliest evidence of efforts to hypostatize the Victorian period, and then to the periodizing claims of modernist historiography, criticism, and fiction, as examples of the continuing drive to define the Victorian period and thereby to declare it definitively nonmodern and utterly dead. From postcolonial criticism, Joyce concludes, Victorianists can learn an important lesson about the heterogeneity and contradictions of Victorian culture, which call for neither its repudiation nor its revival but lead us to recognize its residual force in our own complex investments in the Victorian period.

Time, temporality, and their place in the formation of national identity is the topic of Ronald R. Thomas's essay, "The Legacy of Victorian Spectacle: The Map of Time and the Architecture of Empty Space." The Millennium Dome, built at Greenwich, near the site where Greenwich Mean Time was established as an international standard in 1884, invites Thomas's reflections on contemporary Britain's self-definition against its imperial Victorian past. Time, rather than space, virtual, rather than concrete material reality, the logic of global capitalism rather than that of nation and empire—represented by the Dome's "spectacular empty space"—are the bases upon which the "New Britain" asserts its national identity in a postnational age. What modern Britons share, however, "is the dream not of a familiar place but of a remembered time." This effort to reorient themselves in time by reference to Victorian signs of British global domination—the Crystal Palace, Greenwich Mean Time—tellingly found its expression in an empty space. The Dome, he concludes, now vacant and the property of foreign investors, is the fitting monument to a vanishing nation.

If the nation that created Victorian culture can no longer call upon that heritage in an unproblematic fashion to project its own future, still its artifacts live in our imaginations, not to mention our living rooms and closets. Part 2 looks at "Victorian Commodities for Postmodern Consumers." The proliferation of businesses, mass-circulation magazines, and websites specializing in the restoration and reproduction of Victorian material culture is the subject of Miriam Bailin's essay, "The New Victorians." Bailin reflects on the marketing strategies of these enterprises, which insist simultaneously on the familiarity of things Victorian and "an irreducible difference that guarantees charm." She sets these texts alongside Victorian decorating books and the Edwardian and later backlashes against Victorian taste in order to tease out the cultural motives of both the Victorians and ourselves. Indeed, Bailin identifies a significant continuity between Victorian methods of production, distribution, and advertising—not to mention their penchant for revivalism—and our own. Living in the disposable culture Victorian technology and capitalism made possible, we too seek to transform discarded objects into treasures in order to reassure ourselves that "in the perdurable world of things, all is not lost."

The problems of reading representations of Victorian commodities in contemporary media is the subject of Ellen Bayuk Rosenman's essay "More Stories about Clothing and Furniture: Realism and Bad Commodities." Rosenman looks at how the visual media of film and television redefine the complex and gendered critique of commodity culture in Victorian fiction. The problems raised for contemporary feminist critics by these popular and commercially successful adaptations are acutely evident in Rosenman's discussion of the BBC's *Middlemarch*. Whereas George Eliot was, like many of her realist contemporaries, proficient at representational strategies that disavowed desire for the very objects on which realism depends, the film adaptation of her masterpiece indulges visual desire and consumer capitalism, abetting such enterprises as *Exposures,* an up-market supplier of Victorian reproduction furnishings. But as Rosenman notes, feminist critics of these phenomena are trapped between an antimaterialist critique and our knowledge that such critiques have typically been deployed against women. In fact, even the reception of film adaptations of Victorian novels reproduces the gender-bias against commodities, snidely referring to their female audiences and deriding them as "costume dramas," "bonnet dramas," and "Big Frock" dramas. Victorian novels themselves, Rosenman remarks, "enact the hybrid position of the modern intellectual, whose job it is to critique commodity culture but who also stands inside it, and not always unwillingly."

Not only do we create Victorian surroundings to live in, but, as the essays in part 3, "The Ways Victorians Live Now," suggest, we may also fashion ourselves in relation to Victorian subjectivities. Jesse Matz takes up the place of Oscar Wilde in gay historiography as an example of a Victorian identity that has become a powerful archetype in our own time and offers evidence of how strong continuities between Victorian and postmodern ways of being are embedded in the repertoire of subjectivities contemporary culture makes available to us. Like the marketable commodities discussed by Rosenman and Bailin, Matz argues in "Wilde Americana" that a nineteenth-century conflation of individual with corporate personhood, instantiated by the Supreme Court's 1882 ruling in *Santa Clara County v. Southern Pacific Railroad,* helped to produce a gay identity available for commercial appropriation. Just as Oscar Wilde himself, who was touring America with his gospel of aestheticism at the time of the ruling, learned that commerce could be beautiful, so too have "members of the gay niche market allowed corporate culture to define their identities—indeed to take on their identities—in exchange for a viable public selfhood." Intervening in debates regarding new gay historiography, Matz does not seek simply to revise the "radical-break" position accorded to Wilde or reverse the reversal by which homosexual acts were allegedly transformed into homosexual identity by the Wilde trials. Rather, through an analysis of the developments that began with "Wilde's self-marketing, with the culture that trained him to defer his selfhood to the system of commodities," Matz finds grounds for urging "the makers of gay lifestyle and gay identity to give up on the acceptability that comes through commercial uniformity—that acceptability so strikingly featured in advertisements that make cultural difference a matter of commercial differentiation." Were they to do so, Matz argues, "they might be able to resist the sort of centripetal force that first converged with such ultimately miserable results around Wilde."

By contrast, the appropriations of Victorian subjects discussed by Sharon Aronofsky Weltman in "Victorians on Broadway at the Present Time: John Ruskin's Life on Stage" suggest that the function of Victorian culture on the contemporary stage is to "validate audiences in their self-satisfaction" by confirming our superiority to our precursors. She cites the 1995 opera *Modern Painters,* the 1999 off-Broadway play *The Countess,* and Tom Stoppard's *The Invention of Love* (2001), each of which uses its Victorian sources to comment on contemporary culture. As particularly telling examples of a phenomenon of Victorian "revivalism" that includes *The King and I, Jekyll and Hyde,* and *Jane Eyre: The Musical,* these works illustrate the tendency to deploy Victorian culture in order to reassure ourselves, especially regarding our own sexual and social liberation. These adaptations achieve their goals by masking the manipulation of their sources, and in some instances, strike audiences as offering unmediated action in a way that overwhelms readings of the various texts—the already highly constructed letters, diaries, and published writings—on which they are based. Aronofsky Weltman comments that these depictions of Ruskin are likely to be contemporary audiences' only encounter with this widely influential, original, and revolutionary thinker, and what they will know of him is the scandal of his failed marriage and sexual neuroses.

The persistence of Victorian methods of disciplining subjectivities is the topic of part 4, "Law and Order, Victorian Style." In "Rounding Up the Usual Suspect: Echoing Jack the Ripper," Kate Lonsdale analyzes the impact of the Jack the Ripper and Sherlock Holmes myths on contemporary criminal investigations and the professional identities of police investigators. In the late 1970s, those myths drove the hunt for the Yorkshire Ripper with fatal consequences, leading investigators to dismiss evidence and even release the prime suspect when facts in the case did not conform to expectations established by the most notorious unsolved crime of the Victorian period. What is more, the heroic stature and celebrated methods of a fictional detective, Sherlock Holmes, with whom police explicitly identified, encouraged the police to narrate themselves in a master detective/archvillain paradigm "at the expense of the abject, the female corpse that succumbs to the Oedipal narrative project of quest and resolution." Lonsdale emphasizes that the Yorkshire police are not alone in their susceptibilities to this narrative; rather, it infuses much of contemporary criminal investigation, influencing profilers, criminologists, and FBI behavioral scientists.

My essay, "Legal Uses of Victorian Fiction: Infant Felons to Juvenile Delinquents," examines Mary Carpenter's unwitting appeal to fictional narrative to mount her influential reform campaign on behalf of children accused of crime. Current penal policy is predicated on Carpenter's insistence that juvenile delinquency must be addressed through an expertise gained by personal experience and empathy rather than by juridical expertise. But the uncertain status of the evidence on which Carpenter relied raises larger problems for contemporary narrative legal theorists, who similarly advocate the substitution of personal stories and imaginative identification with accused criminals for forensic evidence and the allegedly objective application of legal rules. Carpenter's use of narrative evidence she believed to be authentic—but proved to be the creation of a sensation novelist—stands as a cautionary tale to present-day critics of traditional legal reasoning, who also inherit the Victorians' mass-media productions of fictionalized sentiment.

The final part of this volume, "Future Reading: Recovery, Dissemination, Pedagogy," addresses the challenges we must meet in order to ensure a historically informed critique of our Victorian inheritance under changing material, technological, and institutional conditions. Of greatest urgency is the recovery and preservation of those artifacts of Victorian culture that have thus far been neglected by our otherwise voracious appropriations. Florence Boos, in "'Nurs'd up amongst the scenes I have describ'd': Political Resonances in the Poetry of Working-Class Women," introduces us to a significant body of Victorian poetry, much of which exists in unique and often fragile copies, that requires the attention of Victorian scholars lest this important facet of our cultural legacy should be lost to us. Precisely because the authors and texts discussed by Boos have yet to benefit from the popular and critical attention bestowed on the materials treated by other contributors, this essay provides substantial biographical information and close readings, as well as suggesting a critical framework for working-class women's poetry, so that we can recognize the importance of inflecting the dominant view of Victorian culture with these Victorian voices. Thanks to the poets we encounter here, working-class women cannot be reduced to "Wragg"—the woman who kills her infant after giving birth in a workhouse, cited by Arnold in *The Function of Criticism at the Present Time* as symptomatic of his culture's ills—but speak compellingly to contemporary readers of diverse experiences and in distinct tones, calling on us to preserve the words of working-class women and disseminate them in our scholarship and teaching.

In "Revisiting the Serial Format of Dickens's Novels; or, *Little Dorrit* Goes a Long Way," David Barndollar and Susan Schorn report on two experiments they conducted aimed at bridging the vast gulf between Victorian reading habits and our own by attempting to recreate the experience of reading serially. In one, titled Dickens by Inches, the authors assembled a group of readers who made their way through *Little Dorrit* from 1996 to 1999, meeting for monthly discussions. In the other, Dickens by Pixels, participants read weekly numbers of *A Tale of Two Cities* on the web and discussed their reading in an online forum. From the difficulties encountered in both projects, Barndollar and Schorn draw out the implications both for critics of Victorian fiction and for teachers, constrained by the structure of college courses, distribution requirements, and academic calendars, which demand new pedagogical strategies for presenting Victorian novels. The authors conclude that the resistance contemporary readers exhibit toward serial reading can be used to emphasize the relationship between Victorian novels and their own social context, as well as the social context of our students, who are familiar with serial texts in the form of news stories and scandals or ongoing reality TV shows.

Finally, in "Disseminating Victorian Culture in the Postmillennial Class-room," Sue Lonoff offers a salutary diagnosis of the challenges we will face as teachers in the next millennium, when technologies and nonprint media further threaten already diminished reading skills. Simply put, if eight-hundred-page novels prove to be beyond the reading capabilities of students in ten- to fifteen-week terms, what will become of our field? What will happen when even the best graduate students hoping to specialize in Victorian culture have read only four or five examples of Victorian fiction? In addition to making suggestions about reading and writing assignments, and uses of the internet and other digital technologies to teach Victorian culture, Lonoff hopes that her own performance in this essay will help students learn about their agency as readers and cultural critics, the value of their feedback, the humanity they share with their teachers. Lonoff brings autobiography to bear on her topic, explaining the genesis of her argument, her anxieties in revising it, and the provisional nature of its conclusions. By demonstrating that engaging with the past is a living process, we can encourage new functions of Victorian culture in future times.

Notes

1. Gary Day, *Varieties of Victorianism: The Uses of a Past* (New York: St. Martin's Press, 1998), 7.
2. John Kucich and Dianne F. Sadoff, eds., *Victorian Afterlife: Postmodern Culture Rewrites the Nineteenth Century* (Minneapolis: University of Minnesota Press, 2000), x.

PART 1

On Victorian Time

Historiographies of Culture

.

The Victorians in the Rearview Mirror

SIMON JOYCE

The initial assumption underlying this essay is that we never really encounter "the Victorians" themselves, but instead a mediated image like the one we get when we glance into our rearview mirrors while driving. The image usefully condenses the paradoxical sense of looking forward to see what's behind us, which is the opposite of what we do when we read history in order to figure out the future. It also suggests something of the inevitable distortion that accompanies any mirror image; thus, the warning that "objects in the mirror are closer than they appear" nicely expresses a feeling we may have about the Victorians themselves, a recognition of a surprising (and perhaps frightening) closeness to our past that occurred at different times and to different people throughout the twentieth century.[1] It is clear, one hopes, that such distortions are often the products of ideology, deliberate misreadings, exaggerations, or simplifications of a complex past. Margaret Thatcher's call for a return to "Victorian values," encoded in a 1983 speech that listed hard work, self-reliance, thrift, national pride, and cleanliness among the "perennial values" inherited from her Victorian grandmother, is perhaps the most famous of these, and incidentally provides us with a good example of the surprising closeness of the past.[2]

The second assumption I am making is that such elaborations of the essence of the Victorians sometimes make it difficult for people like me to work and call ourselves "Victorianists." This may equally be the case with other periods, of course, each of which have suffered from the processes of simplification that are the necessary starting point for descriptions of anything like "the Elizabethan World Picture" (in E. M. Tillyard's phrase) or other versions of the periodic zeitgeist or weltanschauung. What John McGowan has recently said of the nineteenth century, that "the Victorians as a group characterized by certain shared features do not exist except insofar as they are produced in that similarity by a discourse that has aims on its audience,"[3] could presumably be said of each of these. With few exceptions, though, those other periods have not had the kind of purchase on the present that Thatcher's appeal had, in part because they are simply more distant in time. This is not to say that Thatcher found unanimous consent for her particular version of the Victorian past, of course; in a strikingly ineffective example of what I will be describing later as a strategy of simple inversion, future Labour Party leader Neil Kinnock responded that "the 'Victorian Values' that ruled were cruelty, misery, drudgery, squalor and ignorance," after which the party went on to lose the next election by a wide margin.[4]

Such counteractive efforts, however well intentioned, do nothing to unsettle common-sense assumptions about what the Victorians represented and may even paradoxically help to consolidate them. There seems to be a prevailing popular consensus about the defining features of the period—among which we could list a confidently triumphalist imperialism, a rigid separation of public and private spheres, a repressive sexual morality, and an ascendant hegemony of middle-class values—that can easily accommodate elements of either argument: Thatcher's personal morality as a by-product of sexual repression and the Protestant work ethic, and Kinnock's painful social conditions as the regrettable flip side of industrialization. (Two press cuttings from 1998 illustrate this dichotomy: in one, Britain is praised for "becoming less Victorian" in the wake of Princess Diana's death, having finally abandoned "the phlegmatic belief in coping, the buttoned-up stoicism [that] were once not the outdated fashion of the ruling class, or only male virtues, but a visible part of the national character"; in the other, a striking manufacturing worker holds up a placard, which simply reads that "BERISFORD/MAGNET ARE VICTORIAN EMPLOYERS.")[5]

Faced with the persistence of what Roland Barthes termed the commonsensical "doxa" of public opinion about the Victorians, what is a progressive Victorianist to do? There is, first of all, the laborious work of opposition, as illustrated here by Kinnock's counterargument or elsewhere by the assorted reviewers who painstakingly redressed the imbalances in Gertrude Himmelfarb's tendentiously Thatcherite diatribe, *The De-Moralization of Society: From Victorian Virtues to Modern Values* (1994).[6] Such corrective efforts clearly shade into ideology critique, asking what John McGowan terms "the Bakhtinian question of whom this discourse addresses (answers, contests, affirms) and to what ends" (23). I want to briefly mention three other strategies which have had some success while nonetheless leaving the basic shape of the doxological Victorian largely intact. The first is exemplified by Steven Marcus's study of nineteenth-century pornography, *The Other Victorians* (1966), which served in part as the impetus for Michel Foucault's more influential reconsideration of Victorian sexuality in volume 1 of *The History of Sexuality*. As Marcus's title makes clear, he is interested in those who don't fit within our received notions of the Victorians, and this approach readily extends to other "others" (feminists, colonial subjects, socialists, sexual minorities, and so on). Implicit in this framework, though, and made explicit in Marcus's text, is the way that it presumes a normative definition against which "otherness" can be measured: indeed, "this otherness was of a specific Victorian kind," Marcus notes, and after exhaustive evidence of this he concludes that "the view of human sexuality as it was represented in the subculture of pornography and the view of sexuality held by the official culture were reversals, mirror images, negative analogues of each other."[7] The problem is that such an approach tends to leave uninterrogated that "official" view as the normative pole of definition, although it should be added that the work of Foucault, Eve Kosofsky Sedgwick, and others has done much to complicate this kind of binary thinking.

A second strategy, with some overlaps with Marcus's focus on Victorian "others," is to stress those elements of nineteenth-century society or culture that most closely resemble our own. In the introduction to a collection of essays called *Victorian Afterlife: Postmodern Culture Rewrites the Nineteenth Century* (2000), John Kucich and Dianne F. Sadoff propose that "rewritings of Victorian culture have flourished . . . because the postmodern fetishizes notions of cultural emergence, and because the nineteenth century provides multiple eligible sites for theorizing such emergence. The cultural matrix of nineteenth-century England," they continue, "joined various and possible stories about cultural rupture that, taken together, overdetermine the period's availability for the postmodern exploration of cultural emergence."[8] Such an approach yields some immediate benefits, enabling a fully fledged narrative (or multiple narratives) of Victorian otherness to be glimpsed beneath the surface, as it were, of our understanding of the period itself. By suggesting that such an attention to emergent formations allows for a reconsideration of the temporality of historical rupture, and by positing multiple and overlapping processes of transition, the approach laid out by Kucich and Sadoff would presumably problematize the conventional meta-history that sees "the Victorian" as superseded by something else, variously termed "the modern," "the Edwardian" or "the Georgian"—about which I will be saying much more in a moment. It is hard, though, to shake the suspicion that "the Victorian" itself has stayed the same, even if (as famously for Marx's version of capitalism) it can be shown to contain within itself that which will come after. We might also see emergence itself as a problematic concept, which only defers the troubled question of definition: after all, if what draws us to the nineteenth century are those ways that it anticipates the postmodern present, then how do we characterize *that?* The kind of progressivist narrative that undergirds such an approach is one that has been critiqued by (among others) Foucault for its imposition of a teleological destination to which all historical roads lead, and by E. P. Thompson for treating with "the enormous condescension of posterity" those formations that did not necessarily emerge into the daylight of the present.[9]

Thompson's point, that "we are not at the end of social evolution ourselves," and as such are scarcely in a position to dismiss past alternatives, is borne out by a third strategy for approaching the nineteenth century as the repository of just such options. In *The End of Utopia* (1999), for instance, Russell Jacoby upbraids critical thinking at the end of the twentieth century for having abandoned the project of utopia, the "belief that the future could fundamentally surpass the present," which is subsumed under the more general idea "that history contains possibilities of freedom and pleasure hardly tapped."[10] Disappointingly, *The End of Utopia* seems more concerned to descant on the limitations of the present than to discuss those other possibilities; in reviewing a new edition of Edward Bellamy's 1888 novel *Looking Backward,* however, Jacoby points to the subsequent portion of the nineteenth century as "awash in utopian books and schemes," with a hundred utopian novels appearing in the twelve years remaining.[11] Far more useful for my present purposes is Regenia Gagnier's *The Insatiability of Human Wants* (2000), which deploys a startling reading of the interpenetrations of aesthetics and economics throughout the nineteenth century to argue, first, that the Victorians were far from concluding that the free market was the best or only way to organize society and, second, that it still isn't: "One purpose of this book," Gagnier writes, "is to recall social visions that challenged modern market society, visions that under current conditions of mass communications are in danger of being erased from cultural memory."[12] Where Thompson writes of the effort to "rescue" forgotten figures (including "the 'utopian' artisan") from the condescension of history, and to place them in the service of a possible stage of future social evolution, we can read the same impulses in Jacoby's return to the traditions of nineteenth-century utopianism or Gagnier's recovery of alternatives to the free market that were articulated by Victorian political economists, feminists, socialists, and aesthetes.

As was the case with Marcus's "other Victorians," though, it's hard to escape the feeling that the norm is getting off the hook here, regardless of whether it is viewed as ultimately transcended by its own emergent possibilities or challenged by its suppressed and dissenting voices. In a way, we're back to Thatcher versus Kinnock, and a logic of split perception that only reaffirms the ways that such binaries get set up in the first place. (Who, after all, would question that periods produce their own others and/or anticipate their successors and/or contain unprocessed elements that might turn out to be potentially useful in the future?) In this essay, I propose to address these issues of period definition, retrospection, and the continued function of "the Victorians" at the present time by looking more closely at where and how our doxological Victorians first appeared, before considering whether we might think about the term itself as a dialectical condensation of the same contrary tendencies that I have been discussing up to now.

As John McGowan notes, it is the so-called Bloomsbury Group of British modernists that did most to advance the view of the Victorians as "nonmodern," in part "by introducing the (subsequently) endlessly repeated narrative of our (ambivalent) progress around sexuality. No restaging of Victorian life is complete without reassuring us that we are more enlightened sexually than those repressed Victorians."[13] While I agree that Bloomsbury acted as a powerful amplifier of anti-Victorian sentiment, my argument here is that it began much earlier (on the Queen's death in 1901, if not sooner) and was not confined to—or even primarily expressed in terms of—sexuality. Journalistic coverage of Victoria's passing at all points on the political spectrum revealed a desire to summarize her reign, the century with which she seemed synonymous, or both, and a simultaneous uncertainty about the future. Some representative examples illustrate these broad generalizations. On the Right, the weekly *St. James Gazette* noted the day after the Queen's death that the "habit of thought" that most characterized the Victorian Age—the idea that "mankind was going to settle everything by logic and common sense"—had recently come to seem less compelling.[14] On the Left, *Reynolds Weekly Newspaper* argued four days later that, while "the world has seen some changes in the Victorian Era," the labeling of these shifts as "improvements" or "progress" merely begs the question of exactly where the nation is progressing *to:* "To loftier ideals, a happier common life, lessening of the strain after sordid things? No; the progress has not been made in that direction; on the contrary, it has been the reverse."[15]

If these excerpts give us some sense of the public discourse at the moment of Victoria's death, others illustrate the difficulty of looking ahead to a new century or a new reign. On the Right, the *Saturday Review:* "Whatever the twentieth century and the reign of King Edward VII may have in store, we may be sure that it will not be quite like the Victorian age, will probably differ much from it."[16] Toward the political center, the *Pall Mall Gazette* (predicting possible disaster in the Boer War): "It is for us to make sure that New Year's Day, 1901, shall not find the Empire of England on the way to the same fate as those out of which it has been built up."[17] On the Left, *Reynolds* again: "In our judgment, the first year of the new century will prove to have been the last year of good trade and we must look forward to a period of lean years and to decline in trade as compared with our two great rivals, America and Germany. Unhappily, instead of preparing for this, we have squandered an enormous sum in South Africa and, if we do not make peace, we shall squander much more."[18] I do not mean here to force any kind of equivalence on these statements or to minimize their very real differences, but rather to suggest that there is a consistent rhetoric of evaluation, retrospection, and incipient panic in each, which dominates whether or not the journal itself is for or against the Queen, or empire, or progress as defined in generally material or scientific terms.

Each of these statements is arguing what I take to be a decisive feature of Bloomsbury—and more generally of modern—anti-Victorianism: the idea that something termed (on the basis of variable determining factors) "the Victorian" has, for better or worse, now come to an end. What is perhaps distinctive about modernism, however, is its ability to keep on making this same statement long after January 1901. Sensing that, at least in the cultural sphere, the Edwardians failed to enact the decisive break with the past that was being predicted on Victoria's death, Virginia Woolf wrote in *Mr. Bennett and Mrs. Brown* (1924) that "on or about December 1910 human character changed."[19] Robert Graves's *Goodbye to All That* (1929) pushed back that assessment to 1918, so that the experience of military service during World War I became the transitional moment.[20] In 1935, George Dangerfield surveyed the recent history of Britain and wrote critically of the idea that it was war itself that finally broke the hold of the past: "It is easier," he notes, "to think of Imperial England, beribboned and bestarred and splendid, living in majestic profusion up till the very moment of war. Such indeed was its appearance, the appearance of a somewhat decadent Empire and a careless democracy. But I do not think its social history will be written on these terms."[21] And indeed, Dangerfield argues that an uneven but decisive shift in the national character had actually been taking place, almost subconsciously, in the early years of George V.

Woolf's *Mr. Bennett and Mrs. Brown,* one of the classic manifestos of Bloomsbury modernism, identifies a shift in the zeitgeist that coincides with the first postimpressionist exhibition in London as well as the first months of George's reign, and thus implicitly criticizes the Edwardians for not making a decisive break with their own Victorian pasts. Where the *St. James Gazette* had predicted in 1901 that any new burst of literary genius (considered "unlikely") would "be on very different lines from those laid down or used by Tennyson, Dickens, Thackeray, Carlyle, Ruskin,"[22] Woolf's judgment of Edwardian high-realists like H. G. Wells, Arnold Bennett, and John Galsworthy was (in the words of Carola Kaplan and Anne Simpson) that they engaged in a kind of Oedipal struggle with the Victorians "in the terms their predecessors had taught them."[23] One telling mark of the new literary consciousness that Woolf sees in such diverse figures as Joyce, Lawrence, Strachey, and Eliot is that they "do not pour out three immortal masterpieces with Victorian regularity every autumn" (24), an assessment that nicely damns with faint praise a model of professional authorship that had been perfected by exactly those Edwardians under discussion.[24] Taking as its defining category the delineation of character, Woolf's essay imagines a woman sitting in a railway carriage, to be confronted by representative figures of Edwardian realism and Georgian modernism. Without wanting to overstate the point or to force a precise parallel between the Queen and her fictional "Mrs. Brown," a number of clues beyond the names suggest that we should have Victoria in the back of our minds. First, the description of her character suggests a suitably diminished version of the monarch brought down to earth: there is "something pinched about her—a look of suffering, of apprehension, and, in addition, she was extremely small. I felt that, having been deserted, or left a widow, years ago, she had led an anxious, harried life, bringing up an only son, perhaps, who, as likely as not, was by this time beginning to go to the bad" (6). If this sounds like Victoria's troubles with the wayward Prince of Wales, more clues appear later, as we learn that the train originates at Windsor and an imaginary Edwardian reader upbraids Woolf herself because "we do not even know whether her villa was called Albert or Balmoral" (19).

It is this stubborn insistence on external details and material facts that still characterizes Edwardian fiction for Woolf, and this is also the sense in which major figures like Bennett, Galsworthy, and Wells remain caught in the mode of high Victorian realism. If the "Edwardian tools are the wrong ones for us to use" because they "have laid an enormous stress upon the fabric of things," the superior Georgian attitude is founded on a new view of human relations that is visible first in new interactions between "masters and servants, husbands and wives, parents and children" and only then extending to "religion, conduct, politics, and literature" (5). This generalization helps to bring together a varied group of modern writers, but in doing so it also fixes a simplified version of both the social structures and literary techniques that now seem to characterize the Victorians as well as their brief Edwardian echo.

Besides its obvious inaccuracies, what troubles me about this approach is that it has a tendency to accrete certain characteristics as representative of "the Victorian," often colluding with the nineteenth century's own favored self-image. While we might understand the urgency of these critiques, they are limited on a couple of counts. First, their insistence on relegating all things Victorian to the remote past suggests the process of distinguishing oneself that Harold Bloom termed "the anxiety of influence," which dictates an almost pathological insistence on the newness of the modern.[25] As we have seen, however, modernist historiographies were also repeatedly engaged in redrawing the precise boundaries of temporal change (at 1901, 1910, 1918, and so on), with each new marker serving as a tacit acknowledgment that "the Victorians" have persisted beyond their appointed time—whether we rename them as "Edwardians" or "early Georgians." Since the desired distance is also always collapsed by the associated revelation that previous assertions of modernity remained tainted by the past, each effort at differentiation seems ultimately self-defeating. The logic here is strikingly similar to one that Raymond Williams describes in *The Country and the City* as a kind of "moving escalator" of literary history. A hallmark of the pastoral, he notes, is its sense that there once existed (usually in childhood) a Golden Age of harmony between nature and society; the problem is that one person's youthful paradise always turns out to be another's debased present—and so, before long, the search ends at Arcadia, Eden, or some other space that strangely exists outside of time itself. The process Williams is tracing persistently backdates a moment of temporal change or social corruption, while the modernists I am looking at move it forward, but these seem to me to be two sides of the same coin, and equally suspect as approaches to history.[26]

Strategically, modernist critiques of the Victorians also relied too heavily on the logic of binary inversion, which—through a simple substitution of negative for positive valuations—sometimes leaves the terms of the opposition in place, much like the temporary overturning of hierarchies in Carnival that then give way to business as usual. In the argument I am making here, periodizing claims about the death of the Victorian era act like those licensed inversions, leaving the term itself intact and enabling the past to be "revived" on much the same terms that it was initially derided, whether by Evelyn Waugh in the 1940s or Margaret Thatcher in the 1980s. As Jonathan Dollimore has suggested, however, there is another use of inversion that is at least potentially more effective in displacing the terms of a binary opposition. "In actual historical instances," he notes, "the inversion is not just the necessary precondition for the binary's subsequent displacement, but often already constitutes a displacement, if not directly of the binary itself, then certainly of the moral and political norms which cluster dependently around its dominant pole and in part constitute it."[27] His key example is Oscar Wilde, and especially the epigrammatic paradoxes in essays like "Phrases and Philosophies for the Use of the Young," many of which—"Only the shallow know themselves," for instance, or "If one tells the truth, one is sure, sooner or later, to be found out"—now seem to be well-worn quotations. For Dollimore, what distinguishes these aphorisms from simple inversion, even as they substitute such scorned qualities as lying, superficiality, and insincerity for cherished Victorian norms, is the way they show the inseparability of such terms from their opposite. Thus, it is not just that superficiality is better than depth, but that one can be deeply shallow, or caught out by telling the truth in some circumstances. "That which society forbids," according to Dollimore, "Wilde reinstates *through and within* some of its most cherished and central categories—art, the aesthetic, art criticism, individualism. At the same time as he appropriates those categories he also transvalues them through perversion and inversion, thus making them now signify those binary exclusions by which the dominant culture knows itself."[28]

This—and not simple condemnation—seems to me to have been Lytton

Strachey's aim in *Eminent Victorians* (1918). It was first conceived as a balanced series of silhouettes that would have represented figures that its author admired as well as those who he felt had been overvalued by history.[29] The published preface also seeks to disavow any particular critical purpose, claiming to select the book's subjects with "no desire to construct a system or to prove a theory," much less to attempt the "futile . . . hope to tell even a *precis* of the truth about the Victorian age."[30] We can of course choose to take this with a pinch of salt, but my reading would agree with Strachey here, that it is not a more accurate truth that he is after but a deconstruction of the Victorians' own cherished notions of themselves.

Strachey has been taken to task for this by the neoconservative historian Gertrude Himmelfarb, who wants to discover a continuity with the Victorian past as much as anyone, as the subtitle of her book, "From Victorian Virtues to Modern Values" makes clear. In an earlier essay in which the real criminal is history from below, Himmelfarb sees Strachey's revision of biographical methods as a deliberate belittling, writing the lives of Newman, General Gordon, Thomas Arnold, and Florence Nightingale in order "to discredit them, to reveal the private selves behind the public facades, the private vices that are presumed to belie their public virtues." In her own terms, however, it is not immediately clear what Himmelfarb is objecting to in Strachey: presumably, it's not historical accuracy, since the Victorians themselves are praised a page later for "human[izing] their heroes, reveal[ing] their private vices without denying their public virtues." If balance is the key, there is no indication given of how it is to be achieved, except perhaps to err on the side of reputation; yet—if we agree that such vices as Strachey depicts do undermine his subjects' claims to eminence—we would need to ask where such reputations arise in the first place, perhaps in those same Victorian biographers who were apt to take the stated virtues at face value. We may glimpse what is really worrying Himmelfarb in a remark that follows, claiming that Strachey's method makes his subjects "seem more individualistic . . . than they actually were."[31] They need to be representative figures of the age itself, then, with illustrative virtues and perhaps even typical vices: with such effective examples as these, she thinks, history from below is rendered entirely unnecessary.

What a nostalgic new Victorianist like Himmelfarb finds unsettling about Strachey is his insistence on taking seriously this representative status, and using it to undermine the Victorians' own view of what counts as virtue or eminence.[32] In the process, he is making a very different historical argument than the others I have been discussing, each of whom seems desperate to consign the Victorians to the dustbin of the past. The opening essay of *Eminent Victorians* on Cardinal Manning begins by presenting its subject as a throwback to the clerics of the Middle Ages, a figure who ought logically to be an anachronism in his own time: "What had happened?" Strachey asks. "Had a dominating character imposed itself upon a hostile environment? Or was the Nineteenth Century, after all, not so hostile? Was there something in it, scientific and progressive as it was, which went out to welcome the representative of an ancient tradition and uncompromising faith?" (4).

The opposite might equally be the case: that what drew Strachey, as a Georgian intellectual, back to the Victorians is their unexpected modernist tendencies—among them self-doubt, contradictory impulses, the clash of ego and moral duty—all of which are shown to coincide with an antithetical public confidence in personal, collective, and national virtue. At times, the conflict is figured in Freudian terms, as when the "demons" haunting Florence Nightingale are elaborated as a kind of irrational id beneath the deceptive public image of "the Lady with the Lamp." At others, what is compelling is the peaceful coexistence of seemingly opposed facets, in what the essay on General Gordon terms "the mingling contradictions of the English spirit" (246)—and which it exemplifies in the controversial image of its subject, seeking solace simultaneously from "an open Bible and an open bottle of brandy" (264).

In such passages, it is not exactly hypocrisy that Strachey is indicating, in which case, pretended public qualities (piety, moral purpose, duty, heroism) would be shown to cover up real, private ones that suggest the opposite (fanaticism, confusion, ambition, tyranny). Instead, what *Eminent Victorians* is arguing is the more Wildean proposition that such qualities are not actually antithetical at all: thus, Gordon's character is said to possess "intricate recesses where egoism and renunciation melted into one another" (260); piety is shown to produce fanaticism just as an overriding stress on personal duty generates massive egos and rampant self-glorification. In a clear echo of Wilde, Strachey writes of Cardinal Newman and his theological hair-splitting prior to conversion that "the possibilities of truth and falsehood depend upon other things than sincerity. A man may be of a scrupulous and impeccable honesty, and yet his respect for truth—it cannot be denied—may be insufficient" (33). In which case, to come back to Gertrude Himmelfarb's complaint, it seems appropriate and representative of the time that its celebrated military hero, General Gordon, was also an addled and self-destructive zealot, or that Florence Nightingale, the poster-woman

for selfless sacrifice, was also a megalomaniac. In a simple move of redefi-
nition, Strachey's "eminent Victorians" turn out to be closer than we imagined to Steven Marcus's oppositional "others."

The argument I have been making about Strachey and Wilde has striking
parallels with that made by postcolonial critic Simon Gikandi in his contribution to the collection *Victorian Afterlife*. In his analysis of the residual
influence of "Victorian" culture and values on the twentieth-century
Trotskyist/Africanist C. L. R. James and the *fin de siècle* black nationalist
Alexander Crummell, Gikandi identifies what he terms "the embarrassment
of Victorianism" in those moments when nineteenth-century "forces, values, and cultures [that were] intended to consolidate colonial conquest
could so easily be transformed into the foundational narratives of black self-
determination and rights" in the twentieth century.[33] In the case of James in
particular, his surprising reverence for high-Victorian figures (Dickens,
Thackeray, Thomas Arnold, in addition to popular heroes like the cricketer,
W. G. Grace) enables him not only to recognize his childhood formation in
the colonial West Indies as quintessentially "Victorian" but also to develop
a powerful critical deconstruction of that term. In Gikandi's argument,
James recognizes that "there was a fundamental contradiction between his
notion of England—derived from books and colonial practices—and the
complex realities of English life"; that Victorianism did not represent an
absolute break with the past, nor was it transcended by modernism—
indeed, "Victorian ideas and practices heralded the irruption of modernity
onto the colonial sphere."[34] All of this requires roughly the same attention
to the heterogeneity of Victorian beliefs, and to the gaps between its theoretical self-image and its practices (nowhere more visible than at its colonial
periphery), that I have been arguing here in relation to Strachey.

One lesson of postcolonial criticism has been that attention to the practices of colonial administration can highlight the contradictions and incon-
sistencies that might otherwise be concealed by hegemonic rule in Britain.
The deconstructive tendency at work in *Eminent Victorians* or in Wilde's
aphorisms provides us with one route by which we can track the paradoxes
of colonial Victorianism back home. The experiences of James or Crummell,
caught between the promises of Victorian values and their failure to live up
to those expectations, might thus be viewed as a useful hypostatization of
a more generalized condition; and their reluctance to abandon the inheri-

tance of the nineteenth century, when such a dismissal was clearly de rigueur among metropolitan modernists, might equally serve as a salutary lesson for contemporary Victorianists. We can, and perhaps should, view the period as one riven with internal fault lines and incoherences, instead of endorsing efforts either to write it off as a completed project or to revive an incomplete and tendentious version of the Victorian past—both of which ultimately concur in their assessments of what it was really like. As an age of contradiction, it was neither a good nor a bad thing, not something that needs to be mourned or derided. To understand it better, though, we need to resist its own self-definitions and equally to be skeptical of critiques that claim to be free of them. To recognize our own investments in the period is also, then, to see the continuing residual force of the Victorian, as a concept that has been repeatedly transcended, negated, parodied, and resurrected ever since its apparent demise.

Notes

1. I am grateful to Richard Nash for pointing out to me the way this phrase has resonated in popular culture, from a song by Meat Loaf to a scene in *Jurassic Park* in which the object in the mirror turns out to be a Tyrannosaurus Rex. The idea of a threatening dinosaur returned to life is surely one of our nightmares of the Victorians!

2. Margaret Thatcher, "The Good Old Days," in Raphael Samuel, "Mrs. Thatcher's Return to Victorian Values," *Victorian Values: A Joint Symposium of Edinburgh and the British Academy,* ed. T. C. Smout (Oxford: Oxford University Press and the British Academy, 1992), 14.

3. John McGowan, "Modernity and Culture, the Victorians and Cultural Studies," in *Victorian Afterlife: Postmodern Culture Rewrites the Nineteenth Century,* ed. John Kucich and Dianne F. Sadoff (Minneapolis: University of Minnesota Press, 2000), 23.

4. Neil Kinnock, cited in Samuel, 13.

5. Andrew Marr, "One Year on, Has Britain Changed," *Guardian Weekly* 30 (Aug. 1998): 13; illustration in the *Guardian Weekly* 25 (May 1998): 19.

6. See (among others) David Bromwich, "Victoria's Secret," *New Republic* 15 (May 1995), and Marilynne Robinson, "Modern Victorians: Dressing Politics in the Costume of History," *Harper's Magazine,* July 1995. For a further discussion of Himmelfarb's rendering of the nineteenth century as a model for the present, see my "Victorian Continuities: Early British Sociology and the Welfare of the State" in *Disciplinarity at the Fin de Siecle,* ed. Amanda Anderson and Joseph Valente (Princeton: Princeton University Press, 1992), 261–80.

7. Steven Marcus, *The Other Victorians: A Study of Sexuality and Pornography in Mid-Nineteenth-Century England* (New York: Bantam Books, 1967), xix; 286.

8. Kucich and Sadoff, xv.

9. See Foucault, especially "Nietzsche, Genealogy, History," in *Language, Counter-Memory, Practice,* ed. Donald Bouchard (Ithaca: Cornell University Press, 1977), 139–64; E. P. Thompson, *The Making of the English Working Class* (New York: Vintage, 1966), 12–13.

10. Russell Jacoby, *The End of Utopia: Politics and Culture in an Age of Apathy* (New York: Basic Books, 1999), xi–xii.

11. Jacoby, "A Brave Old World: Looking Forward to a Nineteenth-Century Utopia," *Harper's Magazine,* Dec. 2000, 73.

12. Regenia Gagnier, *The Insatiability of Human Wants: Economics and Aesthetics in Market Society* (Chicago: University of Chicago Press, 2000), 5.

13. McGowan, 11. Foucault's revisionist history sets out to challenge the position being parodied here, that the Victorians held a repressive attitude toward sex from which we have since been liberated. See *The History of Sexuality,* vol. 1, especially parts 1 ("We 'Other Victorians'") and 2 ("The Repressive Hypothesis").

14. *St. James Gazette,* Jan. 23, 1901, 5.

15. *Reynolds Weekly Newspaper,* Jan. 27, 1901, 1.

16. *Saturday Review,* Jan. 26, 1901, 100.

17. *Pall Mall Gazette,* Dec. 30, 1899, 1.

18. *Reynolds Weekly Newspaper,* Jan. 27, 1901, 1.

19. Virginia Woolf, *Mr. Bennett and Mrs. Brown* (London: Hogarth Press, 1928), 4. All future references are to this edition and are incorporated in the text.

20. See, for example, chapter 27, when Graves returns to Oxford after the war to find that the students are oddly committed to their studies rather than childish pranks and drunkenness. "I can't make out my pupils at all," remarks one master. "They are all 'Yes, sir' and 'No, sir.' They seem positively to thirst for knowledge and scribble away in their note-books like lunatics. I can't remember a single instance of such stern endeavour in pre-War days." Robert Graves, *Goodbye to All That* (New York: Doubleday, 1957), 291–92.

21. George Dangerfield, *The Strange Death of Liberal England* (Stanford: Stanford University Press, 1997), 315.

22. *St. James Gazette,* Jan. 23, 1901, 5.

23. Carola M. Kaplan and Anne B. Simpson, "Edwardians and Modernists: Literary Evaluation and the Problem of History," in *Seeing Double: Revisioning Edwardian and Modernist Literature,* ed. Kaplan and Simpson (New York: St. Martin's Press, 1996), xii.

24. The attitude that Woolf has in mind here is exemplified by Bennett, who wrote in the preface to *The Old Wives' Tale* (1911) that "I calculated that it would be 200,000 words long (which it exactly proved to be), and I had a vague notion that no novel of such dimensions (except Richardson's) had ever been written before. So I counted the words in several famous Victorian novels, and discovered to my relief that the famous Victorian novels average 400,000 words apiece." Arnold Bennett, *The Old Wives' Tale* (Garden City: Doubleday, 1928), vii–viii.

25. See Harold Bloom, *The Anxiety of Influence: A Theory of Poetry* (Oxford: Oxford University Press, 1973).

26. Raymond Williams, *The Country and the City* (Oxford: Oxford University Press, 1973), 9–12. A perfect illustration of Williams's thesis (and one that equally accords with the argument I am making here) occurs at the beginning of Evelyn Waugh's *Brideshead Revisited* (1944). As its narrator, Captain Charles Ryder, looks out at a modern world that he characterizes as "the homogeneous territory of housing estates and cinemas," the chance encounter with an old country house transports him back to "a cloudless day in June" of 1923 and Oxford. "In her spacious and quiet streets," Ryder recalls, "men walked and spoke as they had in Newman's day; her autumnal mists, her grey spring-time, and the rare glory of her summer days—such as that day—when the chestnut was in flower and the bells rang out high and clear over her gables and cupolas, exhaled the soft vapours of a thousand years of learning." Sure enough, however, as soon as Ryder projects himself back to that timeless Oxford of youth, his scout is complaining about modern manners: "For this was 1923 and for Lunt, as for thousands of others, things could never be the same as they had been in 1914." Waugh, *Brideshead Revisited* (Boston: Little, Brown and Co, n.d.), 21–22.

27. Jonathan Dollimore, *Sexual Dissidence: Augustine to Wilde, Foucault to Freud* (Oxford: Clarendon, 1991), 66.

28. Oscar Wilde, "Phrases and Philosophies for the Use of the Young," in *The Complete Works of Oscar Wilde* (London: Collins, 1966), 1205–6; Dollimore, 15 (emphasis in original).

29. See Michael Holroyd, *Lytton Strachey: A Critical Biography* (New York: Holt, Rinehart and Winston, 1968), 2:66.

30. Lytton Strachey, *Eminent Victorians* (San Diego: Harcourt Brace, n.d.), viii. All future references are to this edition and are incorporated in the text.

31. Gertrude Himmelfarb, "Of Heroes, Villains, and Valets," *On Looking into the Abyss: Untimely Thoughts on Culture and Society* (New York: Alfred A. Knopf, 1994), 35–36.

32. It is a symptom of the very instability of current definitions of the Victorian period that the same phrase ("New Victorian") that I am using here to describe Himmelfarb's neoconservative call for a return to an earlier code of values has also been applied to modern feminism, in a wide-ranging diatribe against its critiques of pornography, date rape, and violence against women. See Rene Denfeld, *The New Victorians: A Young Woman's Challenge to the Old Feminist Order* (New York: Time Warner, 1995), especially chapter 7.

33. Simon Gikandi, "The Embarrassment of Victorianism: Colonial Subjects and the Lure of Englishness," in Kucich and Sadoff, 167.

34. Gikandi, 161–62.

The Legacy of Victorian Spectacle

*The Map of Time and the Architecture
of Empty Space*

RONALD R. THOMAS

On June 19, 1997, Prime Minister Tony Blair, wearing a hard hat and knee-high rubber boots, delivered an address at the polluted industrial site and deserted gas works that occupy the narrow peninsula stretching between the northern and southern banks of the Thames River. In that address, he identified this derelict parcel of British soil as "the home of time."[1] Signs posted around the area reading "This Is Where Time Began" echoed the proclamation. Like Blair's speech, those signs referred to the immense construction zone set aside for "The Millennium Dome," the ambitious building project that would produce the largest enclosed structure in the world and the most expensive cultural project in the history of England. Twice the size of its closest competitor, over a mile in circumference, and covering more than twenty acres of land, the Teflon-covered structure boasted an exhibition space large enough (according to the promotional materials describing it) to contain thirteen Royal Albert Halls and eighteen thousand double-decker London buses. As Blair's remarks indicated, however, the significance of the structure was to lie not in its command over space but in its claim upon

Fig. 1 The Millennium Dome under construction, spring 1998, showing polluted industrial site and deserted gas works occupying site on the peninsula between the northern and southern banks of the Thames River. (Brian Harris, used with permission of THE INDEPENDENT/SYNDICATION.)

time (fig. 1). The dome was designed to mark Britain's spectacular celebration of the new millennium, which epoch, we were reminded in those same marketing materials, also would begin in this place. "We may no longer have an empire," a *New York Times* article quoted one Londoner as saying with reference to the Dome, "but we still own time."[2]

Such assertions found their justification in the fact that the Millennium Dome was being built just downriver from the Royal Observatory in Greenwich, the site of the prime meridian of longitude and the place where Greenwich Mean Time was established as an international standard in 1884. From that point onward, this spot would mark the official ground zero from which the earth was mapped into geographic coordinates and divided into so many time zones. The Millennium Dome, proclaimed as a harbinger of the future era and of the "New Britain," also looks backward to this moment in British imperial history when London was officially acknowledged as the center of the civilized world. As such, the structure was planned to serve as a collective memory of other great monuments of British global domination in the nineteenth century—not just the Royal Observatory at Greenwich, but also the midcentury Great Exhibition at the Crystal Palace of 1851 and the celebrated clock tower of Big Ben completed with such fanfare in 1859. Part urban renewal project, part commercial venture, part patriotic shrine, part Anglo-Disney, the Dome was offered as a monument to the national memory—to the time when Britain owned an expansive empire of territory and trade routes upon which the sun never set, and therefore owned time as well.

The high-sounding claims spoken in anticipation of the Dome's completion ring rather hollow in light of its notorious debut on New Year's Eve of 2000 and in the context of Tony Blair's visit to the Dome at the end of the year, when he admitted that the visions for the Millennium Dome back in 1997 were, in fact, "too ambitious." He proceeded to thank the staff for its extraordinary achievements and dedication to the project amidst all the controversy it generated and announced plans to close the attraction in light of its being purchased by an international high-tech consortium.[3] Denounced in the press as a "great white elephant," "the butt of all jokes," the amazing "Blunderdome," and (by Prince Charles) as "a monstrous blancmange," the Dome of the Millennium ran out the clock of its short life under a cloud on the prime meridian where, one newspaper headline proclaimed, it had only succeeded in bringing "Mean Times in Greenwich."[4] In fact, while attendance fell far short of its inflated expectations, the Dome was immensely successful by any other standard and (like its predecessor the Great Exhibition of 1851) was always intended to be closed after the first year of operation. In that year, it attracted nearly six million paying customers, ranking it the most popular paid attraction in Britain and one of the five or six most popular in the world.[5] My concern in this essay is not so much with the success or failure of the enterprise but with the terms in which its overly ambitious visions were originally conceived and the way they represent a modern retelling and revision of the story of the Britain of the Victorian Age, perhaps best symbolized by the Great Exhibition of 1851 and by the outcome of the circumstances surrounding the Prime Meridian Conference of 1884.

The Millennium Dome, poised astride the prime meridian of longitude as the putative home of time, was offered to the world as a giant narrative that would retell and revise the story of the British Empire as the story of the line of time itself. This monument to Britain's self-declared geographical and political centrality in the world is also a reminder that the designation of a universal prime meridian in 1884 not only confused thorny nineteenth-century political and economic controversies with scientific and geographical debates about providing a universal grid for mapping the earth's surface, it also marked the end of the age of romantic nationalism. In the Prime Meridian Conference of 1884, this critical moment in the history of the map, nationalist imperatives would be replaced by the demands of new internationalist economies that depended upon the mapping of national boundaries and global territories primarily as convenient market designations. By invoking the authority of its "possession" of the prime meridian now, a century after the fact, as the most potent event to invoke in order to redefine itself as a *nation*, the "New Britain" seems to concede that modern transnational economies must rely upon maintaining a necessary fiction of national authenticity in order to carry out their ambitions. It was a gesture of particular significance at a time when Britain was so thoroughly "devolving" its national identity and engaging in such a strained and equivocal relationship with the European Economic Community.

The Royal Observatory at Greenwich was established by Charles II to address the longitude question and was charged to apply "the most exact Care and Diligence to rectifying the Tables of the Motions of the Heavens, and the Places of the fixed Stars, so as to find out the so-much desired Longitude at Sea, for perfecting the art of Navigation."[6] The founding of the Royal Observatory at Greenwich, like its predecessor (and principal competitor) observatory in Paris, was a scientific project quite explicitly conceived to address a political and commercial problem, a heavenly directed effort to map the globe and chart international trade from its proper origins in British soil. By assembling the most dependable and widely used astronomical tables for navigation and publishing them in the *Nautical Almanac*, Greenwich also subsequently became the nation's official timekeeper in 1833, when it provided the world's first visual time signal. Each day, at precisely 1 P.M., a large red ball would descend from atop a time turret constructed on the eastern end of the observatory, signaling the hour to all the navigators on ships harbored in the Thames so that they could accurately set their chronometers. The Royal Observatory, founded as Britain's official surveyor of space, had become the nation's official keeper of time.

The daily signal announced at 1 P.M. from the Observatory was Greenwich time, however, which differed from London time by some twenty-three seconds, and from Plymouth time by another sixteen minutes. These differences were vigilantly noted and preserved in each locality. The very technological advances that had brought these places closer together in the nineteenth century—like the railroad and the telegraph—had also created a new problem. As the midcentury expansion of the railroad system combined with an increasingly efficient postal system and developments in rapid communication, local time differences had become increasingly significant and troublesome. While local times were staunchly and even patriotically adhered to throughout Britain (and across Europe), railroad companies voiced increasingly urgent demands to establish a more generally accepted "British time" to avoid the tremendous confusion created by recognizing so many distinct local times on increasingly complex train schedules. Consequently, in 1840 the Great Western Railway issued a controversial decree that London time would be kept exclusively in all its stations throughout the country and would be published in all its timetables. Five years later, the Liverpool & Manchester Railway Company petitioned Parliament to establish "uniformity of time for all ordinary and commercial purposes throughout the land," a proposal that was met with considerable opposition in local municipalities.[7]

By 1855, due largely to the profound impact of train travel throughout the nation, 95 percent of the clocks in Britain would be set by the agreed standard of Greenwich Mean Time. It would take another thirty years for Parliament officially to establish a uniform time for the nation, however, reflecting the customary response to what David Harvey has called the phenomenon of "time-space compression" in modern society. This implosion of social space advanced by new technologies of travel and communication commonly engenders what Harvey refers to as a collective "crisis of identity," a phenomenon that reacts against the shrinking of the world and the erasure of differences with an enhanced level of devotion to localized memories of place, nation, region, or ethnic grouping.[8] In this instance of the phenomenon, an increasingly extended and complex map of railroad lines gradually imposed a standardized experience of space (calculated station by station) as an increasingly frequent and precise schedule of operation regimented one's sense of time (according to departure and arrival timetables). By the time the Prime Meridian Conference convened in Washington in 1884, space had quite literally become a matter of time both in Britain and throughout the modern industrialized world.

Prior to 1884, London was only one of over a dozen widely recognized prime meridians by which navigators would chart their location at sea. The zero point of the earth was, for various reasons of commerce and politics, sometimes calculated from Paris (the principal rival to Greenwich) but also from Rome, Madrid, Lisbon, Washington, Jerusalem, Cape Verde, the Canary Islands, the Bering Straits, and Copenhagen, to name a few of the other frequently used sites. Because of Britain's long-standing naval superiority, the Royal Observatory in Greenwich had historically produced and published the most accurate astronomical tables in its *Nautical Almanac*, and Greenwich had therefore become by custom one of the most frequently used first meridians for *maritime* purposes. But there remained these several other claimants to the home of time for other cartographic purposes. At the time of the 1884 Washington conference, for example, the United States Congress had for more than thirty years officially maintained *two prime meridians:* the first located at the naval observatory in Washington, which was to be used for setting time and for all astronomical and land survey purposes; and the second at Greenwich, used for nautical calculations only (Howse, 123). Several other nations, most vociferously France, looked to their own capitals as the proper location for the meridian in much the same way, sometimes using Greenwich for nautical calculations.

At the same time, many geographers had advocated a more "neutral" scientific approach that would transcend these political loyalties, invoking the Newtonian ideal that the earth be treated as "a rotary globular clock" with a universal meridian. This scheme usually situated the first meridian at a line running from pole to pole through the Atlantic Ocean at Palma in the Canary Islands, the defining point of the Renaissance prime meridian because it formed the line separating the eastern and western hemispheres. Since this line would split the continents of Europe and Africa from North and South America and passed almost entirely through ocean rather than land, it seemed to present itself as a more universal and "scientific" first meridian than those several "domestic meridians" that ran through so many national capitals and invariably invoked a kind of cultural patriotism as part of the argument for advocating them.[9] At stake in these protracted debates about establishing a universal first line of longitude in the late nineteenth century were not only the sensitive issues of national sovereignty and competitiveness but the cultural potency enjoyed by the map in modern civilization. When scientists and diplomats agreed in the 1884 conference that the identification of the prime meridian was an *imaginary* geometry determined not by science but by diplomatic treaty, they acceded to a fundamental conceptual shift from the enlightenment ideal of geographic knowledge. They admitted that the map reflects the contingencies of political circumstances at least as much as it does the facts of the physical world. Acknowledging that "prime meridians signify spatial structures which in turn signify political figurations," as M. H. Edney has put it, the delegates to the Prime Meridian Conference in 1884 embraced the idea that "the choice of a prime meridian is a political discourse"(393).

It is important to note that a number of ineffectual international gatherings had been held prior to the Washington Conference for the purpose of establishing a universal first meridian, gatherings attended primarily by scientists and geographers rather than politicians—four between 1881 and

1884 alone. The first such International Geographical Congress was held in Antwerp in 1871, and concluded by proposing that Greenwich be officially adopted as the first meridian, since it was already widely used by merchants and traders. That proposal offered as a concession to the other most obvious claimant, Paris, that the nod to Greenwich be linked to the adoption of the metric system throughout the world, seeming to admit quite explicitly that this entire question was one of political negotiation and trade-offs. The same recommendation came out of subsequent International Geographical Congresses: the one in Rome in 1875, a second in Venice in 1881, the 1883 International Geodesic Conference in Rome, and, finally, the Washington Conference of 1884.[10] One of the most immediate causes of this sudden urgency for solving the prime meridian problem and establishing a universal time system was the proliferation of the railroad throughout the world, requiring agreed-upon universal timetables in order to function effectively. But there were larger cartographic issues at stake as well.

The year of the first of these gatherings corresponded to the outbreak of the Franco-Prussian War, for example; the second with Britain's acquisition of major holdings in the Suez Canal and Victoria's being proclaimed Empress of India; and the third with the establishment of a German presence in South Africa to rival Britain's. During the same period that these conferences were being convened, London and several other European capitals would also witness international gatherings of anarchists and social revolutionaries to coordinate their efforts at overthrowing state governments. In light of the geopolitical circumstances of these events and the international realignments (and threats to nationalism) they signaled, the earlier ineffectual scientific congresses on the prime meridian made it quite clear that the question of how to map the globe would not be resolved by scientists but was a matter for politicians to negotiate.

For this reason, when the American government convened its International Conference in 1884 for the express purpose of "fixing a prime meridian and a universal day," the delegates were limited almost entirely to official diplomats and politicians rather than geographers and scientists (Malin, 203). The political and practical aspects of establishing the meridian *as opposed to* the scientific aspects of the project structured the entire debate of the Washington congress, a debate that sometimes veiled (and sometimes did not) the manifest competition between the French and British delegations on the matter. From the outset, the United States justified locating the conference in Washington, as the invitation explained, on the basis that America possessed "the greatest longitudinal extension of any country traversed by railway and telegraph lines" (Howse, 140). Notably, all North American railroads had adopted a standard time based on Greenwich time only eighteen days before the invitations to the conference were sent out, a fact that underscores how deeply the issue of establishing a universal ordering of space and time was driven by the need to foster the movement of goods and the enhancement of trade than by anything else. In his welcoming address, accordingly, the president of the conference, Admiral C. R. P. Rodgers (U.S. Navy), offered a statement of reassuring condescension to the other delegates about situating the conference in Washington: "Broad as is the area of the United States," he boasted, "vast as must be its foreign and domestic commerce, its delegation to this Congress has no desire to urge that a prime meridian shall be found within its confines."[11]

The case for Greenwich was won, finally (despite the adamant opposition of the French), on the basis of the American argument that "as a matter of economy as well as convenience" Greenwich should be selected because more than 70 percent of all the shipping of the world uses this meridian for purposes of navigation (*Protocols*, 40) (fig. 2). In opposing the motion to name Greenwich as the prime meridian, the French delegation first argued that the congress should be limited to making only the political decision of establishing *some* universal meridian, leaving the identification of naming a proper location for it to the scientists. Failing to convince on this point, the French then substituted their own motion, declaring that Greenwich was an inappropriate choice because it would be "at variance with the exclusively scientific principles which we are instructed to maintain," principles that called for a site with "a character of absolute neutrality," that would "cut no great continent—neither Europe nor America" (29, 36). Failing to win that point as well, the French then pressed the case that historically *and* scientifically, Paris had a stronger claim than Greenwich for the honor. At the conclusion of the conference, amid accusations from France (and with less zeal, Brazil) that the choice was an expression of "national rivalries" rather than geographic precision, a majority of delegates adopted Greenwich as the official site of the prime meridian and the place where the universal day would begin; and they agreed to pass this resolution on to their individual governments to be put into effect, an outcome none of the predecessor conferences could claim (47–57). French resistance to the notion has endured, as is evident in the way the French celebrated the first Bastille Day of the new millennium: by organizing a massive national *pique-nique* on the Paris Meridian; planting some ten thousand trees along the line that runs from the North Sea to the Mediterranean through the Paris Observatory, two

Fig. 2   This composite of views of the Greenwich Observatory appeared in *The Graphic* on August 8, 1885, soon after the Washington conference designated Greenwich as the prime meridian of longitude. The domestically styled exterior views in the center show the time ball that daily announced Greenwich mean time and the public clock that displayed the "real" time to the world. The framing interior views illustrate the elaborate scientific apparatus within for observing the heavens and calculating the precise time, warranting Greenwich as "the home of time." (J. R. Preston, *The Graphic*, Aug. 8, 1885. Courtesy of the Watkinson Library, Trinity College, Hartford, Conn.)

degrees, twenty minutes, and fourteen seconds east of Greenwich; and dubbing the line (in order to distinguish it from that fraudulent version) "the Green Meridian."[12]

This background forms the foundation for the combination of transnational entrepreneurial extravaganza and monument to British primordial space that became embodied in the planning for the Millennium Dome nearly a century later. As at once a precedent and counterpoint for the Dome, the Great Exhibition of 1851 is the other shadow event that this postmodern structure both invokes and deconstructs. The official purpose for the 1851 Great Exhibition had been (according to Prince Albert) "the encouragement of arts, manufactures, and commerce" through the display of "products of all quarters of the globe" expressly for the "stimulus of competition and capital" among all nations.[13] The Crystal Palace set the standard for the modern Great Exhibition and World's Fair, which, as Walter Benjamin put it, stood as "places of pilgrimage to the commodity fetish."[14] But there was an equally powerful British nationalist agenda undergirding Prince Albert's understanding of the Exhibition, an effort, as Jeffrey Auerbach has described it, to put "A Nation on Display" and demonstrate British industrial superiority to the world in dramatic fashion.[15] "It is not merely to witness the triumphs of our industry," an editorial in the *Times* claimed of the Great Exhibition, "but the still more solid and durable progress of our constitutional and social organization, that we have called all the world around us. We are the normal school of nations, and are bound, for our own sake as well as theirs, to keep the machine which we are exhibiting in good working order" (May 22, 1851, 5).

But in addition to offering the world a model for how the machinery of the nation-state should operate, Auerbach goes on to claim that "the Great Exhibition itself was a force for the creation of the Liberal party" and a symbol of "the integration of all parts of the United Kingdom" (31). Tony Blair's comparable adoption of the Dome 150 years later for the purposes of defining and symbolizing the New Britain and the New Labour party, however, makes use of this exhibition to advance the agenda of British "devolution" rather than British integration, and in doing so strategically emphasizes the importance of time over place. The Millennium Dome (according to Blair) would be designed to present an entertainment experience rather than a display of objects or industry. Accordingly, he described the Dome *not* as a place but as "a *time* for the nation to come together to be excited, entertained, moved and uplifted."[16] The emphasis upon products and territory in the Great Exhibition, organized as it was as a virtual commodity map of the world with individual exhibits displayed nation by nation, has been replaced in the new millennium by the Dome's emphasis upon experience and time in a series of entertainment events and on redefining what it means to be a nation in a world defined by spectacle and simulation. World exhibitions like the Crystal Palace had always glorified the exchange value of the commodity by creating a framework in which its use value recedes into the background, as Benjamin has argued. But the Dome functions somewhat differently and becomes the perfect embodiment of what Benjamin calls the "entertainment industry," which takes the process one step further by "elevating the person to the level of the commodity" and enhancing the sense of distraction he experiences: "he surrenders to its manipulations while enjoying his alienation from himself and others" (7) (fig. 3).

If the Great Exhibition (like the establishment of the prime meridian and home of time itself) was created as a compromise between the demands of new economic forces and old political competitions, the Dome of the

Fig. 3   This George Cruikshank illustration of "all the world going to see the Great Exhibition of 1851" seems to place the Crystal Palace itself at the prime meridian, a spectacular beacon (like the Millennium Dome that will follow) drawing the entire world to its display of commodities. (From Henry Mayhew and George Cruikshank, *1851; or The Adventures of Mr. And Mrs. Sandboys, Their Son and Daughter, Who Came Up to London to Enjoy Themselves and See the Great Exhibition* [London: D. Bogue, 1851]. Courtesy of the Watkinson Library, Trinity College, Hartford, Conn.)

Millennium enacts a postmodern version of the same conflictual issues. Since Britain's millennium project was first proposed by the conservative government under John Major as a vague celebration of British private enterprise to take place in Birmingham, most social commentators were certain that New Labour would kill the idea when Blair took office. Once the New Labour government was elected, however, Blair surprised everyone, viewing the idea as an opportunity to symbolize the New Britain that formed the central theme of his campaign and a place to stake a claim for the nation as the cutting edge of modern technology and productivity. The new prime minister instantly became an ardent champion of the project, relocating it from Birmingham to the Greenwich site on the meridian and, coincidentally, in an area of London that needed economic redevelopment. Blair awarded the design commission to architect Richard Rogers, codesigner of the Pompidou Center in Paris, the impressive skyscraper headquarters for Lloyd's insurance company, and a number of visionary architectural schemes for the City of London.

With the Crystal Palace Exhibition as his explicit model, Rogers consciously conceived of the Millennium Dome as a monument to Britain's significance in the world, if not by its domination of territory then by its control of time. He even referred to himself as the heir, architecturally speaking, of Sir Joseph Paxton, the noted Victorian designer of the controversial Crystal Palace, a design that received a level of ridicule and scorn when it was first proposed comparable to that the Dome garnered in the modern press.[17] Blair then appointed Minister without Portfolio Peter Mandelson as his "Dome Secretary" to take over arrangements for the project. Mandelson, the grandson of Herbert Morrison, who had organized the 1951 Festival of Britain (itself modeled after the Crystal Palace Exhibition of one hundred years earlier), also saw himself in the line of the producers of grand British national events and festivals. The real difficulty was that while they were both enthusiastic advocates of the Dome plan, neither Mandelson nor Rogers had any clear idea about exactly what should go into the Dome, only that there should be one.

When Mandelson flew to Disney World for inspiration on the subject, therefore, he invoked the wrath of the British populace and press, who wondered why the symbol of the New Britain should model itself after the quintessential American fantasyland. But if we understand the Dome as a celebration of the simulacrum of national sovereignty, of the nation's ghostly memory of itself rather than its actual presence, Disney World is the perfect reference point for a strategy of celebration. It would be only fitting, then, that two years later, in February of 2000, after the disappointing debut of the Dome caused its chief executive to be sacked, the person named as the new CEO of the Dome should be Pierre-Yves Gerbeau, the former executive of Disneyland Paris, formerly named EuroDisney. Offended by the combination of a direct link not only to Disney, Inc., but also to France, the British press roundly denounced the appointment and mercilessly derided Gerbeau, referring to him only as "Mickey the Gerbil." Those developments could not have been foretold (though perhaps they should have been) a few months before the Dome was to be opened, when the actual content of the Millennium experience still remained unclear. Nevertheless, at that time the governing corporation set up for the project—the New Millennium

Experience Company—announced a vague sketch of a plan that could be accessed on the web at *millennium.greenwich2000.com*. With the theme "Time for a Change" unifying the site, the plan called for twelve separate theme exhibitions or "zones" (as in time zones, later extended to fourteen) within the dome, including such exhibits as The Body Zone, Serious Play, The Spirit Level, Dreamscape, and, finally, "Trans-Action," later dubbed "The Money Zone," a place in which the visitor would "see how money and finance are changing your life." The official brochure for the Dome offers an enticing invitation to the exhibit that suggested the Dome's embodiment of the principles of global capital: "Blow a million pounds in a wild spending spree. Discover what happens when everyone else behaves that way. See how events on the other side of the world affect the cash in your bank account." In another zone, called "uk@now," visitors would be able to "decide what being British means for all our futures." Throughout, some two thousand high-tech commodities of the future called "Millennium products" were to be featured in each of the sites, invoking the commodity theme of the Great Exhibition. But in this case, the commodities were not the explicit focus of the event but served as background to the larger entertainment experience provided by the Dome itself, where a visitor could, for example, enter the Journey Zone and "take a wondrous journey from one end of existence—the Big Bang—to the present," an amusement ride, quite literally, through the history of time, which begins and ends *in this place*, where time was both born and where it resides, where history, in effect, makes its home ("Europe" travel brochure, American Express, April 1999).

In a 1998 *New Yorker* article about the Dome when it was in the process of construction, architecture critic Paul Goldberger referred to the structure simply as "The Big Top," emphasizing not only the circus-like, theme-park character planned for the structure but also the fact that it had been designed as a geometric form following form rather than as a form following any particular function.[18] Like many British critics, Goldberger lamented this plan for making London a theme park for presiding over primordial time; but he maintained his admiration for the *form* of the Dome itself, which "wants to be a pure monument," he contended, though "the present government appears to see only wastefulness in that" (158). But even in its inevitably crass celebration of commodities and empty British neojingoism, I would like to suggest that the Dome *is* a pure monument—to the idea of the nation renewing itself as a nation in the context of the new global capital. Ritualizing the movement through space as a repetition of capitalist exchange expressed in the vague discourse of unspecified nationalistic pride, the Dome is fashioned as the great emblem of what we might call postnational space, the nation as cybermemory of itself. It seemed to be offered as a palimpsestic recollection of the empire upon which the sun never set, of the Great Exhibition, of the Big Ben clock tower, of the prime meridian of the earth, and the place by which the world still sets its clocks.

Designed as an exhibition space without a specific plan for an exhibition, the Dome emerged as the perfect (and perfectly empty) signifier for controlling space by asserting control over the story of time. And it spins this tale at the very moment when the territory of the United Kingdom is less united and less of a kingdom that it has ever been. Indeed, as the title of a more recent *New York Times Magazine* article announced, "The End of Britain" is at hand, swallowed up by the European Union, the independence movements of Scotland and Wales, the gutting of the British Constitution in the current "reform" of Parliament through the strategy Blair calls "devolution," and the possible loss of its prized national currency.[19]

If the elaborate Victorian architecture of the Big Ben clock tower has stood since the middle of the nineteenth century as the icon of old Britain's timeless imperial reign, the gigantic watch face of this postmodern geodesic dome—punctuated at its circumference by twelve looming steel stanchions as if to mark the hours of the day—will stand as the New Britain's claim upon the postnational space of the twenty-first century by identifying itself as the place where time began. It marks the nation as global trademark commodity in the process of a new transaction in which the politics of money and finance are changing its life and redrawing its boundaries. At the Dome's completion, Goldberger had predicted, the structure would stand as "the world's most spectacular empty space," a place that will allow the people of the New Britain to "sustain some illusion that they possess common ground" (159). The ground they share, of course, is the dream not of a familiar place but of a remembered time. It is the memory of a time to which the British cling tenaciously (if ambivalently) as they enter a strange new world in which they may yet cash in their pounds and shillings for the universal currency of the Euro and finally abandon the nineteenth-century map of nation states for the new millennium's arrangement of economic communities (fig. 4).

In the final months of the Dome's existence, it adopted a new theme by which to define itself. Rather than "Time for a Change," it would now take as its motto "Essentially British," in an effort to bolster attendance from

Fig. 1   This view of London's Millennium Dome appeared on January 1, 2000, in the *New York Times* and other newspapers around the world. It was taken at the stroke of midnight as Greenwich time recorded the birth of the new millennium. (Hugo Philpott, used with permission and courtesy of Agence France Presse.)

the "domestic market." In this respect, the Dome remains the national monument to an essentially vanishing nation, the modern translation of Britain's nineteenth-century Crystal Palace domination over territory for its pleasure-dome-like dream of dominion over time; the dream for a time became the possession of a high-tech transnational conglomerate, then a futuristic housing project, a possible sports stadium, and finally an abandoned site once again. It seems only fitting, then, that the Dome of the Millennium, this globelike structure poised at the so-called center of the world and offering itself as the so-called home of time, may be best remembered for its starring role in the opening sequence of the 1999 James Bond film, so aptly signaling the insufficiency of space as a category for domination in its all-too-fitting title: *The World Is Not Enough.*

Notes

1. Warren Hoge, "Where Time Begins, a Millennium Pleasure Dome," *New York Times,* July 28, 1997, A-4.
    2. Ibid.

3. *Financial Times,* London Edition, Dec. 20, 2000, 2. That plan, like several others that preceded and followed, came to naught, and the site at this writing remains abandoned.

4. See *Observer,* Jan. 9, 2000, 13; *Times* (London), Feb. 22, 2000; *New York Times,* Feb. 18, 2000, 1.

5. Michael Specter, "The Blunderdome," *New Yorker,* Jan. 29, 2001, 46–51.

6. Dava Sobel, *Longitude: The True Story of a Lone Genius Who Solved the Greatest Scientific Problem of His Time* (New York: Walker and Co., 1995): 39–40.

7. Derek Howse, *Greenwich Time and the Discovery of the Longitude* (New York: Oxford University Press, 1980), 87.

8. David Harvey, "Between Space and Time: Reflections on the Geographical Imagination," *Annals of the Association of American Geographers* 80 (1990): 427.

9. Matthew H. Edney, "Cartographic Culture and Nationalism in the Early United States: Benjamin Vaughn and the Choice for a Prime Meridian, 1811," *Journal of Historical Geography* 20 (1994): 387.

10. S. R. Malin, "The International Prime Meridian Conference," *Journal of Navigation* 12 (1985): 203.

11. *Protocols of the Proceedings of the International Conference Held at Washington for the Purpose of Fixing a Prime Meridian and a Universal Day* (Washington, D.C.: Gibson Brothers, 1884), 6.

12. *Washington Post,* July 15, 2000, A14.

13. Quoted by Theodore Martin, *Life of the Prince Consort,* 2 vols. (New York: D. Appleton and Company, 1877), 2:205.

14. Walter Benjamin, *The Arcades Project,* trans. Howard Eiland and Kevin McLaughlin (Cambridge: Harvard University Press, 1999), 7.

15. Jeffrey A. Auerbach, *The Great Exhibition of 1851: A Nation on Display* (New Haven and London: Yale University Press, 1999), 31.

16. Quotation attributed to Tony Blair on the Greenwich Millennium Dome website: www.londonnet.co.uk./ln/guide/about/dome.html.

17. See Asa Briggs's account of the reaction to the Crystal Palace in *Victorian People: A Reassessment of Persons and Themes, 1851–1867* (Chicago: University of Chicago Press, 1955), 35–37. The popular reaction to Paxton's structure, notably, was much more generous than that of the critics and the press.

18. Paul Goldberger, "The Big Top," *The New Yorker,* Apr. 27 and May 4, 1998, 152–59.

19. Andrew Sullivan, "The End of Britain," *New York Times Magazine,* February 1999, 39–78. See 70, 78.

PART 2

Victorian Commodities for Postmodern Consumers

The New Victorians

MIRIAM BAILIN

The following quotation from a book of wallpaper samples called "The New Victorians" is typical of the marketing of the so-called Victorian Revival in home decorating:

> Who are the New Victorians? "We are," Cynthia explains. "Everything is changing, just as it did a century ago, and like the Victorians, we have a real need to feel anchored in family. And home sweet home. The Victorians did a wonderful job creating an oasis in the home, and today we are too. I've tried to translate this sensibility into my designs. . . . romantic, comfortable, lush and not afraid to mix and match."[1]

There are at least five mass-circulation magazines and scores of websites capitalizing on recent consumer interest in the material comforts and what is invariably called the graciousness and elegance of Victorian taste. Builders and architects now cater to period living by specializing in retrofitting and restoration, and innumerable shops and specialized suppliers offer period advice and reproduction features like moldings and stained glass, tiles, fabrics, and wallpapers. The advertising and editorial copy that accompanies the marketing and promoting of Victorian decor and furnishings tends to emphasize our similarity to the Victorians and at the same time to insist on an irreducible

difference that guarantees charm; there is nothing alien in this borrowed
past and at the same time nothing smacking of the world that's too much
with us. One shop, for instance, is billed as a place "where the past feels like
the day before yesterday." An article in *Victorian Homes* on "late-Victorian
shopping" notes that "it's that curious familiarity across the century that
accounts for the bond so many of us feel for 19th-century life."[2] The website for *Wings and Roses*—purveyor of period garments for everyday
wear—declares that its merchandise is "for those of us who wish to return
to a gentler more romantic time," while the ad for the magazine *Victoria*
begins: "Return to Graciousness with Victoria, endearing fashions, a touch
of lace. Old-fashioned delights. The charm of yesteryear. . . . Let us take you
to a time when elegance and graciousness touched every part of your life."[3]
It is in the unexpected insertion of the pronoun "your" and the repeated use
of "return" in such copy generally that this romantic, elegant, gracious,
serene, mellow, and above all "quiet" past is rendered retrievable—retrievable because it exists in a space that is neither history nor lived experience
but rather a neutral "timelessness" of imputed essences—enduring friend-
ship, the magic of childhood, the romance of moneyed leisure. It seems
hardly necessary to point out that the "romantic, comfortable, lush, and
not afraid to mix and match" sensibility touted by the Victoriana trade is
largely a creature of contemporary nostalgia for the not here and not now.
It is not difficult to find contrary accounts of Victorian decor against which
to juxtapose these plangent tributes to "bygone times." I will content myself
for the purposes of contrast with this quotation from H. G. Wells's description of a gentleman's study in his novel *Kipps:*

> It was a gaunt, Victorian room, with a heavy, dirty cornice, and the
> ceiling enriched by the radiant plaster ornament of an obliterated gas
> chandelier. It held two large glass-fronted bookcases, one of which
> was surmounted by a stuffed terrier encased in glass. There was a
> mirror over the mantel, and hangings and curtains of magnificent
> crimson patternings. On the mantel were a huge black clock of
> classical design, vases in the Burslem Etruscan style, spills and tooth-
> picks in large receptacles of carved rock, large lava ash-trays, and an
> exceptionally big box of matches. The fender was very great and
> brassy.[4]

It is, of course, that terrier under glass that strikes one most forcibly in this
description of a typically furnished Victorian room. But lest you think
Wells is having us on, the stuffed or skinned household pet was, in fact, a

frequent feature of mid-Victorian decor. In *Beetons Household Treasury* of
the 1870s there comes this description of a bedroom: "In the room the skin
of a favorite brown setter of Irish breed lay before the washstand in perfect
harmony and keeping with the time-tempered browns of the bedside carpet."[5] And that's not even mentioning the much-favored stuffed grizzly
bear that served as a card rack stand in many a Victorian entrance hall.
Taxidermy was one of the crafts that women were encouraged to take up
as a hobby along with such things as waxwork and photograph painting.
In a home handicrafts manual of 1863 one finds this tip on stuffing small
birds: "after taking out the entrails open a passage to the brain which
must be scooped out through the mouth."[6] A "gentler and more romantic
time" indeed.

The Wells passage not only reminds us that the typical Victorian middle-
class interior could appall as well as charm, and that the past is decidedly
not like the day before yesterday, but also that the rosy glow shed over the
age by today's Victoriana buffs is quite a recent phenomenon, dated most
often from the early 1980s. Invective was rather the order of Wells's anti-
Victorian day, but throughout the first half of our century the interest in
Victorian things was decidedly a minority taste. Even those who wrote on
Victoriana from the 1930s through the 1960s did so in the same apologetic
tone with which books on Tennyson used so often to begin. Ralph Dutton
writes in *The Victorian Home* (1954), "it is necessary to search carefully
amidst much that offends and dazes to find the scattered features which are
rewarding," finally concluding that "the charms of the Victorian age are
mental rather than visual" (4).

The usual brief against Victorian decor was that it was altogether too
much of a good, and more often of a vulgar, thing. Vita Sackville-West writes
of the older Victorian style in her novel *The Edwardians:* "There were too
many chairs, too many hassocks, too many small tables, too much pampas
grass in crane-necked vases, too many blinds and curtains looped and fes-
tooned about the window—the overmantel bore its load of ornaments on
each bracket, the mantel-shelf itself was decked with a strip of damask
heavily fringed."[7] Even contemporary observers, such as Thackeray, found
the middle-class drawing room an occasional object of satire:

> But what could equal the chaste splendor of the drawing room? . . .
> about the room were high chairs, bandy-legged chairs . . . marqueterie
> tables covered with marvellous gimcracks, china ornaments of all ages
> and countries, bronzes, gilt daggers, Books of Beauty, yataghans,

Turkish papooshes and boxes of Parisian bonbons. Wherever you sat
down there were Dresden shepherds and shepherdesses convenient
at your elbow; light blue poodles and ducks and cocks and hens in
porcelain; there were nymphs by Boucher and shepherdesses by
Greuze, very chaste indeed.[8]

Such superabundance was, however, actively encouraged by many Victorian
guides to taste. Harriet Spofford pronounces in her *Art of Decoration
Applied to Furniture:* "provided there is enough space to move about without walking over the furniture, there is hardly likely to be too much within
the room."[9] Although by the last two decades of the century the trend was
toward simplification, more often than not the exhortation to simplify usually meant that elaboration moved from one aspect of house design to
another, to, for instance, "the richly ornamented collector's ambience" of
the late-Victorian "artistic home."[10] The prevailing taste was for an excess
of ornamentation, dim lighting, dark colors, heavy draperies; size, opulence, and quantity were the order of the day. The effect was, in Ralph
Dutton's phrase, "crowded and crepuscular" (145). And though Gordon
Roe wrote *Victorian Corners* to aid collectors of Victoriana, he confesses,
"to put it bluntly, I have written in this book of persons and things I
admire, and of persons and things in whose company I would not choose
to be found dead."[11] According to Walter Benjamin, however, being "found
dead" is the only imaginable stance to take in high Victorian interiors. As
he puts it in his essay "One-Way Street," the "bourgeois interior of the
1860s to the 1890s, with its gigantic sideboard distended with carvings, the
sunless corners where palms stand, the balcony embattled behind its
balustrade, and the long corridors with their singing gas flames, fittingly
houses only the corpse."[12]

The homes of both the upper-middle classes and the aspiring middle
classes were built for display, for a highly formal and routinized social
life—morning At-Homes, afternoon teas, elaborate dinner parties. "There
was a rule for everything," Virginia Woolf noted in "A Mark on the Wall":
"The rule for tablecloths at that particular period was that they should be
made of tapestry with little yellow compartments marked upon them. . . .
Tablecloths of a different kind were not real tablecloths."[13] The Georgian
ideal of proportion "succumbed to the pretensions and increase in scale
that marked the aggrandizement of the Victorian era"—reflecting the social aspirations and anxieties of the newly rich or in the case of the landed
aristocracy the need to distinguish themselves from the steadily encroach-
ing parvenus (Gere, 67). Floor plans were determined by the demands of

respectability and status and the correspondent need to segregate the household inhabitants. Houses were divided by class hierarchy, by gender, by age. Rooms, corridors, and entrances multiplied to keep upper servants from lower, servants separate from family or guests, children from adults, men from women. Those middle-class homeowners who strove to emulate more affluent models on a much smaller scale had to endure dark, narrow passageways, small rooms, and uncomfortable makeshift arrangements. On the other end of the social spectrum, the English country house, for all its manifest splendor, was, in David Cannadine's words, often "cold, gloomy, eerie, filthy, smelly and insanitary."[14] And of course the maintenance of these large, crowded, and inconveniently laid-out homes rested on the battalions of servants who dusted and swept and black-leaded and hewed and carried and polished. Lady Dorothy Nevill recalls in her memoir "that no less than six men were kept constantly employed at nothing else but looking after the [oil] lamps" at Belvoir Castle (quoted in Gere, 54). In *The Country House Remembered*, Lady Mander writes that Wightwick, her Victorian country house, was "a monument to Victorian standards of conspicuous inconvenience, which meant that it was prestigious to make no concessions to easy running."[15] The gradual trend toward a relative austerity in home furnishings and more convenient floor plans was as much the result of a gradual revolution in taste as it was a response to the emergence of what became known in the periodical press as the servantless household.

If the past does feel like the day before yesterday, then the similarities clearly do not lie in the cultural motives and design priorities of the Victorians themselves but in the very technical and commercial developments that today's aficionados of yesteryear seek to escape or ignore. It is to the Victorians that we owe the mass manufacture of household goods and cheap decorative materials and the development of new processes that made possible "the adaptation of even the most exotic aspirations" to the convenience of the domestic consumer (Gere, 54). The label "machine-made" had its historical moment as an encomium, much as "store-bought" had in midcentury America (Dutton, 146). The greater sophistication and efficiency in the marketing and distribution of manufactured goods made the furnishing and refurnishing of homes easier and more desirable. The enormous increase in books and periodicals providing advice in home decor to insecure consumers led to an emphasis on decorating as a measure of the successful wife—an emphasis that the journalistic practices of women's magazines did much to create and exploit. These publications, as Margaret

Beetham points out in *A Magazine of Her Own,* encouraged and benefited from the presentation of commodities "not simply as made objects but as objects with 'value,'" with "a measure of cultural and symbolic worth" distinct from their function.[16] And in a turn of events that has been most fully realized by the period decor magazines of our own era, the 1880s saw the rise of the practice of sending the reader to named shops or suppliers. According to Beetham, "brand-name products sold nationally began to take over from small-scale locally produced goods," enabling more extensive advertising and more investment in advertising to control a greater share of the market (146). Periodicals like *Home Chat, Queen,* and *Hearth and Home,* and books like *Cassells Household Guide* and Mrs. Haweis's *The Art of Interior Decoration,* kept people up-to-date, directed them to suppliers, and instructed them on taste, thus producing a pattern of consumption that we can all recognize: they aroused anxiety and provided the means to overcome it. Some of the women who provided consultation on furnishing and decoration, in books or through correspondence columns in periodicals, would even travel to the homes of individual buyers to give advice.[17] The readers of periodicals for women came to be addressed first and foremost as consumers, a merging of identities that was repeatedly underscored by the gradual merging of editorial content and advertisements.

These aspects of modern life and consumer capitalism are what most enduringly form "that curious familiarity across the century." Our connection to the Victorians may, in short, be attributed to their marketing and manufacturing ingenuity rather than in a shared taste for cretonne, rep, and lincrusta. And it is finally, in a minor but salient irony, the nineteenth-century invention and promotion of labor-saving devices and new technologies that have allowed us to indulge our own taste in the past, just as they did for the Victorians. The nostalgic re-creation of the elaborately furnished and decorated interior of the nineteenth century would have been unthinkable without the introduction of such amenities as central heating, double-glazed windows, and thermostatically controlled boilers, which, in Raphael Samuel's words, "at a stroke turned large rooms into comfortable living spaces and transformed the servantless, uneconomic mansion into a potential family home."[18] Here again we simply follow in the footsteps of the Victorians, whose own penchant for revivalism, for baronial interiors in new houses, for instance, was enabled by industrial advances and technological know-how.[19]

The marketing challenge of those magazines that celebrate the romance and serenity of the past, so far from our "fast-paced world," is how to make their own origins and reliance on commerce seem fully compatible with the authenticating values of tradition—how to achieve, in other words, what *Victoria Magazine* calls "the perfect marriage of entrepreneurship and reverence for the past." The contemporary world constructed by these magazines in response to this essential contradiction is one of small businesses that have grown out of hobbies and pastimes shared by families and linked to the past. One woman makes angels out of shells she has gathered on the beach with her eleven-year-old daughter, which, we are informed, are now in many family collections. From my hobby to your heritage, as it were. More often than not the businesses are owned and operated by husbands and wives we are invited to meet in their own picture-perfect homes—Tim and Carol, Kate and Joe, Alan and Francis, Tricia and Gary who met at a flea market, who share a taste for calligraphy or for refurbishing old furniture, and who now find themselves with forty stores nationwide (for shopping information see p. 118). A seminar offered by *Victoria* and sponsored by Apple Computer and Mary Kay, Inc., is called "Turning Your Passion into Profit" (Nov. 1997). An article on a designer of "vintage" clothing proclaims, "Kevin's hobby turned into a business by popular demand" (*Victoria,* Aug. 1997). Or there's the owner and restorer of a Victorian home who can't find the right door furniture and ends up opening his own business to provide it for others in his predicament.[20]

The emphasis is most often on the personal, the individual, the creative production, use, or collection of the purely aleatory and incidental—no market research here. Hobbyists find the decorative in the neglected accumulations of everyday life, or even better, of someone else's everyday life. And it is in such accumulations and their recovery I think that one finds another sustaining link between Victorian domestic life and current preoccupations—in the combination of acquisitiveness and amplitude that might be called, using Derek Walcott's wonderful phrase about the nineteenth-century novel, "an appetite for inventory."[21] The raw material for indulging this appetite is readily found in the hyperbolic abundance of Victorian things. Tea caddies, card cases, candle-shades, handkerchief cases, hat brushes, penwipers, needle books, pincushions, hair tidies, watch pockets, netting boxes, key baskets, letter cases, blotting books, handbells, paper knives, forkrests, fire screens, door-porters, foot-scrapers, napkin rings, scrap-albums, watchstands, inkblotters, doilies, and antimacassars, all of them decorated by the lady of the house with seedwork, beadwork, conework, shellwork, hairwork, waxwork, leather work, and burnt work. For the most part ornamental clutter in their own day, these objects have provided the inexhaustible inventory of artifacts in our own, to be collected and reclaimed, itemized and pored over, authenticated, photographed, reproduced, and displayed. Belonging to another time and to other circumstances, and thus ineluctably value-laden, they also have the talismanic power to evoke whatever we long for as if it were something we've lost. "Collecting Memories" is the apt title of a feature story in *Victoria* (Nov. 1997). Whereas the revivalism of the Victorian age itself was predicated on the self-confident adaptation of antique styles and cultural borrowings to new things and requirements with the emphasis on the original and the "brand-new," the current mania for reproduction and revival is characterized by a reverent attachment to the past as aura and ideal. In the more serious period magazines this takes the form of a painstaking attention to detail and authenticity in the refurbishment or reproduction of period homes and fittings; in the more mainstream "lifestyle" magazines the emphasis is on the quality that Walter Benjamin called, with specific reference to the deep and velvety enclosure of nineteenth-century interiors, "dwelling."[22]

The stock-in-trade of period marketing and of the appetite for inventory it taps is, at bottom, the promise of redemption experienced in the mute and glorious certainty of the material realm. It is, perhaps, this aspect of what the British call "heritage" that accounts for its popularity across class and political lines. Disinterred from contexts that once marked people according to a hierarchy of taste and privilege, of nationality and class, the miscellaneous "things"—a doorknob, a piece of lace, old playing cards— that circulate from auction to thrift shop to website are "collectibles," not commodities. As Raphael Samuel argues, "heritage offers an ideal home which is defined not by pedigree but by period, and which can be decked out with make-believe family heirlooms" (246–47).[23]

In a curious example of transference, the process of redemption is seen as reciprocal. A recurrent narrative found in all of the publications for the devotee of Victorian household decor and furnishings is of things, crafts, collections, ways of life that have been lost, scattered, or left to decay, that are then retrieved, restored, resituated. They are, like us the readers, "returned." Things "live" in drawers and "wait" to be discovered. In one shop the owner "creates starring roles for the oddments so often left layered in the drawers and trunks of our lives" (*Victoria,* Jan. 1994). She sells pillows stitched from found bits of a child's dress, a bureau scarf, old linens. One store makes jewelry from old, broken china and another sells handbags made from old, discarded frames found in thrift shops, auctions, and estate sales. The emphasis is often on remnants, fragments, oddments made suddenly meaningful through the act of discovery and incorporation. The owner of a vintage fabric store tells readers that fine swatches can "pop" out of a drawer or be found in the family attic. Neglected old homes are lovingly and painstakingly restored to their original state.

All of these stories of salvage and their implications are epitomized by an article in *Victoria* recounting the story of Alice Austen, the daughter of a leading Staten Island family and an amateur photographer of the leisurely and opulent life of the nineteenth-century country house. Alice, over the course of the years, loses her family, house, objects, and photographic plates (we are not told how), and the 1940s find her living in poverty and silence. "But the story didn't end there" the article continues after this brief whiff of desuetude. The plates are found, developed, published, exhibited. The home she lost becomes a museum and the things in it searched for and restored to their original places. Even Alice herself is retrieved from the poorhouse, restored to peak condition, and celebrated in her great old age.[24]

There is in this fantasy of retrieval something not unlike that stuffed terrier under glass, despite my earlier use of it to exemplify Victorian otherness. The beloved pet becomes, through a special kind of transmutation, not a dead pet but a cherished object. The neglected and impoverished woman is "restored" and commemorated in a museum bearing her name. In our disposable culture, the ability to transform the discarded objects of another century into the "found" treasures of our own may offer some reassurance that here, at least, in the perdurable world of things, all is not lost.

Notes

1. "The New Victorians," Imperial Home Decor Group, marketing copy.
2. *Victorian Homes*, 1994 (issue unknown).
3. Http://www.wingsandroses.com. The *Victoria* copy appears in each issue of the magazine.
4. H. G. Wells, *Kipps: The Story of Simple Soul* (London: J. M. Dent, 1993), 112–13.
5. Ralph Dutton, *The Victorian Home: Some Aspects of Nineteenth-Century Taste and Manners* (London: B. T. Batsford, Ltd., 1954), 135.
6. L. B. Urbino, et al., *Art Recreations* (Boston: J. E. Tilton and Co., 1863), 260.
7. Vita Sackville-West, *The Edwardians* (London: Hogarth Press, 1960), 132–33.
8. William Makepeace Thackeray, *The History of Pendennis* (New York: Scribners, 1917), 429–30. I am indebted for this quotation to Thad Logan, "Decorating Domestic Space," in *Keeping the Victorian House*, ed. Vanessa Dickerson (New York: Garland, 1995), 221–22.
9. *Art of Decoration Applied to Furniture* (1878). Quoted in Judith and Martin Miller, *Victorian Style* (London: Mitchell Beazley International, 1993), 139.
10. Charlotte Gere, *Nineteenth-Century Decoration: The Art of the Interior* (New York: Harry N. Abrams, 1989), 18.
11. F. Gordon Roe, *Victorian Corners: The Style and Taste of an Era* (London: George Allen and Unwin, 1968), 13.

12. Walter Benjamin, *Reflections,* ed. Peter Demetz, trans. Edmund Jephcott (New York: Schocken, 1978), 64.

13. Virginia Woolf, *A Haunted House and Other Stories* (New York: Harcourt, Brace, 1994), 41.

14. David Cannadine, *The Pleasures of the Past* (New York: W. W. Norton and Co., 1989), 101.

15. Lady Mander, *The Country House Remembered,* ed. Merlin Waterson (London: Routledge & Kegan Paul, 1985), 136.

16. Margaret Beetham, *A Magazine of Her Own* (London: Routledge, 1996), 146.

17. Nicholas Cooper, *The Opulent Eye* (London: Architectural Press, 1976), 8.

18. Raphael Samuel, *Theatres of Memory* (London: Verso, 1994), 76.

19. Charles Newton, *Victorian Designs for the Home* (London: V&A Publications, 1999), 8.

20. A how-to manual of crafts from 1910 gives the hobby-to-career angle of contemporary Victoriana journalism a different perspective: "the author has endeavoured to show how certain crafts may be done quietly in the home by mother or daughter, in town or country, as a relaxation, and to drive away the dreariness that comes from a lack of congenial occupations, or as a means of earning money." Mabel Tuke Priestman, *Handicrafts in the Home* (London: Methuen & Co. Ltd., 1910), 1.

21. Derek Walcott, "Signs," in *The Bounty* (New York: Farrar, Straus and Giroux, 1997), 20.

22. Walter Benjamin, "Convolute I: The Interior, The Trace," in *The Arcades Project,* trans. Howard Eiland and Kevin McLaughlin (Cambridge: Belknap Press, 1999), 220.

23. The "escape from class" that Raphael Samuel sees in the heritage movement (246) is not, however, absolute. Peter Howell, chairman of the Victorian Society, offers this bit of advice to those contemplating period restoration: "It is to be hoped that those restoring Victorian houses will respect the social hierarchy. . . . those living in Mr. Pooters modest home should not aspire to the greater luxury of houses decorated by Robert Tressells." "Ragged Trousered Philanthropist," *The Victorian House Catalogue* (New York: Sterling Publishing, 1992), 6.

24. The article about Alice Austen appeared in *Victoria* in 1994. Issues from that year are no longer available, so I was unable to specify the date of the story. In another of the ironies I have encountered in writing this article, in an effort to trace the month the story appeared I looked up Alice Austen on the Internet and discovered that many of the sites devoted to her, as distinct from the Alice Austen Museum on Staten Island, are lesbian sites. The story in *Victoria* failed to mention that Austen is now celebrated as a "lesbian icon" by those less interested in poignant stories of Victorian retrieval.

More Stories about Clothing and Furniture

Realism and Bad Commodities

ELLEN BAYUK ROSENMAN

Surveying her tasteful home, newly redecorated by the architect Owen Jones, George Eliot remarks with satisfaction and relief that Jones "has determined every detail so that we can have the pleasure of admiring what is our own without vanity."[1] Pleased with the beauty of her surroundings, Eliot is nonetheless suspicious of her investment in "what is our own," associating it with a disturbing self-promotion. In her private ambivalence, Eliot voices one of the central problems of the realist novel, the public discourse she helped to construct: how to relate to commodities. Certainly one defining feature of this genre is its faithful rendering of the objects of domestic space—its "forensic attention to the tangible components of the environment at hand," the writing desks and muslin gowns that crowd every scene.[2] Indeed, the home life that the realist novel seems designed to celebrate is inseparable from its material markers.[3] But if the realist novel depends on objects, a second defining feature is its ambivalence about those objects. I want to explore the representational strategies by which the novel attempts to disavow what Eliot calls vanity and to distance itself from the commodities that, of necessity, it furnishes itself, with specific attention to those "bad" commodities—clothing and furniture—that are associated with women. Then I want to consider the translation of this material culture, modern films and television, whose claims to high-cultural status redefine these commodities and the relationship between gender and genre.

The novel's uneasy, many-sided relationship to commodities is well documented.[4] As works of art, novels undergo a process of "singularization" that defines them as "singular, unique, unexchangeable"; the aesthetic value of *Adam Bede* cannot be quantified or measured objectively against that of *Dombey and Son*.[5] And, with their humanistic values, Victorian novels critiqued a burgeoning materialistic culture. But at the same time, they were also mass-produced, bought, sold, marketed, and distributed like any other commercial object; indeed, their emergence as the premier literary form of the period depended on advances in print and paper technology, on the rise of advertising, and on new distribution networks. Facing "their own implication in what they opposed," novels dwelled on commodification as a central, unresolved theme:

> In the narrative form of these texts one can see most clearly the complicated set of attitudes, conscious and unconscious, entertained by writers about the process of commodification—and one can also see most clearly the fundamental significance of those attitudes for our understanding of the Victorian novel.[6]

When we pick up the hint Eliot drops in the word "vanity," with its special application to women, we see a further complication. In negotiating their position between art and intellectual critique on the one hand, and commodity culture on the other, novelists contended with the interrelated gendering of commodities and fiction. Prototypical consumers, women were understood as "natural" shopping experts and as addicts consumed by the desire for more things.[7] Moreover, since women were responsible for managing the signifiers of bourgeois identity, as many critics have argued, then an intimate knowledge of these signifiers is a gendered knowledge.[8] When G. H. Lewes derided the "detailism" of realist art forms that slavishly described waistcoats rather than illuminating character or dwelling on philosophical abstractions, he subtly implicated the genre in the trivialities of everyday life that are women's special province, as feminist critics have noted.[9] The link between private life, commodities, and women gives novels a hybrid identity: they are part high art and cultural critique but also work hand in glove with conduct books, fashion plates, and women's magazines to feed consumer desire. Eliot herself makes this judgment, though she abjects it onto a specific kind of fiction: the "Silly Novels by Lady Novelists" that gives her famous essay its title. For their sin of yoking together philosophy and material culture, Eliot dubs them "mind-and-millinery" novels, neatly capturing their hybridity.[10] Purveying the delights of fashionable clothes and accessories, these novels provide the guilty pleasure of "knowing that [the heroine's] sorrows are wept into embroidered pocket-handkerchiefs, [and that] her fainting form reclines on the very best upholstery" (141). Writing on the eve of her career as a serious novelist, Eliot is eager to distance herself from the feminine coding of commodity-filled fiction.

Eliot's examples are not random. She identifies two key areas in which the stakes of commodity-worship are especially high: women's clothing and furniture. The decoration of self and home engage most directly the commodity fetishism from which the novel, no less than Eliot, attempts to distance itself. These are two areas in which female vanity displays itself most brazenly, as women arrange their appearance and their surroundings to garner admiration, declare their social position, and advertise their personal worth. Precisely because they are so obviously linked to female consumption, clothing and furniture preoccupy novelists and often form the ground on which novels stake their claim to high art. Novels relentlessly critique characters who know and care too much about these objects, implicitly declaring a superior detachment. Moreover, by censuring certain kinds of clothing and furniture—the fashionable, the nouveau riche, the ostentatious—novels mark them off as bad commodities, mis-valued objects with illusory appeal that betray the bad taste of their admirers. Then other objects can be rescued from commodity status and represented in such a way that their appeal seems genuine and timeless, reflecting the good taste of the characters who possess them, the reader who admires them, and the novel that has created its fiction world from them. The category of bad commodities allows "good" objects to define themselves by contrast, to flourish without implicating the novel in the female vanity of commodity fetishism.

We can see one strategy for repudiating commodities in Trollope's *The Way We Live Now*, in which Paul Montague tries to disengage himself from Mrs. Hurtle, the seductive American adventuress. Mrs. Hurtle has dressed to perfection in a simple black dress, knowing that "There are times . . . in which a man would prefer that his companion should be very quiet in her dress—but still pretty; in which he would choose that she should dress herself for him only. All this Mrs. Hurtle understood accurately; and Paul Montague, who understood nothing of it, was gratified."[11] Unlike the hapless Paul, the narrator is knowledgeable enough about the semiotics of women's clothing to demystify them. But he cannot know too much. While he can convey the effect of Mrs. Hurtle's costume precisely, he does not describe the costume itself but instead repeats the generic tags "simple" and "pretty," identifying the dress's material as "a fabric which the milliners I think call grenadine" (214). I call this strategy "under-detailing." Its purpose is to disavow the fetishistic interest of the fashion expert. To specify the fabric, or cut, or trim would be to align the narrator with Mrs. Hurtle, or—even worse—with her milliner. While he must know the material culture of his world, including the degraded category of women's dress, the narrator cannot know too much without betraying an embarrassing overinvestment, as if he is taking women's clothing as seriously as women take it themselves.

A similar moment occurs in Eliot's *Middlemarch,* when the narrator remarks, "Let those who know tell us exactly what stuff it was that Dorothea wore."[12] While the narrator declares her ignorance, the servant Tantripp dwells on the tasteful design of Dorothea's half-mourning costume: "three folds at the bottom of your skirt and a plain quilling on your bonnet—and if ever anyone looked like an angel, it's you in net quilling" (847). Detailed sartorial knowledge is left to milliners and servants, whose gender and class both permit and are signified by their obsession with the technicalities of fashion. In fact, there is no quicker way to vulgarize a character than to align her taste with the professional eye of the milliner. In Wilkie Collins's *Basil,* the social-climbing Margaret Sherwin describes clothing in "exact millinery language," a vocabulary that her suitor, the aristocratic Basil, does not deign to repeat,[13] while Rosamond Vincy's elegant outfit is "so perfect that no dressmaker could look at it without emotion" (*Middlemarch,* 471). Abjecting knowledge of fashion onto servants and milliners serves two purposes. First, this knowledge serves as a status marker, not only displaying the inferiority of these working-class women but also damning ambitious, middle-class women by association, identifying them with their inferiors and invalidating their claims to social distinction. Second, while novels distance themselves from fashion knowledge by stigmatizing it with these class-and-gender markings, working-class experts serve as middlemen—or women—by providing details about beautiful clothes without directly implicating the novel in them. Thus Tantripp obligingly takes responsibility for counting the folds on a skirt or noticing how becoming a half-mourning outfit might be, while readers who would not stoop to such vulgarity can filter their interest in Dorothea's appearance through a lower-class female surrogate.

Underdetailing is also part of another technique: the promotion of an aesthetic of simplicity. To furnish one's home or to dress simply, no matter how conscious the effort or how becoming the effect, is to display one's lack of vanity, one's indifference to making an impression, and therefore one's moral superiority to fashionable people. Thus, the aesthetic of simplicity is presented as if it were categorically outside the realm of fashion rather than a stylistic preference within it. Gaskell's *North and South* employs this aesthetic in its description of the homey drawing room of the genteel Hales, in contrast to that of the nouveau-riche Mrs. Thornton, "twenty times as fine; [but] not one quarter as comfortable."[14] This conventional contrast is so ubiquitous that it simply seems right: of course it is better to furnish a room for comfort and use than to stuff it full of expensive, shiny baubles. But at the same time the Hales' simplicity makes its effect, and it does so in part because of the narrator's spare depiction. As with Mrs. Hurtle's outfit, almost nothing is described in its particularity; instead, the room is composed of

> a warm, sober breadth of colouring, well relieved by the dear old Helstone chintz-curtains and chair covers. An open davenport stood by the window opposite the door; in the other there was a stand, with a tall white china vase from which drooped wreaths of English ivy, pale-green birch, and copper-coloured beech leaves. . . . Behind the door was another table, decked out for tea, with a white tablecloth, on which flourished the cocoa-nut cakes, and a basket piled with oranges and ruddy American apples, heaped on leaves. (79)

There is no mention of style, size, or color, except for the white vase and tablecloth; a brightly patterned cloth, the chintz is never given a color or design. Only the ivy and the fruits appear in any detail, foregrounded by their rich hues. In contrast, Mrs. Thornton's drawing room is described with attention to color and design: "The walls were pink and gold; the pattern on the carpet represented bunches of flowers on a light ground" (112).

Here, underdetailing exempts the Hales from fetishizing their own decor, implying that it is somehow not composed of specific pieces of furniture, and particular fabrics and colors, that had to be chosen and purchased with the idea of their effect in mind. In the absence of detail, the room seems to consist primarily of ivy and apples. These descriptions advance a fragile contrast between good and bad drawing rooms, good and bad davenports, good and bad color schemes, the loving creation of a home and the style-conscious purchase of commodities. The narrator must give

the Hales a drawing room, but it must seem to be a different *kind* of drawing room from that of the Thorntons, one whose individual furnishings are
subsumed in a general feeling of comfort. It is as if articulating any single
object would distract readers into considering whether they liked the Hales'
taste, dismantling the home and turning it into a kind of furniture showroom. The lure of desirable furniture—simple as well as ornate—threatens
to overwhelm the novel's moral scheme and collapse the careful distinction
between these two domestic spaces.

   This anxiety is even more acute in Eliot's *Middlemarch*. The famous
opening sentence of the novel proper complicates the meaning of women's
dress, layering attitudes and motivations until Dorothea's clothing *as* clothing nearly disappears. As everyone knows, "Miss Brooke had that kind of
beauty which seems to be thrown into relief by poor dress" (29). While this
statement leaves no doubt that Dorothea favors—and is favored by—the
aesthetic of simplicity, the rest of the paragraph places her appearance in a
series of contexts apart from contemporary fashion, and indeed apart from
clothing at all. Her "plain garments" resemble "a fine quotation from the
Bible," with sleeves "not less bare of style"—an interesting formulation—
than those of Madonnas in Renaissance paintings (29). In contrast, what
Eliot disdainfully calls "provincial fashion" evokes the slick, up-to-the-
minute trendiness of "to-day's newspaper" (29). Next, we discover that
Dorothea's gentle birth causes her to regard finery as "the ambition of the
huckster's daughter" (29). Her own desire to look like a gentleman's daughter through plain dress is not seen as "ambition" but as the lack of ambition, a refusal to jockey for social position, while at the same time it
establishes her superiority, marking her as a subtle, expert reader of fashion codes who knows that the aesthetic of simplicity best conveys an elevated class status. Last, we are told, Dorothea's religious fervor makes her
suspicious of ornament. Dorothea's stylistic choices are removed from the
realm of style, with its implications of superficiality and built-in obsoles-
cence, and placed in older, weightier traditions of art, religion, and nobility.
Moreover, while Dorothea is entirely innocent of any desire to promote her
own beauty, her outfit is sublimely becoming. To dress like the Madonna of
an Italian master is not exactly to be "bare of style." Here the narrator
serves as a middleman for Dorothea, dressing her to perfection while
exempting her from the charge of vanity.[15]

   But, for all her notorious brutality toward fashion-conscious women,
Eliot does not entirely disavow the appeal of commodities; rather, she
thematizes her ambivalence in Dorothea's own ambivalent rejection of her

mother's jewels. Taken by their beauty, Dorothea spiritualizes them as "fragments of heaven," much as Eliot spiritualizes her heroine (35). But then she remembers that they are commodities—precisely commodities, in the sense of having exchange value, when she thinks, "'Yet what miserable men find such things, and work at them, and sell them!'" (36). These jewels are the perfect figure for the potential doubleness of objects: they have undergone Kopytoff's process of "singularization" as a unique family inheritance, yet, as Dorothea realizes, this does not absolutely exempt them from being fungible objects that can be—and have been—bought and sold. In fact, Kopytoff uses the example of the heirloom to point out the fluidity of the art/commodity relationship, arguing that an object can move back and forth between these categories at different points in its "biography" and even occupy both categories at once, depending on the beholder. Dorothea's ambivalence about the jewels acknowledges the difficulty of asserting the categorical distinction between good and bad objects—exactly the distinction the novel attempts in describing Dorothea's plain dress.

This ambivalence also reveals Eliot's distinctive understanding of the dangers of commodities. Of all my examples, this episode comes closest to the classic understanding of commodity fetishism as a process that draws desire to objects, endowing them with symbolic power. Marx variously called this power "metaphysical," "mystical," "fantastic," and "magic" to evoke the extraordinary psychic investments people make in things, well beyond their actual use value (82, 82, 83, 87), while Wolfgang Haug explicitly treats commodities as sexual fetishes, arguing that "commodities borrow their aesthetic language from human courtship," flirting with their human admirers.[16] While for Trollope and Gaskell domestic objects are implicated in the maneuvering for social position, Eliot discerns what is perhaps a deeper potential, since it goes to the heart of subjectivity: the ability, at once horrifying and enlarging, to set erotic energy in motion. Thus the gems unlock a "new current of feeling" in Dorothea: "'It is strange how deeply colours seem to penetrate one, like scent'" she remarks, before she disparages her attraction to them (35). Just as she repudiates horseback riding because it gives her so much pleasure, Dorothea suspends her sensuality by putting aside the jewels—a suspension that is undone when she finds the proper object, a man. Eliot reverses the process Haug describes, looping commodity fetishism into romantic love by channeling this "current of feeling" into Dorothea's fervent response to Will Ladislaw. When lightning flashes illuminate the scene in which they declare their love, the power of the gems seems directly naturalized into passion.[17] In a sense, then, Eliot grants objects their mystical power, regarding them as repositories of human desire that, though misdirected, is also potentially productive. In Eliot, commodity-worship undergirds social climbing, as it does in Trollope and Gaskell, but it also models erotic love.

What becomes of these novels when the twentieth century takes them up in films and television shows? Most obviously, adaptations serve a particular function: to stand as an oasis of art within the wasteland of popular culture, understood as mass-produced entertainment designed first and foremost with market considerations in mind. Conceived in terms of previous commercial successes (the "Pretty Woman meets E.T.!" mentality parodied in Altman's film *The Player*), test-marketed on focus groups, obsessed with the bottom line, popular films and their market orientation have been criticized as the antithesis of original art. In contrast, adaptations of Victorian novels borrow the cachet of their literary sources to claim a higher cultural standard: they are seen as providing "a certain intellectual and visual sophistication" and cater to a "patrician" audience.[18] Ironically, in view of its own struggles with commodity-fetishism, the Victorian realist novel invokes an ideal art that stands outside the marketplace. These novels supply contemporary films and television programs with a comforting if inaccurate frame through which to protest the commodification of mainstream television and film.

In such productions, objects are sacred; they stand for history. If the physical world of the period has been faithfully (or better yet, obsessively) re-created, the integrity of the past has been fully realized. Setting *Middlemarch* in the quaint town of Stamford, a good match for 1830s Middlemarch, still required the BBC to disguise front-door mailboxes, which did not come into being until—prepare for a shocking anachronism—the 1840s.[19] Who would know such information except a small handful of Victorian scholars? Authenticity resides in material culture, a belief that exalts the objects of everyday life to high-art status. Women's clothing no longer falls within the realm of fashion; instead, it has become a museum piece, dignified by the simple fact that it existed in the past. (In fact, the costumes for the BBC's *Pride and Prejudice* literally did so when they joined touring exhibits of authentic historical costumes from museum collections.)[20] Such an attitude makes a fetish of every stick of furniture, every article of clothing, every front door. As Andrew Higson argues in his trenchant critique of "heritage films," adaptations function to provide "a space for the display of heritage properties" in which objects, even more than characters and action, catch the camera's eye.[21] At the same time, the assumptions that foreground them aesthetically also relegate them to the background of narrative. Frozen as tokens of history and high art, they are no longer problematic; removed from issues of ethics and class conflict, they require no special representation strategies. Reducing history to a collection of beautiful period objects, adaptations flatten out the novels' uneasiness about lush commodities in the lush production values that recreate the past with indiscriminate reverence.

Adaptations do honor novels' thematic distinctions between good and bad clothes while eliding representational ambivalence. In *Middlemarch,* for instance, Dorothea is dramatically set off from the other female characters by that fashion oxymoron, the natural look. While Eliot framed her clothing in the past with the invocation of Renaissance Madonnas, the adaptation lifts her out of her own period and the now-ism of fashion by making her look modern. Her simple hairstyle is a natural-looking upsweep, in contrast to the stiff curls that adorn every other female character; even Mary Garth has a fancier 'do. And, however simply she is dressed, Dorothea is always in perfect color harmony with her environment, whether wearing a snow-white nightgown in a pastel bedroom, a deep russet-colored dress in Casaubon's wood-paneled study, or a quiet gray cloak in the dim hovel of a tenant farmer. Favoring brighter hues, Rosamond the fashion plate often clashes with the wallpaper, wearing a tangerine gown in a blue room to signify her lack of real taste and real heart. Here, the production designer is the middleman, arranging Dorothea so that she always appears to best advantage. But this packaging is simply an atavistic trace of its original. Unlike the novel, this opulent *Middlemarch* has no anxieties about its beautiful images. Indeed, it manages to make even poverty attractive, for while the tenant farm is nearly empty, it is beautifully color-coordinated, as the farmer's collar perfectly matches the ticking on his ragged mattress.

In such a visually pleasing, exquisitely detailed world, how could Dorothea's snow-white nightgown and pale blue bedroom be anything but objects of desire? As Higson observes, these productions appeal, in part, by offering "a fantasy of conspicuous consumption" (113). Precisely because they appropriate the high-cultural status of literature and gesture so emphatically toward historical accuracy, adaptations authorize viewers to feast on such beautiful furnishings without guilt or anxiety. Dignified by the edification promised by such productions, viewers can also indulge in the less admissible pleasure of virtual shopping. The interiors these works serve up are so artfully burnished and framed that they might be displayed in upscale catalogs that capitalize on our modern taste for retro styles, harvesting the past for items that signify not the rejection of materialistic values but wealth, leisure, and self-indulgence. Admirers of Dorothea's bedroom can purchase a similar setting from *Exposures,* which promises to "transform your bedroom into a visual and personal paradise."[22] The BBC *Middlemarch* is just a step away from the furniture showroom so feared by Gaskell. If novels suggest that some objects are exempt from the commodity circuit, these modern contexts insist that even tasteful objects have their price. Neither bed comes cheap: the *Exposures* bed, canopy, duvet cover, dust ruffle, and organdy overlay (described as a "nice accent" at $179) cost over $1,700, plus $95 shipping, while *Middlemarch* was repeatedly noted as the most expensive BBC production ever, as if its cost automatically signified quality.[23] Its forerunner in the "most-expensive" category, the 1987 version of Thackeray's *Vanity Fair,* was unself-consciously praised in completely commodified terms, as a "product" with a "price tag," distinguished by its conspicuous cost:

> The BBC is set to spend like never before—coughing up a whopping 8 million pounds for a lavish new production. The price tag of the 16-part adaptation of the classic *Vanity Fair* is believed to make it one of the costliest British products ever.[24]

Genuflecting to the past with their expensive production values, adaptations are breathlessly described as "sumptuous," "lavish," and "opulent."[25] It is precisely this opulence that is assumed to represent their superiority. Reflecting on recent productions of Jane Austen novels, one critic, himself the screenwriter for a television version of *Clarissa,* observes with obvious ambivalence, "her style [is] visually translated into production values."[26] Performing the magic that Marx describes, material luxuries are used to express the cultural substance associated with canonical literature. In a further irony, the novel's aesthetic of simplicity has been trumped by *nouveau riche* standards of taste.

Selling the past as a succession of beautiful objects has provoked a backlash that recapitulates the troubled gendering of commodities in the original novels. The celebration of bad commodities also implicates films in a disdained (if lucrative) cultural category, the "woman's picture."[27] In other words, modern adaptations elide Victorian ambivalence toward commodities only to have it return in the politics of reception. In this backlash, adaptations are not high-art enough precisely because they appeal to a "female-based audience" with their emphasis on the decor of Victorian culture.[28] All of these objects are conflated with women's clothing in the pejorative term "costume drama"—also known as "bonnet drama" and "Big Frock" drama, to clarify exactly whose clothing is being sniffed at (Kavanaugh, 86, 87). Likewise, *The New Statesman* chooses as its mocking synecdoches for expensive production values "tastefully lit crinolines," "the rustling of skirts and the rattling of teacups," manifesting a properly modernist, Prufrockian contempt for the whole "women's" culture of such productions and their originals: not only clothing and furniture but the world of the drawing room and social life.[29] Such reviews tend to consider BBC productions in particular as a specific kind of "woman's picture," the soap opera.[30]

Sometimes this contempt washes back over the novel itself. One review proudly exposes the "soap-operaish quality" of the novel *Middlemarch,* which is "disguised from all but the most penetrating critics"—not including the author of the review, of course ("Nixon," 55). Another accuses *Middlemarch* of not being dramatic at all, consisting of "an excess of minute psychological analysis" rather than the sweeping action and "elan" of Stendhal's *The Red and the Black,* another recent adaptation. What *Middlemarch* has going for it, according to this reviewer, is its "soap value": "in-fighting, gossip, marital breakdown and failing medical services, in which everyone is related to, or owes money to, or is being blackmailed by, everyone else" (Baldick, 33). The willful misogyny of this assessment can be measured against Virginia Woolf's *A Room of One's Own,* published in 1929. In her famous literary history, Woolf seems to affirm the reviewer's critique, comparing Eliot's limited experience to the freedom enjoyed by Tolstoy, who, as a man, had access to a vast historical stage of travel, war, and unfettered sexual adventure.[31] With her particular gifts and ambitions, Woolf speculates, Eliot might have been a better writer if she had been able to live on a wider scale. But Woolf also questions the value judgment implicit in the privileging of male over female experience: "Speaking crudely, football and sport are 'important'; the worship of fashion, the buying of clothes 'trivial'" (74). By now, this argument is commonplace for any feminist critic, but it seems not to have reached Baldick, who insists on innate superiority of history's "elan" over the "unhistoric acts" of Eliot's heroine (*Middlemarch,* 896). In his formulation, Eliot herself belongs not to the tradition of canonical fiction, whose proper representative is Stendhal, but to television: in writing *Middlemarch,* "she . . . became the godmother of 'Neighbors' [an Australian soap opera]" (Baldick, 33). This is Eliot's worst nightmare: to have her writing gendered feminine and absorbed into popular culture, a silly novel by a lady novelist. Thus, the ambivalence of Victorian novels becomes split into two opposing camps of reviewers: the reverential admirers, for whom Victorian clothing is exalted into history, and the haute-intellectual critics, for whom it is synonymous with—and degraded into—women's culture.

When I read Victorian novels—especially Eliot novels, so damning of fashionable women when their noble heroines are just as fetching, thanks to Eliot's keen eye for striking costumes—I sometimes resent their presentation of clothing and furniture as a kind of bad faith. But adaptations such as *Middlemarch* remind me that ambivalence is also a form of complexity. The novels I have discussed enact the hybrid position of the modern intellectual, whose job is to critique commodity culture but who also stands inside it, and not always unwillingly. The defensiveness of these novels insists that the desire for things is deep and compelling, and not only for others with bad taste and bad values. Eliot's gratitude for the middleman Owen Jones and her representation of Dorothea's infatuation with emeralds compel attention because they imply a self-critique as well as a critique of culture—something that is lost in the gorgeous television *Middlemarch*. The ease with which all clothing and furniture becomes fully commodified in modern adaptations suggests the fragility, even the deludedness, of the novels' original distinctions, but also a greater wariness and sensitivity about issues of consumption and culture.

The example of Eliot also reminds us that women in particular occupy that conflicted position. As college professors, we are tied to the antimaterialist values of the university but recognize that to repudiate bad commodities is to participate in the misogyny that has structured these values at least since the emergence of the "public sphere" of disinterested, rational discourse. Feminist critics have argued that this sphere fashioned itself in contrast to the feminine, defined as "pleasure, play, eroticism, artifice, style, politesse, refined facades, and particularity" (a version of the "detailism" with which Lewes charged the realist novel).[32] These critics have usefully exposed the ways in which, "bracketing" social differences to encourage the free exchange of ideas, this arena actually masked and perpetuated inequalities instead; what Nancy Fraser calls "unequally valued cultural styles" remain marginalized (120). Fraser remarks, "In most cases it would be better to *unbracket* inequalities in the sense of explicitly thematizing them" (120).

The idea of unbracketing underlies the dramatic self-presentation of an "intellectual woman in patriarchy," to quote Deirdre David's felicitous phrase:

Her height was good, her figure remarkably supple; at moments it had an almost serpentine grace . . . she used to wear black velvet, then seldom adopted by unmarried ladies. I can see her descending the great staircase of our house in Savile Row (afterwards the Stafford club), on my father's arm, the only lady, except my mother, among the group of remarkable men, politicians, and authors of the first literary rank. She would talk and laugh softly, and look up into my father's face respectfully, while the light of the great hall-lamp shone on the waving masses of her hair, and the black velvet fell in folds about her feet.[33]

This seductive charmer in the drop-dead black velvet dress is George Eliot herself, dressing for effect as she crashes the serious-male party. While I suspect that most readers identify Eliot with her noble, educated heroines— Dorothea Brooke or Romola, for instance—the characteristics of her co-quettes are eerily mapped onto her body: the serpentine grace, the flowing hair (she particularly criticizes the heroines of "Silly Novels" for their "redundant locks"), the killing outfit.[34] This moment reinforces the impression that the conflict between the feminine world of women's clothes and the masculine world of intellectual discourse was a live one for Eliot, continually refigured in her pairing of coquettes and noble women: Hetty and Dinah in *Adam Bede,* Dorothea and Rosamond in *Middlemarch,* Gwendolen and Mirah in *Daniel Deronda.* Eliot's dismissive attitude toward her coquettes— so trivial, pixielike, and puny in their aspirations—and her visible contempt for women's culture so ably dissected by Langland seem to simplify the conflict by brushing aside clothing, jewelry, and furniture as so much girl-ish detritus. But Dorothea's movement from jewelry to love and Eliot's own self-fashioning as a brainy femme fatale subtly recuperate the discarded feminine, unbracketing the gender dissonance of the "intellectual woman in patriarchy." If critics of *Middlemarch* can still express their condescen-sion with terms such as "soap value" sixty-five years after Virginia Woolf's critique of literary sexism, clothing and furniture remain highly politicized objects through which women's "unequally valued cultural styles" assert themselves. It is not surprising that Eliot's self-presentation has found its own modern "adaptations" in the self-conscious glamour of power and "do-me" feminists.[35] That these fashion statements confuse, distress, and offend their audiences (myself included) points directly to the unresolved tensions that cluster around women's clothing as a cultural signifier.

A rich site for cultural conflict, bad commodities force us to reckon with the exclusions and hierarchies that underwrite our gender identities, our class allegiances, our cultural aspirations, our tastes, our pleasures. When they submerge these issues in beautiful facades, modern adaptations eviscerate one of the most challenging aspects of Victorian novels. Of course, film is a different medium with its own representational strategies, which should not be expected to duplicate linguistic worlds. Its dominating visual register cannot avoid fetishizing beautiful objects—a perverse project even if it could be achieved. But even this difference might serve a productive ambivalence: used self-consciously to highlight the fetishizing of commodities, it might thread a vein of discomfort through the viewer's enjoyment, sustaining one function of Victorian novels into the present time: not to resolve these tensions in some ideal, untroubled purity but to model self-reflection, to hold up a mirror—that endlessly recurring trope for female vanity—to our own divided selves.[36]

Notes

The title of this chapter is used with apologies to the Talking Heads.

1. George Eliot, *Letters*, ed. Gordon Haight, 9 vols. (New Haven: Yale University Press, 1954–78), 4:124.

2. Katherine Kearns, *Nineteenth-Century Literary Realism: Through the Looking Glass* (Cambridge: Cambridge University Press, 1996), 11.

3. See, for example, Karen Chase and Michael Levenson, *The Spectacle of Intimacy: A Public Life for the Victorian Family* (Princeton: Princeton University Press, 2000), on the "ever increasing profusion of domestic signs" that articulate domestic values in culture and fiction (89).

4. See, for example, Terry Lovell, *Consuming Fiction* (London: Verso, 1987), 19–46, and Jonathan Freedman, *Professions of Taste: Henry James, British Aestheticism, and Commodity Culture* (Stanford: Stanford University Press, 1990). For discussions of Dickens see Jennifer Wicke, *Advertising Fictions: Literature, Advertisement, and Social Reading* (New York: Cornell University Press, 1988); David E. Musselwhite, *Parts Welded Together: Politics and Desire in the Nineteenth-Century English Novel* (London: Methuen, 1987); and N. N. Feltes, *Modes of Production in Victorian Novels* (Chicago: University of Chicago Press, 1986); and see Feltes and Daniel Cottom, *Social Figures: George Eliot, Social History, and Literary Representation* (Minneapolis: University of Minnesota Press, 1987) on Eliot. For a discussion of the antimaterialistic ethos of Victorian intellectuals, see Regenia Gagnier, *The Insatiability of Human Wants: Economics and Aesthetics in Market Society* (Chicago: University of Chicago Press, 2000), 27–40.

5. Igor Kopytoff, "The Cultural Biography of Things: Commoditization as Process," *The Social Life of Things: Commodities in Cultural Perspective* (Cambridge: Cambridge University Press, 1986), 73, 69.

6. Andrew H. Miller, *Novels Behind Glass: Commodity Culture and Victorian Narrative* (Cambridge: Cambridge University Press, 1995), 7.

7. Erika Diane Rappaport, *Shopping for Pleasure: Women in the Making of London's West End* (Princeton: Princeton University Press, 2000), 5. See also Lori Anne Loeb, *Consuming*

Angels: Advertising and Victorian Women (Oxford: Oxford University Press, 1994), and Lovell.

8. See Nancy Armstrong, *Desire and Domestic Fiction: A Political History of the Novel* (New York and Oxford: Oxford University Press, 1987); Elizabeth Langland, *Nobody's Angels: Middle-Class Women and Domestic Ideology in Victorian Culture* (Ithaca: Cornell University Press, 1995); Leonore Davidoff and Catherine Hall, *Family Fortunes: Men and Women of the English Middle Class, 1780–1850* (Chicago: University of Chicago Press, 1987); and Loeb.

9. George Henry Lewes, *Principles of Success in Literature* (Boston: Allyn and Bacon, 1891), 83. The genealogy of this argument includes Naomi Schor, *Reading in Detail: Aesthetics and the Feminine* (New York: Methuen, 1987), Laurie Langbauer, *Women and Romance: The Consolations of Gender in the English Novel* (Ithaca: Cornell University Press, 1990), and Langland.

10. George Eliot, "Silly Novels by Lady Novelists," *Selected Essays, Poems, and Other Writings*, ed. A. S. Byatt and Nicholas Warren (London: Penguin, 1990), 140.

11. Anthony Trollope, *The Way We Live Now* (London: Penguin, 1994), 214–15.

12. George Eliot, *Middlemarch* (London: Penguin, 1965), 470.

13. Wilkie Collins, *Basil* (Oxford: Oxford University Press, 1990), 107.

14. Elizabeth Gaskell, *North and South* (Oxford: Oxford University Press, 1982), 78–79.

15. While I depend on Miller's analysis of novels and commodities, I disagree with his reading of *Middlemarch* in general and of this paragraph in particular. While he understands Dorothea's third, "personal" rejection of finery as "quickly and firmly" subordinating the merely "social factors" advanced by the narrator, I see no such distinction; all three exempt Dorothea from concern about clothing while assuring the reader of her impeccable appearance (193). My interpretation of Eliot's representation of clothing and women's culture is much closer to Langland's critique.

16. Karl Marx, *Capital: A Critique of Political Economy*, vol. 1: *The Process of Capitalist Production*, trans. Samuel Moore and Edward Aveling (Chicago: Charles Kerr and Co., 1908), 82–83, 87; Wolfgang Haug, *Critique of Commodity Aesthetics: Appearance, Sexuality, and Advertising in Capitalist Society*, trans. Robert Bock (Minneapolis: University of Minnesota Press, 1986), 17.

17. I don't want to suggest an extended pattern of imagery at work here, but it is clear that Dorothea's puritanical impulses early in the novel, symbolized in part by her repudiation of the jewels and of riding, are happily undone by her love for Will, who is consistently described in terms of light and brightness (see for instance the "gush of inward light" that illuminates his smile [237]). It is perhaps worth noting that the lightning-enhanced love scene is a forerunner of Lou Christie's classic hit "Rhapsody in the Rain."

18. Andrew Higson critiques this appeal to "literary culture and the canons of good taste" ("Re-presenting the National Past: Nostalgia and Pastiche in the Heritage Film," *Fires Were Started: British Cinema and Thatcherism* [Minneapolis: University of Minnesota Press, 1993], 110). I have lumped together these adaptations where a British audience might make distinctions. BBC-1 productions, such as *Vanity Fair*, are seen as lighter fare than BBC-2 productions, such as *Middlemarch*. Moreover, since I address American viewers, I have omitted the significant dimension of Higson's argument that focuses on the political context of Thatcher's Britain. See, too, Betsy Sharkey, "Patron of the Arts," *Mediaweek*, Jan. 1, 1996, 18, and Michael Kavanaugh, "Is Costume Drama Going Out of Style?" *Electronic Media*, Jan. 19, 1998, 86.

19. Ros Drinkwater, "On Location: Middlemarch," *In Britain* 151, no. 5202 (Mar. 1997): 26.

20. Imelda Whelehan, "Adaptations: The Contemporary Dilemmas," *Adaptations: From Text to Screen, Screen to Text*, ed. Deborah Cartmell and Imelda Whelehan (London: Routledge, 1999), 14.

21. See Higson's fascinating description of the camera work of the Merchant-Ivory film *A*

Room with a View: "Lucy, the ostensible focus of *narrative* interest, sits in the background, while artifacts and furnishings fill and frame the foreground; the camera gracefully, but without narrative motivation, tracks slowly around one splendid item of furniture to reveal it in all its glory" (117).

22. *Exposures Homes Catalogue,* Spring 2001, 9.

23. Harry F. Waters, "By George, We've Got It," *Newsweek,* Apr. 11, 1994, 70; Mick Imlah, "Let's Hear it for Casaubon," *Times Literary Supplement,* Feb. 4, 1994, 17; Louis Menard, "Eliot without Tears," *New York Review of Books,* May 12, 1994, 5; and Sharkey, 18.

24. *Star,* Mar. 21, 1987, qtd. in Robert Giddings, Keith Selby, and Chris Wensley, *Screening the Novel: The Theory and Practice of Literary Dramatization* (New York: St. Martin's Press, 1990), 162.

25. "Sumptuous": Waters, 70; David Hiltbrand, "Picks and Pans," *People,* Apr. 11, 1994, 16. "Lavish": "Television Winners," *Broadcasting and Cable,* May 11, 1998, 12; John J. Connor, "Trollope's Novels Stylishly Produced," *New York Times,* Jan. 30, 1977, sec. 2, p. 29. "Opulent": Waters, 70; Imlah, 17; Lewis Segal, "Television," *Los Angeles Times,* Jan. 31, 1977, sec. 4, p. 12.

26. David Nokes, "It Isn't in the Book," *Times Literary Supplement,* Apr. 26, 1996, 12.

27. "Dressed to Shoot," *Sight and Sound* 4, no. 2 (Feb. 1994): 3.

28. Ibid., 3.

29. Christopher Baldick, "Middlemarch," *New Statesman and Society,* Jan. 14, 1994, 33.

30. Sally Beauman, "Encounters with George Eliot," *New Yorker,* Apr. 18, 1994, 86; John Leonard, "Middling," *New York Magazine,* Apr. 11, 1994, 60; "Nixon and 'Middlemarch': New Versions for the 90's," *New Criterion* 12, no. 10 (June 1994): 55.

31. Virginia Woolf, *A Room of One's Own* (New York: Harcourt Brace Jovanovich, 1981), 70–71.

32. See Joan B. Landes, *Women and the Public Sphere in the Age of the French Revolution* (Ithaca: Cornell University Press, 1988), 46. Landes's analysis is specific to the rise of the public sphere in France as a consciously fashioned alternative to feminized salon culture, but her general points are relevant in other contexts. See Nancy Fraser, "Rethinking the Public Sphere: A Contribution to the Critique of Actually Existing Democracy," in *Habermas and the Public Sphere,* ed. Craig Calhoun (Cambridge, Mass.: MIT Press, 1992), 120, quoted here, and Geoff Eley, "Nations, Publics, and Political Cultures: Placing Habermas in the Nineteenth Century," in Calhoun, 307–19.

33. Bessie Rayner (Parkes) Belloc, *In a Walled Garden* (London: Ward and Downey, 1895), 16–18.

34. Note the "undulations" of Rosamund's figure in *Middlemarch* (139) and Gwendolen's Lamia-like grace in *Daniel Deronda* (London: Penguin, 1967), 11.

35. I can still remember my elation at seeing Jane Gallop deliver an address at conference in the early 1980s, where she wore a black cocktail dress, heavy makeup, and dangling earrings (though Gallop might not accept the designation "power feminist").

36. The example I have in mind, of course, is Scorcese's *Age of Innocence,* which frames jewelry in extreme close-ups and unceasingly tracks the beautiful objects in every room with its mobile, restless camera.

PART 3

The Ways Victorians Live Now

Wilde Americana

JESSE MATZ

Gay historiography singles out 1895 as its watershed year. That was the year of the Wilde trials, which, according to the influential account derived from Foucault, invented homosexual identity. Prior to 1895 same-sex desire expressed itself in *acts:* there were not homosexuals as such, but just homosexual things that people did. Then in 1895 Wilde's conviction gave an identity to these acts, personifying homosexuality. Ever after, for better and for worse, the homosexual was a type—a type to be reviled, disciplined, or exalted, outlawed or (eventually) sold as a lifestyle.

Many now contest this account, most notably David Halperin, whose 1998 "Forgetting Foucault: Acts, Identities, and the History of Sexuality" rejects any such radical epistemic break and says Foucault himself never really thought it had occurred. Whereas the account that makes 1895 a watershed moment and Wilde a pivotal figure would have us believe that one could not have been a homosexual before or indulge in simply homosexual acts after, the revisionist account disallows any such clear distinction between identities and acts. Moreover, it disputes the manicheanism of the identities/acts account, by refusing to believe either that identity meant the salvation of same-sex desire or that it meant its ruin. The identities/acts account tends at once to deplore the way the identity model restricts homosexual possibility and to exalt the way it made homosexual culture possible. The revisionist account, by contrast, wants more subtle descriptions, not only of the history of homosexuality but of its structure.

It is not simply the case, then, that the new gay historiography rejects paradigm shifts and epistemes; rather, it wants these to take more nuanced forms, and it wants them to eschew the extremes of paranoia and advocacy into which they have tended to fall. But how to take this more nuanced, less extreme approach to Wilde and what he represents? These terms themselves hardly seem apt; Wilde has been such a magnet for radical-break arguments because of his own radicality, and his flamboyance and his fate make it hard to place him in any very nuanced version of gay history.

But I think we might put Wilde in his place by focusing our attention on another year: not 1895, but 1882, when Wilde had not yet become the very figure of radical breakage—indeed, when he was only just learning how to become a person who could *personify*. I think we might place Wilde into a better version of gay history by saying more precisely *how* he came upon his power to personify homosexuality, to the extent that he does, and by finding a less manichean way to describe what the Wildean persona means for gay identity today.

I want to fix our attention on 1882 not because the year marks a radical break but because it marks a crossing. In 1882, Wilde went on tour in America, to teach America about art. But he also learned how to do business, from a culture that had just begun to redefine the relations among business, culture, and personhood. Crossing America in 1882, Wilde crossed paths with a Supreme Court case that would give corporations the rights of persons. In this combination (the early combination of Wilde's aspirations and America's corporations) we get the conditions that would enable Wilde to personify homosexuality—conditions that not only made him what he was but continue to manufacture gay identity at the present time.

Wilde went to America with three goals: to publicize *Patience,* by giving America an example of the sort of aesthete the play parodies; to make some money; and to spread a fairly simplistic aesthetic gospel. Beyond his employer's use for him he hoped to beautify what he thought would be a country misled by the pursuit of wealth, and he hoped to get some wealth himself, in order to enrich his own notorious pursuit of the beautiful. His hopes were dashed, however, when it turned out that Americans were just then trashing the mode of aesthetic production Wilde had hoped to promote. Whereas his own compatriots were perhaps primed for the "English Renaissance of Art" by years of mechanical reproduction, Americans had only just begun their glad escape from the sort of hands-on, unalienated, artful living to which Wilde wanted to return. They could not hear with enthusiasm Wilde's glorification of "hewers of wood and drawers of water," having too recently been hewers and drawers themselves.[1] As one assessment had it, "the Aesthete had come to preach handicraft arts to a people who regarded their own handicraft arts as tedious, boorish, and old-fashioned . . . unworthy to be compared with the new marvels of science, invention, and mechanism."[2] Wilde had not known that the Aesthetic would sound, to many of his listeners, like work, and that its opposite, the mechanizing materialism Wilde deplored, had just become the path to pleasure. What ready aesthetes existed (and there were many already caught up in some version of the aesthetic craze) were most often elites interested mainly in knowing the latest thing from London or sensation-seekers interested mainly in flashy spectacle; what open minds there were wanted by contrast to fill their heads with dreams of a modern future.

Wilde quickly adapted, though, and in the way he adapted we see the changes that would have such impact on the nature of gay identity. Rather than fight American materialism, he learned what it could do for art; he who came to teach, learned—specifically, that commerce could be beautiful. As his friend Robert Sherard put it, "America had taken the nonsense out of him . . . [brought him] into contact with the most energetic of men, roused his latent energy, sharpened and stimulated him to a degree that made him almost unrecognizable. . . . The dealings he had with men, the struggles both social and commercial in which he had, in the main, triumphed, had given him experience which years of life in London might never have afforded. He had a sound commercial training" (Lewis and Smith, 443). These last words are key. Wilde got "sound commercial training": he came to America a derivative aesthete who mumbled a message unsuited to its audience, but left a man of commerce and became a marketing genius. That he was one is of course well known, for no one more than Wilde represents the advent of public relations, or the coming of the culture impresario. Less well known, however, is the way a specifically American proto-corporate culture taught Wilde business, and the way Wilde's commercial training in America set the pattern for the combination of corporate and personal identities that informs gay identity today.

What was this specifically American proto-corporate culture? Much might be said about nineteenth-century commercialism and its relation to the arts and to people like Wilde, but I have in mind the more specific thing called the "doctrine of corporate personhood." In 1882, the Southern Pacific Railroad neglected to pay taxes in the amount of $13,366.53 to

Santa Clara County. The county's efforts to recover the money led to the Supreme Court case that, infamously, conferred upon corporations the rights of persons—the right, specifically, of "equal protection" against taxation. Extending the fourteenth amendment and the equal-protection clause to corporate bodies, the court unleashed the massive growth in corporate power that today characterizes the more threatening aspects of globality. But the courts also affirmed what we might call a *chiasmus of corporate and minority personhood*, a change in the very nature of personhood crucial not only to the rise of corporate power but to the history of gay identity.

In *Santa Clara County v. Southern Pacific Railroad* (1886), the defense mounted a number of justifications, but one in particular set an astonishing precedent:

> That the provisions of the constitution and laws of California, in respect to the assessment for taxation of the property of railway corporations operating railroads in more than one county, are in violation of the fourteenth amendment of the constitution, in so far as they require the assessment of their property at its full money value, without making deduction, as in the case of railroads operating in one county, and of other corporations, and of natural persons, for the value of the mortgages covering the property assessed; thus imposing upon the defendant unequal burdens, and to that extent denying to it the equal protection of the laws.

What is now so astonishing about this argument (and the precedent it sets) is that it makes a constitutional provision meant to protect minority rights a means of corporate deregulation. The fourteenth amendment was of course designed to see to it that ex-slaves did not lose rights of citizenship in the way laws were locally and specifically administered. But by claiming, successfully, that corporations were also entitled to equal protection, the defense in *Santa Clara County v. Southern Pacific Railroad* abrogated to strong corporate entities the rights of weak minority persons, effecting a base reversal of corporate and minority identities. Symbolically remarkable, the result also had real-world chiasmic results, as the distinction between persons and corporations and their respective cultural priorities got blurred—as corporate culture began its long successful appropriation of the personal and its peculiar tendency to poach upon the distinctions afforded to the particular persons of minority culture.

Proof that this chiasmus characterized the culture from which Wilde learned business appears in the ease with which the court accepted the doctrine of corporate personhood. As David Korten points out in his *The Post-Corporate World: Life after Capitalism,* the doctrine was "introduced into this 1886 decision without argument": "according to the official case record, Supreme Court Justice Morrison Remnick Waite simply pronounced before the beginning of argument . . . that 'the court does not wish to hear argument on the question whether the provision of the fourteenth Amendment to the Constitution, which forbids a State to deny to any person within its jurisdiction the equal protection of the laws, applied to these corporations.' We are all of the opinion that it does."[3] Implied in the court's opinion is a readiness on the part of the larger culture to extend the personal into the corporate—to encourage the growth of corporate power by imagining it to be a personal prerogative, and thereby also to allow that persons define themselves according to commercial negotiation.

The problem here has been amply explained in recent efforts to roll back extensions of global corporate power. Representative of a new critique of capitalism in this vein are Thomas Frank's *One Market under God: Extreme Capitalism, Market Populism, and the End of Economic Democracy* (New York: Doubleday, 2000), and Kalle Lasn's *Culture Jam: How to Reverse America's Suicidal Consumer Binge—And Why We Must* (New York: Quill, 1999). Frank and Lasn decry a late result of the doctrine of corporate personhood: the fact that it is by now unquestioned that the "market" best serves human need—that we vote with our pocketbooks, express ourselves through our consumer choices, and expect that this mode of political participation outweighs in efficiency and accuracy any sort of voting we might do by conventional means. Both Frank and Lasn trace the ascendancy of this "market populism" to *Santa Clara County v. Southern Pacific Railroad,* noting that our current total faith in markets could not have happened were their corporate masters not endowed, long ago, with the powers necessary to outstrip government control and, moreover, to justify their powers through appeals to personhood. Frank and Lasn note the irony at work in the fact that corporations gained their power through a constitutional amendment designed expressly to protect the rights of the disenfranchised. Were they to have extended their sense of this irony to insight into its necessity—had they, in other words, recognized that the chiasmus of corporate and minority identities was to no small extent the absurdist logic upon which "market populism" is based—they might have noted the special significance of figures like Oscar Wilde.

So what exactly did Wilde learn, in his "sound commercial education," from the culture so ready to confuse corporations and persons? I think

Wilde learned, first, that it didn't matter what he said: perhaps the strangest thing about the response Wilde got from America is the way America made him out to be so much more than what he was. What he said was unremarkable, and often unhearable; as Jonathan Freedman notes, "Americans were by and large disappointed with Wilde, in part because he delivered his lectures so indifferently, in part because he dressed like an English gentleman, not an Bunthornian aesthete, and in part because, far from bringing Americans anything new, Wilde preached the familiar Ruskinian gospel of the moral value of art, especially the moral importance of handicrafts."[4] Nevertheless, oddly, Wilde was well received, despite the irrelevance of his message and the indifference of his manner. "Americans did not hesitate to recreate Wilde in their image of him" (Freedman, 102); and Wilde seems therefore to have learned that the message hardly mattered: he saw that his aesthetic gospel fell on ears bored by it or gladly deafened by the commercial machine, but then he saw that he could become more beautiful as a part of that machine itself. Wilde sold in spite of himself; this is what he learned, a lesson perhaps best represented by an advertisement that ran in the local Savannah newspapers on July 8, 1882: "Oscar Wilde could not please the Savannah public, but Jacob Cohen of 152 Broughton Street can, as he has sent us since being in New York, the best and cheapest assortment of DRY and FANCY GOOD ever seen" (Lewis and Smith, 373). Such an ad, in addition to those more directly using Wilde to sell things, consolidated an identity that made personality marketable. It reflects the way Wilde's persona could detach from his intentions and become at once figurative and commercial. And if we recall that Wilde then made this form of detachment a means to market himself—if we recall, that is, what Jonathan Freedman and others have told us about the strong connections among aestheticism, commodity culture, and the "culture of professionalism" (55)—we might consider the doctrine of corporate personhood the best context in which to understand the sort of personification that would later enable Wilde to circulate as an identity.

We might, in other words, fill in some of the prehistory to the trials. No longer would the trials seem to have invented homosexual identity out of instant public discipline; rather, they would have behind them a history in which that means of personification prepared itself, according to the corporate model of indistinction between persons and things. Moreover, we might fill in some subsequent history here in a fashion similarly more attentive to the specific problems of personal identity in corporate culture. Much more pertinent to the current state of gay identity than anything that went on in Wilde's trials is what went on before them, insofar as gay identity is ever more conditioned by corporate selfhood. Seeing how Wilde himself was thusly conditioned might help us better understand what makes us who we are today.

Many have noted that greater tolerance for homosexuality in the latter half of the twentieth century is as much a result of market forces as of activism or social liberalization. Homosexuality has been able to go mainstream to the extent that it has largely because advertisers and marketers have found in the homosexual public a lucrative niche market, with the result of greater visibility, greater public sanction, and (most important) advertising revenue for gay and lesbian "lifestyle" magazines. As I turn now to discuss this trend I do so out of a sense that it continues what began with Wilde—that the gay identity ever more manufactured for corporate gain has its roots in the chiasmus of corporate and minority identities that made Wilde who he was in the first place.

Prior to the 1990s, gay and lesbian publications had to support themselves primarily with ads for sex-related business. Mainstream advertisers stayed away—just as mainstream media and morality refused to think that homosexuality could be anything other than the special interest of an unpalatable minority. But with the 1990s changes took place that have been, as some cultural critics have noted, instrumental to the better fortunes of gay politics and culture. Mainstream advertisers discovered that gay people could be a great source of revenue—that they were a substantial, credible, and active niche market. Whereas before advertisers had presumed both that targeting gays would tarnish their image and that targeting gays could not have the focus adequate to produce returns, now advertisers found that gays could be a lucrative market, for reasons not unrelated to those that produced Wilde's popularity in the first place. First, the approbation of advertising itself could help wear away the very stigma advertisers feared: corporate identity could itself help to mainstream minority identity so that it would not in turn make corporations look bad. Second, the gay niche market, in the interest of promoting its own identities, would take care to support gay-friendly businesses: in the spirit of "market populism," they would reward advertisers with their business in order to promote their own interests. Like Wilde before them, the members of the gay niche market allowed corporate culture to define their identities—indeed to take on their identities—in exchange for a viable public selfhood; and the corporate sponsors in question continued to reap the rewards they had begun to reap long ago when such interchange of identities began.

Gay publications made a shift from marginal to mainstream advertising, with huge results for circulation, production values, and influence. But for the gay movement, "going to market" has been a kind of devil's bargain—in the words of many, a "selling out." As John D'Emilio, Alexandra Chasin, and Sarah Schulman complain, emergence as a niche market has meant more power only with the expense of a mainstreaming that has disempowered many of the movement's constituencies. As Chasin puts it, "gay politics, in collaboration with identity-based consumption, tends to under-represent women, people of color, poor people, sick people, and very young and very old people"; and "when gay men and lesbians were targeted as consumers, difference in sexual orientation became not only marketable, but less different."[5] As Schulman puts it,

> a fake public homosexuality has been constructed to facilitate a double marketing strategy: selling products to gay consumers to meet their emotional need to be accepted while selling a palatable image of homosexuality to heterosexual consumers that meets their need to have their dominance obscured. Rather than elevating the centuries-old underground gay and lesbian culture to the level of mainstream visibility, straight people have invented their own homosexual culture and placed it front and center.[6]

In becoming something United Airlines and Subaru (for example) can relate to, gay identity had had to become something that has much more to do with the interest of corporate America and much less to do with the interests of real, diverse, and often radical gay people. So we get Gay Pride marches "dominated by arrogant, corporate-style, money-driven organizations geared toward assimilation through the marketing of acceptable gayness."[7] And so we get, in Michael Warner's words, gay media "increasingly dominated by highly capitalized lifestyle magazines, which themselves have been drawn into close partnership with the mass entertainment industry" against the interests of the public cultures that once set gay men and women apart.[8]

Were we to recall the 1882 convergence of Wilde's tour of America and the provocation for *Santa Clara County v. Southern Pacific Railroad* we might find one way to understand the pernicious essence of such developments. If it is true that Wilde initiated our current state of gay identity less through his trials than by the "commercial education" he received at the hands of America's growing willingness to confuse corporate and minority identities, then it might be true as well that such confusion is the essence, today, of what makes gay identity more and more a corporate brand. And such confusion does in fact seem to be behind what may be the most bothersome trend in contemporary "lifestyle magazine" advertising. Many mainstream ads appearing in gay magazines tend to appropriate gay difference to dramatize the difference between brands; they speak as if the language of gay rights and gay desire can easily apply to the language of corporate marketing. Replaying something like the chiasmus put into play with *Santa Clara County v. Southern Pacific Railroad*, they allege that corporate beings and minority identities share common selves. One such ad shows a naked body happily reclining, with the words, "No one should be made to feel uncomfortable," as a way to explain the impetus behind the creation of more legroom on United Airlines. Here the right to tolerance becomes a justification for the demand for greater consumer satisfaction. Another example (fig. 1) has a Subaru vehicle claiming that its all-wheel driving system is "not a choice" but "just the way we're built"—extending justifications for tolerance, in this case the argument-from-nature, to a false modesty about consumer luxury. A third example says, to a pack of Bud Light, "nice package"—rather surprisingly using the language of lewd proposition to admire advertising itself. And finally, in perhaps the most brazen appropriation of the rhetoric of minority rights, an ad for tequila transposes the activist chant, "We're here, we're queer," into "We're here, we're Cuervo." These ads are funny enough and perhaps not at all unusual in their way of appropriating popular sayings. But they are disturbing when put in the context of the chiasmus of corporate and minority identities, for they show how easy it is for advertising to co-opt the language of identity, and not just in order to sell any important messages that turn up in the rest of the magazines they occupy. For, as Chasin and Schulman observe, the messages in the rest of these magazines—the features, articles, editorials—have changed to line up with the sort of statements these ads want to make. They too have become glib, superficial in their style of connection, and alarmingly certain that consumption is the best means toward assertion of minority selfhood.

What might be the alternatives? Could there be any way to have homosexual identity, now, apart from the corporate culture that has grown so pervasively fundamental to self-expression? And would homosexual activists and citizens want to give up on the new power and acceptance that has come through the power of the purse? These questions are not at all unlike those raised by critics of corporate culture more generally—by Frank and Lasn and any number of others who deplore the extent to which the

Fig. 1   Courtesy of Subaru of America, Inc.

market has co-opted personal expression and yet admit that such co-opting must extend perpetually beyond any attempts to limit it. The "culture jammers," however, do have their "campaigns": through "buy nothing day" and "TV-turnoff week," Lasn and his fellow culture jammers have made attempts to decouple what was coupled initially with *Santa Clara County v. Southern Pacific Railroad,* and while the attempts no doubt smack of excessive idealism, they may ultimately have an impact on advertising that would in turn have an impact on the way homosexual identity gets marketed. If we turn now to the culture jammers' main efforts at "corporate crackdown," we might discover activities very interestingly opposite to those that began with Oscar Wilde's trip to America.

Lasn has published a "Culture Jammer's Manifesto" that fairly well captures the spirit of the activities in question. The manifesto is stale, perhaps, in its affect, but when read as a challenge specifically to the producers of gay culture it has a fresh vigor of the kind once typical of but more and more absent from the gay scene:

> We will take on the archetypal mind polluters and beat them at their own game.
>
> We will uncool their billion-dollar brands with uncommercials on TV, subvertisements in magazines and anti-ads right next to theirs in the urban landscape.
>
> We will seize control of the roles and functions that corporations play in our lives and set new agendas in their industries.
>
> We will jam the pop-culture marketeers and bring their image factory to a sudden, shuddering halt.
>
> On the rubble of the old culture, we will build a new one with a non-commercial heart and soul. (Lasn, 128)

This manifesto extends into Lasn's *Adbusters,* a "journal of the mental environment," which consists of various editorials and articles attacking corporate and consumer culture, but mainly of mock advertisements: the magazine features a number of images that look like advertisements for McDonald's, Nike, and other major corporations but on closer inspection turn out to be indictments of the various ways such corporations dehumanize, deface, and delimit world culture. These mock-advertisements tend mostly to seem to want to defamiliarize the deeper structures of consumer culture and to point up the absurdity of the spaces in which we choose to live and express ourselves. In a way they are the opposite of the ads that frequently appear in gay lifestyle magazines, and not only because they attack what those ads promote. They are opposite to such ads in that they propose a reverse relationship between self-expression, or identity, and the image-structure of consumer culture. *Adbusters* perpetually denies the now natural effort of the consumer eye to identify with what is advertised—the effort ever more encouraged by those ads in gay lifestyle magazines that try to give their products themselves gay identities. *Adbusters* therefore commits itself not only to an effort to criticize consumer culture but to retrain the consumer eye and accustom it to seeing the way expressions of consumer culture must always contradict the interests of human beings. Were these efforts to work—and such an outcome is obviously the culture jammer's great hope—the apparently totalizing power of corporate culture to co-opt whatever is cool or compelling would be neutralized, by the tendency of the consumer eye to see disjunctions where corporate culture projects identity.

For gay identity, the change would be particularly salutary, and peculiarly revolutionary. For the change would cease the promotion of "identity" as the best hope for happiness and would do so in such a way as to undo a century of developments toward self-commodification. I speak here of the developments that began with Wilde's self-marketing—with the culture that trained him to defer his selfhood to the system of commodities. In place of gay identity we might get something like a return to gay acts, those acts being, like the debranding gestures of culture jamming and adbusting, by definition resistant to the centripetal forcing of corporate personhood. Abandonment of corporate gay identity in favor of disparate gestural actions would not require us to believe that some abrupt shift has, a century ago, turned us from the former to the latter; it would not, that is, require us to think in terms of reversing the reversal that allegedly happened with Wilde's conviction. Rather, it would be of a piece with the view that acts and identities exist perpetually as different models for selfhood, and it would in fact help us to see that identity only seems inevitable because of the way corporate personhood has come, in the era of "market populism," to deglamorize and disenfranchise other sorts of selves.

I speak here in terms, I hope, distinct from those that cultural critics have long used to expose and critique commodification. For the commodification at work here is not that which has been so extensively remarked in the critique of capitalism; or if it is that, it is also something more specific, because it is a commodification with key distinct features: it is one that happens not only as a result of the fundamental means of production but in choices actively made to shift the boundaries of production—in this case, so that they extend further into the realm of the human. And it is one that happens precisely such that people not typically considered fully to participate in the realm of the human can partake of that norm. When, in other words, the makers of gay lifestyle and gay identity welcome corporate definition, they do so because such commodification restricts the range of the very personhood they are alleged to lack, and the result is mixed. On the one hand, what had been problematic social difference becomes a matter of very acceptable commercial uniformity; but on the other hand, of course, what had been truly personal becomes a feature of the corporate body, in much the way that rights of minority persons got absorbed as a result of the doctrine of corporate personhood. Were the makers of gay lifestyle and gay identity to give up on the acceptability that comes through commercial uniformity—that acceptability so strikingly featured in advertisements that make cultural difference a matter of commercial differentiation—they might be able to resist the sort of centripetal force that first converged with such ultimately miserable results around Wilde.

The argument here is finally an argument against gay identity as such. Not so much against its existence, although my argument is meant as contribution to that revisionist gay historiography that would deny that gay identity got invented in 1895. Rather, the argument here sets itself against the focusing of personhood that happens through identity, and it does so out of a sense that such focusing follows models not only not amenable to minority selfhood but in fact developed mainly by the corporate system out to co-opt minority distinction. Others have spoken against the demands made by gay identity—their participation in suspect liberal-humanist values, their ghettoizing tendencies, their simplifications and conventionalities. But for the most part these complaints have been made in the name of subversion, in the name of the "full range of play and waste" that identity would have to delimit (Warner, 110). We might also reject identity in the name of the "mental environment," not so that we might play and waste but so as to halt corporate inroads into that space of selfhood that Wilde (for example) ceded and that others yet cede in their will to be heard.

Notes

1. Oscar Wilde, "The English Renaissance of Art" (1882), in *Aristotle at Afternoon Tea: The Rare Oscar Wilde,* ed. John Wyse Jackson (London: Fourth Estate, 1991), 26.

2. Lloyd Lewis and Henry Justin Smith, *Oscar Wilde Discovers America [1882]* (New York: Harcourt Brace, 1936), 71.

3. David Korten, *The Post-Corporate World: Life after Capitalism* (San Francisco: Berrett-Koehler, 1999), 185–86.

4. Jonathan Freedman, *Professions of Taste: Henry James, Aestheticism, and Commodity Culture* (Stanford: Stanford University Press, 1990), 102.

5. Alexandra Chasin, *Selling Out: The Gay and Lesbian Movement Goes to Market* (New York: St. Martin's Press, 2000), 27, 53.

6. Sarah Schulman, *Stagestruck: Theater, AIDS, and the Marketing of Gay America* (Durham: Duke University Press, 1998), 146.

7. Joshua Gamson, "Whose Millennium March?" *The Nation* 270.15 (Apr. 17, 2000): 15–20.

8. Michael Warner, "Zones of Privacy," in *What's Left of Theory?* ed. Judith Butler and John Guillory (New York: Routledge, 2000), 85.

Victorians on Broadway at the Present Time

John Ruskin's Life on Stage

SHARON ARONOFSKY WELTMAN

Contemporary American theater exhibits a fascination with Victorian culture as a vehicle to explore current concerns. The 1990s brought us several blockbuster musicals based on Victorian materials, such as an opulent revival of *The King and I* (1996), the pop phenomenon *Jekyll and Hyde* (1997), and *Jane Eyre: The Musical* (2000). Both *The King and I* and *Jane Eyre* reach back to their nineteenth-century sources for examples of spirited feminism, appealing strongly to turn-of-the-twenty-first-century audiences. Plays showcasing the wit and tragedy of Oscar Wilde, such as *Gross Indecency: The Three Trials of Oscar Wilde* (1997) and *The Judas Kiss* (1998), have found an avid audience off and on Broadway. More surprisingly, the story of Victorian sage and critic John Ruskin has inspired two major American stage adaptations, also offering a feminist reading of Victorian culture, indicting a patriarchal Ruskin for the failure of his marriage. While playing to more limited audiences than the hugely popular musicals, both the 1995 opera *Modern Painters* and the 1999 off-Broadway play *The Countess* use their Victorian sources to make statements about contemporary culture, one to the packed open-air opera house in Santa Fe, the other to enthusiastic

New York audiences. A third show, Tom Stoppard's *The Invention of Love* (2001), also brings Ruskin—as well as Wilde—to Broadway.

Ruskin's importance in his own time can hardly be overestimated. His ideas influenced Victorian artists, architects, writers, and social theorists, promoting economic and educational reforms, defending Turner, advancing the Gothic revival, inspiring and championing the Pre-Raphaelites, and indirectly starting the Arts and Crafts movement. Among his most famous acolytes were William Morris, Charlotte Brontë, Leo Tolstoy, Marcel Proust, and Frank Lloyd Wright. In the twentieth century Mahatma Gandhi credited him for changing his life, and in the twenty-first, Ruskin remains immensely important for the British Labour party. But despite the fact that three towns in the United States are named for Ruskin,[1] hardly anyone in America outside the academy now knows who he was. His relevance, according to these staged versions of his life, is as a sexually repressed and patriarchal madman. Even Ruskin's renowned eloquence and his recognized status within these dramas as someone important to the history of ideas serve only to emphasize his prudish chauvinism. In both cases, the point of Ruskin's story is to allow contemporary audiences to feel good about how far we have come since 1854. As John Kucich and Dianne F. Sadoff explain in *Victorian Afterlife,* at work here is "postmodernism's privileging of the Victorians as its historical 'other.'"[2] Broadway's glance back at Victorian sexuality allows ours to stand out in greater relief; indeed, these revisions construct a teleology in which present-day sexual relations and sex roles are quite simply more advanced than the Victorians'. Thousands of theatergoers viewing Ruskin's repression as quintessentially Victorian find it easy to feel self-righteously complacent about today's more relaxed sexual attitudes.

Unlike *The Invention of Love,* which I will discuss briefly at the end of this article, the opera *Modern Painters* and the play *The Countess* draw from Ruskin's and his wife Effie Gray's letters and diaries as well as from Ruskin's autobiography and criticism to depict their miserable wedded life. Despite their common sources, *The Countess* and *Modern Painters* approach their materials very differently. The play is a straightforward, accessible, realistic drama with a gripping plot and engaging dialogue, focusing tightly on a very short period of Ruskin's life, from June 1853 to April 1854. The opera is a musically minimalist yet philosophically expansive look at all of Ruskin's adulthood, less factually accurate but more committed to communicating the beauty of Ruskin's language, organized thematically rather than chronologically. Both adapt works that are often about ideas into staged representations of a life, resulting finally in plots about domestic interaction rather than in the questions of art and social justice that animate Ruskin's own work. Both locate the failure of Ruskin's marriage in his idealization of women.

The Countess is Gregory Murphy's off-Broadway play about the dissolution of Ruskin's unhappy union. With excellent reviews from the *New York Times,* the *New York Post,* the *New Yorker,* and *Time Out: New York,* this small costume drama ran for more than six hundred performances.[3] Based on the Bowerswell papers housed at the Pierpont Morgan Library in New York, *The Countess* depicts the disintegration of Ruskin and Effie Gray's marriage and the mounting attraction between Effie and their friend, the young Pre-Raphaelite painter whom Ruskin mentored, John Everett Millais, deserving the *New York Times*'s comment that the play is "erotically charged" (Gates, E1). While Ruskin omitted his marriage from his autobiography altogether, the play uses other kinds of life writing with meticulous care, culling details and even dialogue directly from Ruskin's and Effie's letters and journals, dramatizing their experiences with considerable historical accuracy.

Of course, the play takes poetic license for dramatic effect, dropping characters, imagining witty conversation and unrecorded sexual advances; but it follows recorded facts we have about these private lives surprisingly closely. *The Countess* includes myriad details from published letters and sketches, most notably those found in Mary Lutyens's book *Millais and the Ruskins.*[4] Any scholar familiar with these materials will find their continual echoes throughout the script almost eerie, but the temptation to judge the opera and play based on their factual correctness is a mistake. They do not aspire to the condition of scholarship: they contain no footnotes; they are not published by university presses. Both productions, but particularly *The Countess,* encourage the audience to take Effie's side against Ruskin; he comes across in this play as cruel and manipulative. Members of the audience audibly gasp and even hiss when Ruskin berates Effie, disdaining her physical person. Critics and historians knowledgeable about Ruskin's contributions often watch with an increasingly heavy heart while the play's Ruskin behaves in such an abominably controlling way; some want to defend or excuse the historical Ruskin, futilely taking sides in a case that was decided 150 years ago. *The Countess* sparked a hot exchange of letters to the editor in the *New York Times,* with readers and writers defending opposite positions.[5] The power of these productions to incite such a reaction is the very reason to remind ourselves of something obvious: the Ruskin and

Effie and Millais in New York or Santa Fe are literary personae, interpreted on stage. Such a play asks us to consider what happens when historical personages become characters, when their own written words become dialogue, when their self-representations become dramas.

Plays drawn from life writing retain a sense of historical authenticity that adds to their appeal. Part of the fun of any show based on a true story is that it is supposed to be true. But as representations of history, such plays are at least as false as the letters, diaries, and autobiographies that they come from. This is not to claim that Effie, Millais, and Ruskin lied outright in their narration and explanation of these events so crucial to their reputations and their happiness, just that their written experiences come to us as artificial constructs, recalled after the fact and related in artfully crafted words, prepared with rhetorical appeal to persuade readers to understand and agree that each was right in what he or she did. Even diaries involve an effort to make sense of one's own actions, to clarify motivation, if only to oneself. As James Olney and others have shown,[6] life writing of all kinds brims with self-justification, failed memories, and misrepresentations. So the first thing to say about plays based on autobiography is that their attractive sense of authoritativeness is illusory. This must be true even of the renditions most faithful to their source texts.

In addition, there remains a problem historians are very familiar with but that playgoing audiences may not realize: any particular collection of manuscripts is preselected for the researcher by the collectors. In this case, the group of documents now at the Pierpont Morgan Library in New York known as the Bowerswell papers, on which Gregory Murphy based *The Countess,* include many manuscripts by Effie, Millais, Ruskin, and their families and friends. But they came from the home of Effie's parents in Bowerswell, Scotland, and so the choice of documents collected reflects their concern with vindicating the Grays' and Millaises' actions regarding the Ruskins' annulment and the Millaises' marriage. While today a wife's decision to sue for annulment of an unconsummated marriage to one famous man and subsequent marriage to another would not require much justification, the Millaises and Grays certainly felt strongly the need to safeguard their relatives' reputations. They conscientiously gathered whatever materials they could in that cause.

Beyond the illusion of authenticity provided by basing a play on life writing, the realistic genre in drama presents additional complexities. A realistic play's nonexistent fourth wall heightens the effect of verisimilitude because the audience observes seemingly unmediated action. Paradoxically, realistic drama feels more objective than the first-person account of a letter or diary or autobiography. When we pick up documents written by husband and wife in the middle of their marriage's collapse, we would be naive to imagine they write objectively. But when we watch a play based on the same letters, the action comes to us as though unbiased by which hand recorded which incident. Added to the biases inherent in the source material are the playwright's selections and omissions for dramatic effect, satisfying our expectations for a realistic plot with tidy cause and effect, clear motivations, and psychological verity. Yet such neatness does not exist in life and certainly does not exist in the cacophony of voices represented in the self-representations of Ruskin, Effie, and Millais. What adds to the audience's sense of realism and objectivity in the portrayal of history is another layer of mediation created by the writer between the historical figures and the performers' action.

According to the theories of several feminist theater critics, *The Countess*'s realism and the cachet of authenticity achieved by adapting autobiographical materials mark it as patriarchal, despite the playwright's stated effort to the contrary. For example, Elin Diamond discusses the limits of dramatic realism and mimesis, ultimately indicting them because they reinscribe the dominant culture they depict:

> Naturalizing the relation between character and actor, setting and world, realism's project is always ideological, drawing spectators into identifications with its coherent fictions. It is through such identification that realism surreptitiously reinforces (even where it argues with) the social arrangements of the society it claims to mirror.[7]

From this perspective, *The Countess,* very much a realistic play, cannot escape the patriarchal ideology that it wants to expose and explode.[8]

Evidence that the play attempts to reject Victorian patriarchy abounds. The play shows Ruskin and his parents unsympathetically as they try to dominate Effie, dramatizing how powerless she is legally as a married woman in early 1850s England.[9] Likewise it demonstrates the problems that arise when people receive too little education in sexual matters, as no doubt happened much more frequently in nineteenth-century Britain than now.[10] It reveals, through Ruskin's disillusioned reaction to Effie, that a cultural idealization of women hampers real relationships; conversely, it makes the modern feminist point that when women internalize the dominant culture's expectations for their bodies and find they cannot measure up, they believe they are physically defective, inadequate, deformed. In addition, the play provides a strong woman character, Lady Eastlake, who recognizes that there is nothing wrong with Effie and encourages her to leave Ruskin. Finally, the play's plot provides Effie with the strength to achieve her freedom.

Nevertheless, the play finally does reinforce the Victorian social arrangements it portrays. *The Countess* replicates a nineteenth-century version of these characters, best explained through Victorian ideology. The clearest example is that the play ends by having Effie leave her husband so that she can marry Millais, reinforcing the marriage plot. More pervasively, Effie remains extremely decorous and domestic throughout. The play relies on a late-twentieth-century sense of the Victorians as so proper that dialogue pulled from written forms does not seem stilted. Similarly, the play's Effie acts uneasy in situations that could be construed as compromising; her discomfort protects her position as a gentlewoman in the eyes of the audience because it proves she is not wanton. She spends her time on needlework and sketching, thoroughly suitable nineteenth-century feminine behavior. Effie is visibly agitated in trying to discuss sex even with Lady Eastlake, reinforcing her role as a stereotypically chaste Victorian lady. Her likableness for the audience depends not on her bucking Victorian convention but on her being a victim of it. The play does not include the historical Effie's flirtatiousness, her love of parties and gallery openings, the duel challenged over her stolen jewels, not only because of time, not only because of focus on the love story between Millais and Effie, but also because these incidents would not show Effie in the light of the oppressed Victorian angel in the house. Outside of that role, as depicted in this play, she would lose even the turn-of-the-twenty-first-century audience's intense sympathy.

The contemporary audience loves Effie because she satisfies all their expectations for a Victorian heroine, even though the historical Effie surely acted less angelically if no less blamelessly. Even the heroines created by Victorian writers take more gambles sexually than this late-twentieth-century play gives Effie: virtually any novel by George Eliot or Thomas Hardy will provide examples. *The Countess* does not risk the possibility of ambiguity for her, as though anyone other than a spotless paragon might not work within the Victorian context for a present-day audience. Other than a passionate and guilt-ridden kiss, the play goes to considerable lengths to resist anything that could sully her within imagined Victorian judgment. In other words, the play commits the same "sin" that it claims Ruskin does, idealizing Effie. So even though Murphy's stated intent is to defend Effie not only from her Victorian detractors but also from her twentieth-century biographers,[11] to help us understand how isolated and frustrated she must have felt, the play exculpates Effie exclusively within Victorian terms.

While the play's defense of Effie as a vindication of her right to a ful-filling sex life seems tremendously modern and feminist and certainly cor-rect, it is in fact no more than what Victorian culture had already granted: Effie got her annulment, and Ruskin got ridiculed. So while Murphy suc-cessfully shows Effie's untenable position with Ruskin and highlights Vic-torian women's vulnerability within marriage, it breaks no new ground; indeed, it recuperates Effie in the most old-fashioned way imaginable. The play signals Effie's reinstatement by having Queen Victoria finally receive her. In Elin Diamond's feminist dramaturgy, the play is as patriarchal as the Victorian world it recreates, not only on stage but also in the approv-ing mind of the audience.

Even people familiar with the tragic soap opera of Ruskin's love life probably never imagined that it would become the topic of a real opera, but with the 1995 world premiere of *Modern Painters* at the prestigious Santa Fe Opera, it did. *Modern Painters* not only tells the story of Ruskin's marriage but also chronicles his doomed love for the very young Rose La Touche and recounts the disastrous Whistler trial.[12] The Santa Fe Opera commissioned minimalist composer David Lang, best known for cofound-ing the "Bang on a Can Music Festival" in New York, and librettist Manuella Hoelterhoff, the Pulitzer Prize–winning culture critic for the *Wall Street Journal*. Francesca Zambella directed, having just won the Laurence Olivier Award for a production at the English National Opera. The opera received positive reviews from *Vogue* and the *Village Voice* but has not been produced since.[13] Although it is very odd to think of an opera as an adaptation of critical texts, this one largely is. Besides the autobiography *Praeterita*, characters often sing lush passages directly from Ruskin's criti-cism, including *Modern Painters, The Stones of Venice, The Seven Lamps of Architecture, The Crown of Wild Olive, Unto This Last, Sesame and Lilies*, and "Storm Cloud of the Nineteenth Century"; but since John Rosenberg has already shown us that Ruskin's criticism is always autobiographical, perhaps it should not surprise us.[14]

Very different issues arise in adapting autobiography to the opera, rarely a realistic form. As a genre it revels in artificiality, often highlighting virtuos-ity over content, always subordinating words to music. Of course, a realistic play is also a study in artifice and convention; William Demastes, Brian Richardson, and others point out that what defines a play as realistic or not changes over time and across cultures.[15] Nevertheless, as a genre, realistic

drama depends upon the audience's acceptance of these established conventions (linear time, reasonable cause and effect, plausible plot, likely dialogue, ignoring the audience), as marking it somehow true to life. In
contrast, opera traditionally depends upon the audience's expectation of
grandeur and excess. Although some of the same issues of authenticity arise
in watching an opera based on life writing as in a play, the historical accuracy of an opera does not significantly increase its appeal. Opera promises
extravagant emotion and mythic circumstances, no matter how prosaic the
narrative it presents. Far from creating an illusion of greater objectivity
than its autobiographical sources, *Modern Painters*—with its stylized sets,
lengthy arias, and richly metaphorical language—seems outside discussions
of subjective and objective portrayal of real events. Neither does opera
offer the same sense of immediacy that a realistic play does; the medium
acts as a buffer between the audience and the character, no matter how
good the acting and singing, because the conventions of realism do not
include song as a likely mode of conversation. Far from following the
record as rigorously as *The Countess, Modern Painters* radically rearranges
chronology, changes facts, and combines circumstances.[16] Highlighting
some of Ruskin's most purple prose as lyrics, its creators often seem more
interested in transmitting the poetry of Ruskin's language than in telling his
story.

Although the opera is named *Modern Painters*, its seven scenes are organized around *The Seven Lamps of Architecture:* Sacrifice, Truth, Power,
Beauty, Life, Memory, and Obedience. The opera provides little direct relationship between the action and the elements Ruskin describes as necessary
for a nation's healthy architecture, but as abstract terms they resonate thematically with the subject matter of each of the roughly chronological
episodes from Ruskin's life. The result of naming and structuring the creative work after the critical suggests that Matthew Arnold was in this
respect right: criticism provides the stream of ideas for artists, quite literally.
The opera also dramatizes art as criticism and criticism as art, insinuating
that the boundary between the two is meaningless.[17] In addition the show
implies that opera is structured like architecture:[18] it is meant to last, to be
worthy of sacrifice, to be a monument and a living, inhabitable cathedral
of music, meant as much for future generations as for us. In organizing
their opera along the *Seven Lamps,* Lang and Hoelterhoff make a very
grand claim.

Nevertheless, although beguiled by the beauty of Ruskin's writing and the
significance of his ideas, the creators are faced with the fact that what is

opera-worthy about Ruskin is the story of his scandalous marriage and the other personal tragedies of his life. The show reveals the tension between their fascination with his language and their attraction to his dirty laundry in that the opera's best moments appear in the juxtaposition of Ruskin's riveting words to a wildly dramatic version of his private troubles.

While *The Countess* reveals the calamitous wedding night retrospectively, only in Effie's halting confession of misery to her older friend Lady Eastlake, *Modern Painters* symbolically enacts what did not happen. The opera renders the failed nuptials in the second scene, "Truth," where it portrays Ruskin's idealization of women as the reason for his marriage's failure. In their bedroom, Ruskin reads aloud from a book, intoning lyrically to Effie of a beautiful woman:

> She lies on her pillow, a hound at her feet
> Her arms folded softly over her breast
> Her dress is simple, of medieval style,
> with flowing drapery, marble white.
> Around her head a fillet of flowers. (12)

However, this blossom-crowned beauty lying on a pillow is not Effie, and she knows it. In fact, although the audience never discovers her identity, Ruskin's pretty song describes a statue on a tomb; the woman's white pillow is marble; she sleeps in her grave. The book he reads from is his own *Modern Painters,* which describes the funeral effigy.[19] Ruskin does not even look at Effie in her nightgown as he recalls this deathly figure—probably a good thing, since Ruskin has suffered enough bad press sexually without adding necrophilia to the list. Instead, the bridegroom reads himself to sleep, fully clothed, serenading his lovely homage to the cold sculpture of a long-dead Renaissance woman, while the living wife covers her face on their unhappy bridal bed.

In *The Countess* Ruskin describes the same sculpture, this time to Millais, emphasizing more fleshly details: "One day we will go to Lucca, and I'll show you della Quercia's sculpture of Ilaria di Caretto. You will not believe the perfect sweetness of her lips and closed eyes, or the way her dress folds closely beneath the curve of her breasts" (12). In the play, Millais is charmed. It is too early in the action for Millais or the audience to realize that these words set the tone for Ruskin's disappointment in Effie. Both playwright and librettist see in this passage, based on an 1845 letter to Ruskin's father, a key to Ruskin's debilitating idealization of women. Hoelterhoff suggests that Ruskin envisions abstracted beauty, whereas

Murphy views it in surprisingly physical terms. He considers Ruskin's focus on the sculpture parallel to problems men still have with unrealistic expectations about women's bodies: Murphy mentioned in interview that today men are taught to want tall, thin models rather than alabaster effigies, but the idea is the same.[20] This almost anatomical interpretation of Ruskin's idealization of women certainly works as a way to understand Ruskin's disillusionment with his wife once he saw her naked; however, it overlooks the substantially more important impact Ruskin's idealized notions of women's role had on Victorian culture. While the opera and the play try to work out Ruskin's private woes by pinning his ideal of womanhood to a marble statue, the empowering effect of his gender mythology on Victorian women (other than Effie) goes unnoticed. When Ruskin writes about housewives' queenship in "Of Queens' Gardens,"[21] he concerns himself with redefining and enlarging the domestic sphere so that women will take on greater responsibility outside the home. Contrary to what the play and opera depict, the historical Ruskin's ideal concerned what women should do rather than how they should look.[22]

The final scene in *Modern Painters,* "Obedience," stages a lecture famously described by A. E. Housman. Ruskin takes a beautiful landscape by Turner, depicting an English scene before it was polluted by heavy industrialization, and paints ugly modern additions—including smoke, factories, railroads, and prisons—over the glass that covers the painting, completely disfiguring its beauty. Housman describes this lecture as brilliant and its effect on students at Oxford as electrifying, but the opera presents it as the ravings of a mad seer failing to convince a crowd of jeering workers. Although the workmen join Ruskin in singing the miseries of their existence, the production gives us an ineffectual Ruskin whose listeners do not respect him and perhaps fear his madness. The libretto's method of describing alternately the wretched state of the environment and the appalling condition of the workers' lives—lifting passages from *The Crown of Wild Olive,* "The Storm Cloud of the Nineteenth Century," and *Unto This Last*—underscores Ruskin's link between a just society and a healthy ecology. These passages report the hideous putrescence of modern life as richly as earlier scenes described Turner's light and shadow or the glittering pinnacles of Venice. Ruskin's song turns into an incantatory mumbling as he goes from singing repeatedly, "There is no wealth but life," to chanting "Blackened sun, blighted grass, blinded man" (31), signifying his final insanity.

Stoppard's play *The Invention of Love,* about A. E. Housman's youth at Oxford, includes Ruskin as a character but omits the famous lecture

Housman recounts. *The Invention of Love* opened at the National Theatre in London on September 25, 1997, premiered in the United States in 2000 at the ATC in San Francisco, and arrived on Broadway at the Lyceum Theater, March 29, 2001. Not a realistic play, the action takes place in Hades; its characters are dead. Ruskin drifts in and out of the first act, playing croquet with fellow don and aesthete Walter Pater, both wearing angel wings, discoursing decoratively on art, life, and society. Ruskin is hilariously pretentious, declaring, "I have announced the meaning of life in my lectures."23 Only one speech closely follows Ruskin's text; the subsequent witty dialogue undercuts its rhetorical effect:

> Ruskin: There is a rocky valley between Buxton and Bakewell where once you may have seen at first and last light the Muses dance for Apollo and heard the pan-pipes play. But its rocks were blasted away for the railway, and now every fool in Buxton can be at Bakewell in half an hour, and every fool in Bakewell at Buxton.
> Pater (at croquet): First class return.
> Jowett: Mind the gap. (14–15)

Just in case anyone chances to feel moved by Ruskin's aesthetic or ecological concern, Stoppard deflates the moment with funny double entendres regarding the game of croquet and railroad journeys. Later, referring to his utopian social project of St. George's Guild, Stoppard's Ruskin cares more about his undergraduate's prettiness than his moral fiber. Ruskin says:

> I had my students up at dawn building a flower-bordered road across a swamp . . . There was an Irish exquisite, a great slab of a youth with white hands and long poetical hair who said he was glad to say he had never seen a shovel, but I . . . taught that work with one's hands is the beginning of virtue. Then I went sketching to Venice and the road sank into the swamp. My protegé rose at noon to smoke cigarettes and read French novels, and Oxford reverted to a cockney watering-place for learning to row. (15)

While the historical Ruskin did set his students to road building and he did make the crack about Oxford as a place for learning to row,24 here Ruskin is a clever maker of empty aphorisms, like a Gilbert and Sullivan parody of Oscar Wilde, not the passionate moralist critics recognize. Very different from *The Countess* or *Modern Painters,* this depiction of Ruskin leaves out women completely; instead of his fear or repression of desire for them, he displaces an attraction for the "Irish Exquisite." But Ruskin's utility in Stoppard's play is not that far off finally from his function in *The Countess* and *Modern Painters*. He acts the faded aesthete, too wrapped up in theories of beauty or impractical social experiments to pay attention to what really matters, which in the dead Housmán's estimation is sex after all. Stoppard's play chronicles Housman's realization that perhaps he should have had the courage to approach the young heterosexual man whom he loved at Oxford, instead of burying himself in classicism. *The Invention of Love* uses Ruskin only to dismiss him as too removed from real feeling to be of any use at all. Oscar Wilde appears at the end of this play as the example of what Housman could have done, had he the courage to choose illicit love over scholarship. Ruskin, along with Pater and Jowett, represents the latter, the sublimation of sexuality for erudition and aesthetics. Again the Victorians—even for Stoppard—serve to establish postmodern identities as sexually and socially liberated.

The historical Ruskin died just over one hundred years ago. He left a tremendous legacy of extraordinary writing, serious ideas, and both documented and incalculable influences. He has also sparked a growing proliferation of Ruskins as literary characters, not only in *The Countess, Modern Painters,* and *The Invention of Love* but also in a variety of films, radio plays, and other kinds of representation. As time goes by, there will be more. How do theatrical Ruskins function in the present time? What cultural work do they achieve? What does Ruskin-as-idea or image represent?[25] Any staged adaptation of autobiography diminishes the subject. Even the most sensitive, nuanced attempt reduces a life to a few hours' span, choosing what is dramatic or entertaining to succeed or fail as a work of art. Ultimately, the sympathetic *Modern Painters* uses Ruskin's own words against him, making him pitiable. *The Countess* not only indicts Ruskin but also renders Effie less complex than her letters reveal her to have been. *The Countess* and *Modern Painters* demonstrate how fragile the selves created in autobiography are, how inevitably words change out of context.

The John Ruskins of *The Countess, Modern Painters,* and even *The Invention of Love* operate primarily to establish the turn-of-the-twenty-first-century audience's superiority to the supposedly frigid Victorians, despite the fact that the historical record shows that the Victorians often do not fit this stereotype of sexual repression. Victorian attitudes toward sexuality were not as monolithic and very often not as puritanical as the Modernists claimed about the previous generation. Beginning at least with Stephen Marcus's *The*

Other Victorians and going on through a long list of books and articles,[26] researchers have drawn a picture of a diverse set of attitudes toward sex, often including for women a warm appreciation for physical love, even most famously (and to non-Victorianists often most surprisingly), from Queen Victoria herself.[27]

For *Modern Painters,* Ruskin is a tragic, brilliant madman; for *The Countess* he is an eloquent, manipulative tyrant; but in both cases he is a quintessential Victorian prude, too wrapped up in ideal beauty to recognize it in the flesh. Although Murphy believes his drama reveals to playgoers that they do the same thing, neither show holds a mirror to its public. Instead, the audience reacts with relief that no matter how bad their relationships are, at least they (probably) consummated their own marriages. The audiences disapprove of Ruskin's failure to appreciate Effie, confirming their complacency about their own enlightenment regarding sex and women's right both to a loving, respectful relationship without psychological abuse and to physical pleasure within that relationship. So in neither case do these theatrical representations awaken audiences to their own faults. Rather the function of Victorian culture on Broadway at the present time is to validate audiences in their self-satisfaction.

Notes

1. James Dearden, *Facets of Ruskin* (London: Charles Skelton, 1970), 128.

2. Dianne F. Sadoff and John Kucich, "Introduction: Histories of the Present," in *Victorian Afterlife: Postmodern Culture Rewrites the Nineteenth Century,* ed. Dianne F. Sadoff and John Kucich (Minneapolis: University of Minnesota Press, 2000), xi.

3. *The Countess* (New York: Dramatists Play Service, 2000), by novice playwright Gregory Murphy and directed by Ludovica Villar-Houser, opened at the Greenwich Street Theater on March 14, 1999, in an off-off-Broadway showcase; it transferred to the Samuel Beckett Theater off-Broadway on June 8, 1999; it transferred again to the larger venue of the Lambs Theater on May 11, 2000. It ran for 634 performances in all (Beck Lee, press release). Positive reviews include Anita Gates, "Theater Review: A Critic Who Takes His Work Home," *New York Times,* Mar. 30, 1999, E1; Jason Zinoman, "The Countess," *Time Out: New York,* June 24–July 1, 1999; Clive Barnes, "'The Countess Has Sex-Scandal Appeal," *New York Post* Theater and Dance Reviews, Jan. 21, 2000; and *New Yorker,* Sept. 20, 1999. *Time Out: New York* also named *The Countess* as one of the ten best plays of 1999 (issue 223). *The Countess* was the longest-running play to open that year.

4. Although Gregory Murphy cites first the popular semi-academic book *Parallel Lives* by Phyllis Rose (New York: Knopf, 1983) and then *Pre-Raphaelites in Love* by Gay Daly (New York: Tickner and Fields, 1989) as his original inspiration (*New Yorker,* Sept. 20, 1999), most relevant documents are published in Lutyens's *Millais and the Ruskins* (New York: Vanguard Press, 1967). The most notorious episode in *Parallel Lives* does not appear in Murphy's account: *Parallel Lives* contends that the sight of Effie's naked pubis horrified her sheltered

bridegroom, whose image of the nude female form supposedly derived from the hairless or at least adroitly covered private parts shown in Renaissance paintings and classical sculpture. In the play, the question of just what Ruskin found repellent about Effie on their wedding night remains a mystery. Nevertheless, the tale continues to dog Ruskin's reputation. A recent Arts and Entertainment special on *The History of Sex* (Aug. 1999) repeats the Freudian "Medusa's Head" explanation. However, virtually no evidence supports the story; some refutes it. For less speculative interpretation, see Tim Hilton, *John Ruskin: The Early Years, 1818–1859* (New Haven: Yale University Press, 1985).

5. *New York Times Book Review,* June 4, 2000; *New York Times,* Arts and Leisure, Letters, June 25, 2000. See also Lucinda Franks, "A Twisted Victorian Love Story That Won't Die Out," *New York Times,* Arts and Leisure, May 28, 2000, sec. 2, pp. 5 and 18.

6. See James Olney, *Metaphors of Self: The Meaning of Autobiography* (Princeton: Princeton University Press, 1972), and Barrett Mandel, "Full of Life Now," in *Autobiography: Essays Theoretical and Critical,* ed. James Olney (Princeton: Princeton University Press, 1980).

7. Elin Diamond, "The Violence of 'We': Politicizing Identifications," in *Critical Theory and Performance*, ed. Janelle G. Reinelt and Joseph R. Roach (Ann Arbor: University of Michigan Press, 1992), 393.

8. Other feminist theater critics who denounce realism as a genre include Jeanie Forte, "Realism, Narrative, and the Feminist Playwright—A Problem of Reception," *Modern Drama* 32, no. 1 (Mar. 1989): 115–27; Sue-Ellen Case, *Feminism and Theater* (New York: Methuen, 1988); and Jill Dolan, *The Feminist Spectator as Critic* (Ann Arbor: UMI Research Press, 1988). Many debate this antirealist position, including Helene Keyssar, *Feminist Theatre and Theory* (New York: St. Martin's, 1995); J. Ellen Gainor, "The Provincetown Players' Experiments with Realism," *Realism and the American Dramatic Tradition,* ed. William Demastes (Tuscaloosa and London: Alabama University Press, 1996), 53–70; and Judith Barlow, "Into the Foxhole: Feminism, Realism, and Lillian Hellman, " in Demastes, 156–71. I disagree that realist theater inevitably inscribes the ideology it portrays; however, *The Countess,* despite its laudable and moving feminist elements, inscribes late-twentieth-century notions of Victorian ideals to create a heroine that remains bound within a very patriarchal vision of womanhood.

9. For the legal status of Victorian women, see Martha Vicinus, ed., *A Widening Sphere: Changing Roles of Victorian Women* (Bloomington: Indiana University Press, 1977); Elizabeth Helsinger, Robin Lauterbach Sheets, and William Veeder, eds., *The Woman Question: Defining Voices, 1837–1883,* vol. 1 of *The Woman Question, 1837–1883,* 3 vols. (New York: Garland Publishing, 1983); and Mary Lyndon Shanley, *Feminism, Marriage, and the Law in Victorian England, 1850–1895* (Princeton: Princeton University Press, 1989).

10. Later in his life Ruskin appears to advocate sex education for boys and girls (*The Works of John Ruskin,* ed. E. T. Cook and Alexander Wedderburn [London: George Allen; New York: Longmans Green and Co., 1903–12], 34:529). For his progressive ideas about education for girls, see Dinah Birch, *Ruskin and Gender* (London: Palgrave, forthcoming 2002), and Sharon Aronofsky Weltman, "Ruskin and the Mythology of Gender" (Ph.D. diss., Rutgers University, 1992), 82–121.

11. Murphy, interview with author, New York, Feb. 28, 2000. Murphy is not the only author whose goal is to vindicate Effie. See Jennifer Lloyd, whose object is "to rescue" Effie from her husband's shadow in "Conflicting Expectations in Nineteenth-Century British Matrimony: The Failed Companionate Marriage of Effie Gray and John Ruskin," *Journal of Women's History* 11.2 (1999): 86.

12. Manuela Hoelterhoff, *Modern Painters: Opera in Two Acts,* David Lang, composer (New York: Red Poppy, 1995).

13. Michael Kimmelman, "Music, Love Victorian Style," *Vogue,* Aug. 1995, 144–45;

Leighton Kerner, "Critic in extremis," *Village Voice,* Aug. 12, 1985, 68. For a scholar's perspective, see Elizabeth Helsinger, "Ruskin on Stage II: Modern Painters in Santa Fe," *Ruskin Programme Bulletin* 17 (Oct. 1998): 4–6.

14. John D. Rosenberg, *The Darkening Glass: A Portrait of Ruskin's Genius* (New York: Columbia University Press, 1963).

15. See Demastes, *Realism and the American Dramatic Tradition.*

16. In the opera Ruskin proposes to Rose when she is only thirteen, rather than when she is seventeen, as he did in real life. The creators made her younger, no doubt, to emphasize overtones of pedophilia. The opera sets the child Rose's first appearance in 1878, in the midst of artist James Whistler's libel suit against Ruskin, when the critic's mental health was already crumbling; not only is 1878 twenty years after they actually met, but also it is three years after the quite grown-up Rose had in fact already died.

17. See George Levine, *Boundaries of Fiction* (Princeton: Princeton University Press, 1968).

18. I am indebted to Jennifer Jones for this point.

19. The tomb of Ilaria di Caretto, by Jacopo della Quercia, at Lucca. This quotation actually comes from Ruskin's letter to his father on May 6, 1845, reprinted by Cook and Wedderburn as a note to Ruskin's *Modern Painters* (*Works,* 4:122n).

20. Murphy interview.

21. Ruskin's wedding toast paraphrases this essay (*Works,* 18:122).

22. For discussions of how Ruskin contributed to women's advancement, see Jeffrey L. Spear, *Dreams of an English Eden: Ruskin and His Tradition in Social Criticism* (New York: Columbia University Press, 1984); Jan Marsh, "'Resolve to Be a Great Paintress': Women Artists in Relation to John Ruskin as Critic and Patron," *Nineteenth-Century Contexts* 18 (1994): 177–85; Sharon Aronofsky Weltman, *Ruskin's Mythic Queen: Gender Subversion in Victorian Culture* (Athens: Ohio University Press, 1998); and Helsinger et al.

23. Tom Stoppard, *The Invention of Love* (New York: Grove Press, 1997), 15.

24. See "The Eagle's Nest," *Works,* 22:274.

25. Other representations of Ruskin's marriage include the fourteen-minute 1994 film *The Passion of John Ruskin,* directed by Alex Chappelle, with Mark McKinny as Ruskin and Neve Campbell as Effie, focusing primarily on the pubic hair issue. Gregory Murphy has also completed a screenplay and entered negotiations for a movie version of *The Countess.* Ruskin's marital troubles have already appeared in other media: on Sunday, September 8, 1968, BBC's Radio Four transmitted a radio play called *Millais and the Ruskins,* based on Lutyens's book of the same title, written by Thea Holme and covering much the same ground as Murphy's more fully realized drama. This radio play was the sequel to a previous radio dramatization of Lutyens's earlier book, *Effie in Venice (Young Mrs. Ruskin in Venice* [first published as *Effie in Venice* in England] [New York: Vanguard, 1965]), similar to *Millais and the Ruskins* in its use of letters and diary entries to tell her story. In addition, Ruskin's famous skill as a lecturer has prompted actor Paul O'Keeffe to perform re-creations of Ruskin's lectures, including an 1853 Edinburgh lecture, the 1858 Cambridge School of Art Address, and the 1854 Bedford lecture "Traffic" (thanks to Stephen Wildman for confirming this information). Besides all these staged versions of Ruskin, every installation of Ruskin's art or of the artists whom Ruskin influenced or championed—and there have been dozens of such exhibits in the last ten years—is another version of Ruskin consumed by the contemporary public. Finally, every Ruskin scholar, critic, or biographer creates Ruskin anew.

26. Stephen Marcus, *The Other Victorians* (New York: Basic Books, 1964). See also Michael Mason, *The Making of Victorian Sexual Attitudes* (Oxford: Oxford University Press, 1994) and *The Making of Victorian Sexuality* (Oxford: Oxford University Press, 1994); Judith Walkowitz, *City of Dreadful Delight: Narratives of Sexual Danger in Late-Victorian London* (Chicago: University of Chicago Press, 1992); and Cynthia Russett,

Sexual Science: The Victorian Construction of Womanhood (Cambridge, Mass.: Harvard University Press, 1989).

27. See her private writing about Prince Albert in Helsinger et al.

PART 4

Law and Order, Victorian Style

Rounding Up the Usual Suspect

Echoing Jack the Ripper

KATE LONSDALE

> "And when you're here, you will visit me.
> We can have conversations. On many topics. I would like
> to learn about the world you come from.
> For example . . . where is Paris, France? And what is a
> Molotov Cocktail? And who is Jack the Ripper?"
>
> —the young Dalai Lama to
> Heinrich Harrer in *Seven Years in Tibet*

In asking the question "who is Jack the Ripper?" the fourteen-year-old Dalai Lama actually makes a statement testifying to the prominence of the Ripper in Western thought. On the one hand, he is posing an unanswerable question since we do not know the Ripper's real name. On the other hand, his question is perfectly understandable since we all "know" who Jack the Ripper is. Interest in the 1888 Whitechapel murders of Jack the Ripper has spawned quite a discursive history, a continuing dialogue that transcends the boundaries of genre, running the gamut from scholarly criminological studies to romance novels, Ellery Queen mysteries, graphic novels, and low-budget horror films. The outpouring of literary and film treatments attempting to *solve* the

Whitechapel murders alone run into the hundreds. These treatments vary "in tone, content and intention from the serious to the sensational,"[1] from proposing yet another "final solution" (Stephen Knight)[2] to claiming to be an authentic confessional diary of the Whitechapel killer (Shirley Harrison).[3] All the conventional markers of Jack the Ripper's identity are undiscovered, including nationality, marital status, age, race, physical appearance, ethnicity, occupation, class, and even, some have argued (albeit unconvincingly), sex. Since he exists outside the known realm of governmentally or legally sanctioned nomenclature, Jack the Ripper remains a definitional paradox: he is both labeled and disembodied, both historical figure and discursive presence, both representation and reality. Almost any resident of London in 1888 can be (and seemingly has been) considered a suspect, susceptible to having his (and even her) history grafted onto the Ripper's, and vice versa. In contrast with his victims, who are figured as almost pure body, Jack the Ripper was and is "'nowhere to be seen'—only a disappearing shadow, whose 'signature' was the mutilated body of a woman."[4] He is simultaneously nobody, somebody, and everybody.

I present this thumbnail sketch of typical Ripper rhetoric not so I can claim immunity from the persistent seductiveness of its nineteenth-century Gothic and mystery story conventions but so I can illustrate the ramifications of this particular Victorian cultural archetype and its accompanying storytelling modes within contemporary discussions of serial murder. Infamous Victorian journalist W. T. Stead's claim in the October 1, 1888, *Pall Mall Gazette* that "there is only one topic throughout all England" (qtd. in Walkowitz, 191), could be shaped to read "there is only one serial killer narrative" in Western cultural studies, a claim to which legions of "Ripperologists" could attest.[5] This collective use of Jack the Ripper as a conduit through which to comprehend all serial killers encourages certain nostalgic myths of the Victorian Era and of the serial killer as master villain while distorting and disavowing the historical specifics of those representations. These distortions not only are detrimental to popular understandings of the Victorian period, they also restrict our abilities to come to grips either discursively or politically with the serial killer.

A complex set of historical circumstances merged in the late nineteenth century to "create" such enormous interest in the Ripper—in particular, the explosion of journalistic outlets coupled with a sufficiently literate population. Furthermore, the competing and often imbricated social sciences that adopted criminality as their subject matter, including psychology and criminal anthropology (now more or less subsumed under "criminology"), were just beginning to gain wide acceptance in that autumn of 1888. Such causative social and political narratives have been largely ignored, however, even by academics (with a few notable exceptions), in order to portray the Ripper as the ultimate in differentiable evil, and 1888 Whitechapel as his fitting backdrop. While individual serial killers are often constructed as discrete purveyors of evil disconnected from a social context, the "representation [of serial killers and their investigators] has a history,"[6] one that is being constantly modified to meet the contemporary motives of its chroniclers as well as the ever-changing needs of legal and psychiatric practice. In spite of its malleability, this history springs from specifically "Victorian" origins steeped in Ripper lore. Not surprisingly, then, these myths of origin engage in a selective nostalgic amnesia

> based on misimpression. In spite of the barbarism [of the Ripper murders], they represent a real-life mystery from the era of Sherlock Holmes—the bygone romantic era of high Victorian society, gaslights and swirling London fog, though where the killings actually took place had little relationship to Victorian splendor and each crime was actually committed on a night without fog. On only one of the nights was it even raining.[7]

Atmospheric details about the "romantic era of high Victorian society" may seem like trivial discrepancies if it were not that this haunted house version of the Ripper murders had practical consequences both for criminologists and cultural critics who find it hard to resist "a real-life mystery from the era of Sherlock Holmes."

Contrary to popular desire, Jack the Ripper was not the first serial killer who "surfaced,"[8] nor the first serial killer to operate in London, nor the first to prey exclusively on women or female prostitutes. He was, perhaps, the first serial killer whose crimes, viewed retroactively, fit our contemporary definition of "sexual murder," the first whose pattern fits the now-familiar list of discursive elements ensuring the continued presence of history's most conspicuously absent serial killer: "the single, territorial and sensationally nicknamed killer; socially powerless and scapegoated victims; a signature style of murder or mutilation; intense media involvement; and an accompanying incidence of imitation or 'copycat' killings" (Caputi, "American Psychos," 101). Pinpointing the "first" serial killer inevitably raises a debate over definitions (or, as Eve Sedgwick has termed it, "definitional leverage"), the recurrent linguistic problem of historicizing the identification and labeling of deviance and transgression. Such identification inevitably can take place only in retrospect. Thus, it subsequently appears that the Ripper murders "occurred at what now seems like a point of transition" since "the idea of a killer being motivated by deviant sexual urges, familiar and obvious as it may appear to us, was regarded by many people as recently as the late nineteenth century with astonishment, distaste and often outright disbelief."[9] Although a transition in criminological discourse probably did occur in the late nineteenth century—the dawn of what Jane Caputi has dramatically termed "the Age of Sex Crime"—Deborah Cameron and Elizabeth Frazer fall into the argumentative trap of using the very language and promoting the very ideologies they want to critique. By defining the "sexual urges" of serial killers as "deviant" and therefore so far removed from the presumed norm as to be unrecognizable to those within that norm (whoever they may be) and by promoting the notion of the sexually repressed and naive Victorian middle class, they nullify in part the import of what they are arguing: that sexual murder arises out of social consensus about gender roles, not deviations from this consensus.

Thus, the contemporary construction of serial killers displaces them on two levels: the cultural and the temporal. As contemporary Jack the Rippers, they are both outside "the norm" and not of our time, like relics of the nineteenth century in the present. With the exception of psychiatric accountings for serial killer behavior (as troublesome as they are), the contemporary serial killers mythos, while it "never cohered into a single version" (Walkowitz, 2), draws on many culturally accepted fictions extant in 1888 as well as some that have originated since.[10] These "faces [of the modern serial killer are] all of them highly recognizable to our culture: the Sadeian libertine, Mr. Hyde, the Gothic villain, the monster, the hunchback; or on the other hand, the social/mental deviant: the madman, the psychopath, the existential rebel" (Cameron and Frazer, 36) and include many of our most prevalent and enduring modern antiheroes.

Similarly, the common image of serial killers arises out of a popular consensus about what the late nineteenth century, the "romantic era of high Victorian society," looked like. In 1888, such a consensus was much harder to come by. Different political constituencies used the media coverage of the murders to offer competing social theories about the deplorable living conditions in Whitechapel. Anti-Semites blamed the influx of Jewish immigrants to the East End, depicting the murderer and his crimes as something of foreign and exotic origin, while political and Christian reformers saw in the dismembered remains the ultimate example of social neglect, as well as their own failure to achieve progress. One theory, dubbed the "scientific sociologist" theory, espoused by many social reformers including George Bernard Shaw, saw the murders as the work of an insane social reformer driven by his desperation to call attention to the conditions in London's East End. Both Walkowitz and Frayling dispute this common perception of Whitechapel in 1888 as economically depressed and riddled with crime:

> the East End had come to be associated with an utterly different 'image' during the previous five years: stories about upper-class 'slummers,' university settlements, charity organizations, and exposés of appalling housing conditions or the sexual immorality of 'outcast London' . . . were thought to be either out of date (harking back to tales of Newgate and the Ratcliffe Highway) or dangerous (just over two years after the unemployed dock and building workers had marched to Trafalgar Square). (Frayling, 188)[11]

While prostitution, homelessness, poverty, and ethnic unrest were certainly grave problems in London's overcrowded East End, some progress had been made on these fronts by late-Victorian social reformers and neighborhood organizations within the area. In 1889, a violence-free dock workers strike would mitigate the memory of the march on Trafalgar Square as well as that of the Ripper.

In spite of this determinedly extravagant villain, the implausible setting, and the passage of time, the generation of "real-life" suspects continues unabated. Promoting their agenda of "solvability," these solutions appear heavily invested in the triumph of teleology, a convention of detective fiction uneasily imposed on a series of historical—and notorious primarily because they are unsolved—murders. The premise of these solutions rests on a paradox that asserts the solvability of the Ripper *murders* while at the same time winking at the notion of putting the Ripper *story* to rest forever. This paradox in turn relies on the double status of Jack the Ripper as unknown person and discursive presence. While the Ripper is "caught" every time, each solution reinforces the dubious aristocratic legend of a master criminal, a "Napoleon of crime"[12] who, like Professor Moriarty, the nemesis of that "other great [late-Victorian] misogynist," Sherlock Holmes (Frayling, 214), will forever elude permanent capture. As soon as each of these fictions of closure is published, its methodologies and authenticity are questioned by criminologists, historians, and Ripperologists alike, and each is condemned on the basis of the ultimate impossibility of ever proving the solution given the paucity of physical evidence and the passage of time. Thus, if these solutions ever really do bring about a kind of closure, these closures exist solely in the minds of their proponents and provide readers with an opportunity to revisit the murders and to relive the enjoyment of this serial narrative, much as the serial nature of the nineteenth-century novel afforded pleasure to its readers through delay and revelation. The ebb and flow of the public release of these solutions—fanfare followed by refutation, followed by yet another published theory that is subsequently discredited—mirrors the serial nature of the Ripper murders themselves:

> in an age which fervently demands explanation, the denial of expla-
> nation requires us to ask again and again. The repetitiveness of his
> representation echoes the repetitiveness of his performance. In the
> same way as the apparent randomness and motivelessness of his
> crimes make him largely undetectable, he evades capture by familiar
> language. (Tithecott, 169)

Like Freud's fort da game of disappearance and return, the pleasure of these solutions is in the constant capture and release, release and capture.[13]

Each Ripperologist's solution is an "unwitting testament" to the "one permanent characteristic of Jack the Ripper: his *unknowability*" (Smith, 163). These solutions offer a kind of uncanny closure that is not a closure: all the well-ordered joy of a Golden Age detective story ending along with the vicarious thrill of allowing the bad guy to go free. In 1888, Jack the Ripper's fame as a murderer was reestablished with each progressively more brutal killing; as a discursive entity, he is reaffirmed through per-forming spectacle, the display of a shared fantasy, and the now established conventions of serial fiction: repeated pattern killings in successive chapters, each with a plot buildup, climax, and denouement of its own. While seeming to participate in a codification of the story of the modern serial killer, these solutions are equally invested, if not more invested, in allowing the "monstrous" to avoid the ultimate nature of teleology, which entails the impossibility of reappearance. More than providing "a common vocabulary for male violence against women" (Walkowitz, 228) or acting out a famous name, Ripper solutions reiterate their paradigmatic story, becoming a "genre" through the repetition of violence, a dismemberment of other largely nineteenth-century genres, such as the urban Gothic, melodrama, horror, and mystery, that mirrors the evisceration of the Ripper's victims. The disappointingly conventional suturing procedure that combines these ingredients within the plot of detection eliminates the potential such a fascinating slippage between genres and modes of representation might bring. Rather than exploring the potential for representational strategies that such a liminal figure as Jack the Ripper might yield, these solutions sidetrack any possibility that a different kind of representational strategy might allow unknowability to become an asset instead of an obstacle to be overcome.

Instead, this unknowability has allowed Jack the Ripper, whoever he was, to become famous—a shorthand in public discourse, a legend, a brand name, a paradigm, a metaphor—while his victims, the most embodied participants in this history, are virtually unknown, stage props for the performance of this discursive role, the necessary victims of the world's most famous sexual predator. Ripperologist Philip Sugden's description of the first "canonical" Ripper murder, that of Polly Nicholls, is almost comical in its adherence to this cliché: "The Buck's Row killer had left nothing except Polly's body to mark his passing" (47). The most glaring omission in representations of the Ripper murders is the scarcity of the victims'—of women's—stories altogether, stories overshadowed by repeated exhibition of their bodies through photographs, diagrams, and courtroom testimony describing their mutilations. The victims are like extras, and as long as they show up at the right time and in the right costume (thereby signifying their social status and occupation, prostitution), the play can continue. In contrast to the killer, the victims in this genre—if they are depicted alive at all—are generally eroticized, made younger and more sexually attractive, and simultaneously more vulnerable, than they were in 1888.

With the possible exception of the last Ripper victim, Mary Jane Kelly, who was considered young (twenty-four) and attractive (and this may go a long way toward explaining her prominent place in Ripperology lore), Jack the Ripper's victims were middle-aged women who had led lives of extreme poverty and poor nutrition and who, in at least two cases, suffered from chronic physical conditions, alcoholism, or both to such an extent that they did not have long to live even if they had never encountered the Ripper. Their appearance reflected the harsh realities of their social positions and occupations. Victorian depictions of the Ripper victims were in many ways more progressive and empathetic in their outlook than those of the present, although the Victorian press also consistently underestimated the ages of the Ripper's victims. When writing about why women turned to prostitution in spite of the risk of arrest and imprisonment, Havelock Ellis wrote, quoting the November 4, 1889, *Pall Mall Gazette,* "So long as there are a large body of women in the East of London, and in other large centers, who are prepared to say: 'It's Jack the Ripper or the bridge with me. What's the odds?' there will be a still larger number of persons who will willingly accept the risks of prison."[14] Another prostitute elicited sympathy from a reporter when she told the *Pall Mall Gazette,* "The people speak so kind and sympa-thisin' about the women he has killed and I'd not object to being ripped up by him to be talked about so nice after I'm dead" (qtd. in Sugden, 360). Sugden includes this exchange as an effort to explain the Ripper's victims' points of view, but his effort here is notable mostly for its singularity.

This appropriation of the Ripper murders for political ends may date back to that infamous autumn of 1888, but it continues to the present as sexual "murder tends to be treated as a peg on which to hang discussion of other issues (prostitution and slum-clearance in the case of Jack the Ripper; cheque-book journalism and police incompetence in the Yorkshire Ripper case . . .)" (Cameron and Frazer, 122). According to Walkowitz, the media during the Whitechapel murders usurped the concerns of female political reformers (primarily prostitution, poverty, sanitation) and reworked them into a male Gothic melodrama closer in tone to the literature of urban exploration, of the flaneur. The media also drew on cultural fantasies of the grotesque and sexually promiscuous female body; the labyrinthine city, including the illicit and squalid Whitechapel setting; and the notion of the deviant lurking inside every respectable person à la Jekyll and Hyde. The media transformed the murders into a dark male fantasy that simultane-ously symbolized national disgrace and provided titillation. Whitechapel "vigilance committees" were formed ostensibly to offer protection to the women of the area; however, they largely aided in policing the movements and sexual activities of the women they were supposed to protect.

If there was ever a Victorian myth to rival Jack the Ripper, that myth is Sherlock Holmes, whose first appearance in novel form (*A Study in Scarlet*) in the autumn of 1888 coincided roughly with the Whitechapel murders. The canonization of Sherlock Holmes as the father of modern detection makes the merger of these two "characters," these narrative-generating titans, seem almost inevitable, culminating in the "genre" of Sherlock Holmes v. Jack the Ripper fictions, which includes such works as Edward Hanna's *The Whitechapel Horrors* (1992), Ellery Queen's *A Study in Terror* (1966, and its film adaptation of the same name), the Bob Clark film *Murder by Decree* (1979), and, most infamously, Michael Dibdin's *The Last Sherlock Holmes Story* (1978).[15] The genre of Sherlock Holmes v. Jack the Ripper posits a world in which the two "characters" not only coincidentally appear but also intersect. At first blush, this genre appears to treat the narrative possi-bilities of Jack the Ripper in a manner similar to that of the Ripperologists' solutions; however, this genre self-consciously perpetuates and expands the Ripper mythos rather than attempting to clarify his "existence." The uncanny repetition of the combination of two such narrative powerhouses performs the ideological work of reinforcing both Jack the Ripper's and Sherlock Holmes's prominence in cultural and criminological discourse. Thus, the continued cultural resonance of one insures the resonance of the other, a form of discursive guilt by association. In spite of the detective novel format that these fictionalizations follow, they are no more interested in conclusively fixing Jack the Ripper's identity than the endless ostensibly fact-based (in some ways, excessively fact-based) "final solutions" are. In particular, Michael Dibdin's novel—which allows for the possibility that Sherlock Holmes *is* Jack the Ripper—is far more interested in playing with our expectations of both characters and of the rules of detective fiction than in pinning down either "character."[16] By troubling these expectations, Sherlock Holmes v. Jack the Ripper fictions mirror the inchoate and mutable quality of their characters' cultural positions more than the real-life solutions do.

While enacting a readerly fantasy of realizing the fictional character of Sherlock Holmes and fictionalizing the real person who was Jack the Ripper, the Sherlock Holmes v. Jack the Ripper genre merges two quintessentially Victorian characters "born" in 1888 whose epistemological methodologies involve the acquisition of knowledge (and notoriety) through fragmentation and dismemberment (physical and metaphorical). The juxtaposition of these two "characters" and the prevalence of the Sherlock Holmes v. Jack the Ripper genre suggest that both are integral to a mode of understanding— women, murder and violence, the Victorian city—through taking, or hacking, things apart. This genre promotes its own version of epistemological "truth" while allowing us to indulge in the Victorian nostalgia upon which this truth depends:

> If the facts don't fit the legend, then today's sleuths, amateur or professional, tend to print the legend; and readers—used to films which show beautiful young victims (the *average* age of the Ripper's victims was 45, before Mary Kelly broke the pattern) wandering through a thick curtain of expressionist winter fog (in September?) to meet a man in a top hat and opera cloak who is carrying a bulky Gladstone bag, pausing only to chat to Lyceum-style "locals" on the way—tend to believe it. (Frayling, 185)

Without this hyperreal, stylized version of the Ripper's victims and the murders' setting, the premise of both the fictional pastiches and the proposed solutions would be greatly nullified. Constructing a "truth" of the

Ripper murders relies first on creating a world in which truth (as Victorian detective fiction defines it) is recoverable.

The danger in romanticizing contemporary "Jack the Rippers" and their "Sherlock Holmeses" lies not so much in the potential for copycat killings, as Caputi suggests, but in the potential for copycat investigations. The danger, especially for women, is that criminological discourse about serial killers will continue to fall into the same traps and repeat the same "detective versus master criminal" narrative glorified in such fictions as those of the Sherlock Holmes v. Jack the Ripper genre. In "There's Only One Yorkshire Ripper," feminist journalist Joan Smith exposes the fatal consequences of seeing Jack the Ripper as "not a person but a *label* connecting a set of related acts" (163), not as one of many serial killers but as *the* serial killer. As a serial killer prowled the Yorkshire area in the late 1970s, the police made a fatal assumption: that the murderer was a modern-day reincarnation of the popular conception of Jack the Ripper, a clever madman bent on killing prostitutes. The result of the Yorkshire police's stubborn adherence to the belief that they were pursuing a "latter-day Jack the Ripper, that *this* was the significant link to look for in establishing which were the man's victims" (Smith, 170, emphasis mine) proved disastrous. By insisting that the Yorkshire Ripper's victims must be prostitutes, the police investigated several murders of prostitutes that were unrelated to the Yorkshire Ripper and discounted actual victims who were considered the "wrong kind of woman," too "innocent" to be this Ripper's victims. Moreover, some victims whose murders were linked to others by physical evidence were incorrectly labeled prostitutes in order to be included in the inquiry. Smith was herself mistaken for a prostitute when she arrived at the police station to interview the detective in charge of the case: "A prostitute, it seems, is any woman in the wrong place at the wrong time" (176). At the same time, the Yorkshire police's profile of the killer was also both formulaic and too restrictive, causing them to eliminate the real killer—the supremely ordinary, working-class Peter Sutcliffe—from their investigation several times in spite of overwhelming circumstantial evidence. Their insistence that the killer would conform to the Jack the Ripper model contributed to the Yorkshire Ripper's death toll: "if you devote your resources to tracking down a figure from myth . . . you are not likely to come up with a lorry driver from Bradford" (Smith, 164).[17]

These presuppositions about both the killer and the victims caused the Yorkshire police to negate crucial physical evidence and to approach the case backwards, trying to make the evidence fit the profile instead of the reverse. Because of their acceptance of the Ripper hypothesis, "they [the Yorkshire police] convinced themselves that they knew the killer in some mysterious and undefined way; that, if they were suddenly confronted with him, they would recognize him at once" (Smith, 170). To the investigators, the Yorkshire Ripper would have to be as simultaneously exotic and familiar as the legendary version of Jack the Ripper. The investigation consistently turned away from suspects who resembled the police detectives' married, blue-collar acquaintances toward that strangely aristocratic fantasy of nebulous value, the Ripper "as genius, artist, core soul of mankind, preternatural demon, outlaw hero, an undefeatable and eternal entity" (Caputi, "American Psychos," 103). For example, the police concentrated almost exclusively on an elusive false lead, the man with the Geordie accent, because they had received a letter and cassette tape from this man repeating phrases supposedly written by Jack the Ripper in the infamous (but now largely discredited) "Dear Boss" letter received by Central News Ltd. on September 27, 1888. The police also believed that they would be able to recognize the killer instantly by some tenuous exhibition of difference that was never clearly stated (transparent insanity, hatred of women, physical deformity or inferiority), much as Sherlock Holmes could glean a person's class or occupation at a glance. Smith argues that "The difficulty in hunting so insubstantial a figure . . . nudge[d] the police in the direction of assigning characteristics to the man they are looking for—to make him into an acquaintance, someone they can talk about as a real person among themselves and to the press" (166).[18] For instance, upon receiving a second letter and cassette recording from the supposed killer, George Oldfield, the assistant chief constable of West Yorkshire, commented, "I would like to talk to this man. And I feel he wants to talk to me. This has become something of a feud. He obviously wants to outwit me, but I won't pack it in until he's caught" (qtd. in Smith, 184). Ironically, the packages from the mysterious man with the Geordie accent did in fact turn out to be sent by someone Oldfield was acquainted with, a former colleague playing a misguided practical joke.

As the Yorkshire Ripper's death toll quickly overtook his Victorian predecessor's, the police visualized themselves not only as tracking down a modern-day Jack the Ripper but specifically as modern-day Sherlock Holmeses pursuing Jack the Ripper. In order to do this, they imagined themselves as detectives who were not police officers, and in this way they managed to combine their fantasy of chasing down a master villain like Jack the Ripper with that of seeing themselves as heroes in the resurrection of "a real-life mystery from the era of Sherlock Holmes." By visualizing themselves as Sherlock Holmeses, the Yorkshire police were able to fantasize operating outside of the boundaries of law—life as a private detective instead of a public servant—while ostensibly embodying the law. Such extralegal supremacy comprises part of the serial killer's allure as well: "Ascribing authority to the convicted serial killer might appear strange if we didn't regard transcending the law as being *in* power. The figure of the serial killer is both outside of society (out of the law) and in authority (*beyond* the law). Because he transcends the law in both cases, there is no contradiction" (Tithecott, 111). In *Of Men and Monsters*, Richard Tithecott identifies two elements essential to the popularity and proper functioning of serial killer fictions, those of "denial (denial that the serial killer has any connection with normality) and of celebration (of the serial killer's perceived transcendence of normality)" (9). In the case of the Yorkshire Ripper investigation, the possibility of the killer's working-class roots was ignored while his distinctiveness was not only taken for granted but relished. Apparently competing with a master villain elevates his opponent.

In *Murder by Decree,* a film based on Stephen Knight's theory about a Masonic conspiracy to kill the five prostitutes who had knowledge of the heir to the throne's marriage to a Catholic, Arthur Conan Doyle's characters are interjected into a Jack the Ripper solution based on theory involving "real," historical suspects, unlike other Sherlock Holmes v. Jack the Ripper fictions, which largely involve fictional suspects. In the film, Inspector Lestrade perpetuates the myth of Jack the Ripper, describing him as being "in league with the devil," motivated by evil, insanity, or both, but not by social forces or by the exaggerated extension of everyday, ordinary misogyny. Lestrade continues, describing the Ripper as someone who "appears, disappears at will"—not just evil, but superhuman. The hyperbole of these descriptions reinforces the notion of Jack the Ripper as unknowable and uncategorizable. The genre of Sherlock Holmes v. Jack the Ripper does not pit the women of Whitechapel against the Ripper; instead the Ripper's nemesis is an upper-middle-class gentleman living far from the East End in the kind of neighborhood that must have seemed like another world to the women who were likely to have been the Ripper victims, as well as to the men who were most likely to be the Ripper. As Frayling rightly argues, "The Ripper was much more likely to have been the victim himself of the syndrome that leads some deeply depressed, and highly impressionable, men to see a 'fallen woman' as the one last person they can push around than to have been one of the more famous 'other Victorians'; the frustrated victim of (apparent) powerlessness rather than the possessor of real power" (205). In other words, he was more likely to be someone just like Peter Sutcliffe.

Paralleling the Sherlock Holmes v. Jack the Ripper genre, the Yorkshire police relentlessly subscribed to an outdated narrative of sexually motivated serial murder: a "one detective/one perpetrator" psychodynamic in which both "characters'" motivations are persistently configured as individual and psychological rather than sociological or economic. Walkowitz mitigates somewhat Smith's criticism of the Yorkshire police, arguing that while feminists "mock[ed] the police's romantic identification with the Ripper's late-Victorian contemporary," they also "exposed the immersion of the police in a fantasy that positioned them, not women, as the Ripper's principal antagonists (citing such statements as 'It's between him and me,' which they attributed to the officer in charge of the first hunt)" (236).[19] The ascendance of the master detective/archvillain paradigm is bought at the expense of the abject, the female corpse that succumbs to the Oedipal narrative project of quest and resolution.[20] Contemporary criminology's view of serial killers "within its framework of thoroughgoing individualism . . . full of autonomous subjects with individual passions and personal relationships" promotes a blind spot when it comes to the gender dynamics of serial murder since, from that point of view, "there is no reason why one social group [men] should be prototypical killers, while their victims cluster in another social group [women]." Instead, like detective fiction, "Criminology seeks to explain why this individual kills that one; yet the facts suggest there is a prior question, why members of some groups kill members of others" (30). In the stereotypical Ripper story, the social background of the killer or his victims is only as relevant as the setting, frosting on the cake. Such complexity may lend interesting detail; however, it is far from vital to the story itself.

The Yorkshire police are hardly alone in looking at contemporary serial killers through the nostalgic lens of Victorian detective fiction or the contemporary Sherlock Holmes v. Jack the Ripper genre. Profilers, criminologists, and FBI behavioral scientists are not immune from this kind of slippery thinking, this desire to see themselves as the heroes of a Victorian detective story. In his memoir, *Mindhunter,* John Douglas, the former head of the FBI's Behavioral Science Unit (now the National Center for the Analysis of Violent Crime, or NCAVC), attempts a history of the practice of criminal psychological profiling. In a chapter titled "My Mother's Name was Holmes" that opens with this personal revelation, "My mother's name was Holmes, and my parents almost chose that as my middle name instead

of the more prosaic Edward," Douglas traces profiling not to any historical law enforcement figure but instead back to

> Sir Arthur Conan Doyle's immortal creation, Sherlock Holmes, who
> brought out this form of criminal investigative analysis for all the
> world to see in the shadowy gaslit world of Victorian London. The
> highest compliment any of us can be paid, it seems, is to be com-
> pared to this fictional character. I took it as a real honor some years
> back when, while I was working a murder case in Missouri, a head-
> line in the *St. Louis Globe-Democrat* referred to me as the "FBI's
> Modern Sherlock Holmes." (20)[21]

In his description, Douglas not only invokes the stereotype he later debunks
in *The Cases That Haunt Us* ("the shadowy gaslit world of Victorian
London") but also reinscribes his position as master sleuth, a gesture at
once both human and frightening in its implications. Almost as if in
response to Douglas's muddling, Smith argues a clear distinction: "The
difference between Peter Sutcliffe and Jack the Ripper is the difference
between fact and fiction" (163). However, while Smith's goal in making
such a distinction is laudable and perhaps even politically fruitful, drawing such a distinction perpetuates a cultural myth even more powerful
than those of Jack the Ripper or Sherlock Holmes: namely, that this divide
exists in any meaningful way in the first place. Even more relevant to current investigations of serial killers is that this insistence keeps alive the
very fictions Smith is trying to undermine, enabling them to be privileged
over other stories we could be telling, stories that might stand such priorities on their heads and affirm the rest of us, the victims and potential victims.

It is not hard to imagine why the Yorkshire police would want to see
themselves as the kind of cultural superhero Sherlock Holmes represents,
particularly since this desire coincides with ours for a "reality satisfying
the demands of fiction" (Tithecott, 123). In order to satisfy the demand
for what the Ripper represents, the Ripper himself "has been constantly
re-invented . . . to accommodate the 'beasts,' 'monsters,' and 'maniacs' of
the moment. Each generation has added embellishments to a genre picture
which was first created out of the West End's fear of the outcast East, out
of a glimpse into the abyss" (Frayling, 214). While I strongly disagree with
Frayling's use of Nietzschean hyperbole—Jack the Ripper is a *performance* of cultural anxieties rather than a displacement of them—it is clear
that such dark dreamings continue to appeal if only to save us from hav-

ing to face the alternatives. As I put the finishing touches on this article, the latest Hollywood version of the Jack the Ripper story is poised for its video release, a film titled *From Hell* (2001). Based on the graphic novel by Alan Moore, the film stars Johnny Depp as the intrepid (and, in this version at least, psychic) Inspector Abberline, the police official in charge of the Ripper investigation, and Ian Holm as chief suspect, royal surgeon Sir William Gull. The trailers repeat the familiar iconography: foggy nights, dank cobblestone streets, quick shots of a knife flashing by gaslight, a killer in a long, black cape, and an attractive young Mary Jane Kelly (Heather Graham). The film's tag line proclaims, "Only the legend will survive" while the character of Jack the Ripper intones in the dark, "I gave birth to the twentieth century." Both statements play on the audience's desires: the tag line implicates us in the repeated escape of the killer while the Ripper's proclamation casts us all as his descendants. But these lines only tell us what we already know, that "the apparent inability of our cops and killers to distinguish fact from fantasy goes along with our inability or lack of desire to do the same. Together we allow ourselves to dream the dream of omnipotence" (Tithecott, 117). More telling, we allow ourselves to dream of a make-believe time before the postmodern, when identity was as readable (and, dare I say, as romantic) as the glow of gaslight, even with the ubiquitous fog.

Notes

I would like to thank the Ahmanson Foundation for providing fellowship support during the writing and research of this article, and John Jordan and the Dickens Project at the University of California, Santa Cruz, for allowing me to present an earlier version of this paper to the generous scholars at the summer conference, the Dickens Universe. I would like to extend my gratitude as well to Elizabeth Archer, Sumangala Bhattacharya, James Kincaid, Jeffrey Langham, and Hilary Schor for their support, constructive suggestions, and expertise.

1. Joan Smith, "There's Only One Yorkshire Ripper," in *Misogynies* (New York: Ballantine Books, 1992), 163.

2. Stephen Knight, *Jack the Ripper: The Final Solution* (New York: David McKay Company, 1976).

3. Shirley Harrison, *Jack the Ripper: The Chilling Confessions of James Maybrick* (New York: Pocket Books, 1995).

4. Judith Walkowitz, *City of Dreadful Delight: Narratives of Sexual Danger in Late-Victorian London* (Chicago: University of Chicago Press, 1992), 1.

5. My work on Jack the Ripper, like all work on this enigmatic cultural phenomenon, is indebted to Judith Walkowitz. I only have space here to include a bare-bones outline of the complex intersections of scientific and cultural discourses that combine to define Jack the Ripper as the archetypal serial killer since the focus of this article is not the Ripper per se but

his continuing resonance in the present. See in particular Jane Caputi, *The Age of Sex Crime* (Bowling Green, Ohio: Bowling Green State University Popular Press, 1987), and "American Psychos: The Serial Killer in Contemporary Fiction," *Journal of American Culture* 16, no. 4 (Winter 1993): 101–12; Christopher Frayling, "The House That Jack Built: Some Stereotypes of the Rapist in the History of Popular Culture," in *Rape*, ed. Sylvana Tomaselli and Roy Porter (Oxford: Basil Blackwell, Inc., 1986); Sander L. Gilman, "'Who Kills Whores?' 'I Do,' Says Jack: Race and Gender in Victorian London," in *Death and Representation*, ed. Sarah Webster Goodwin and Elisabeth Bronfen (Baltimore: Johns Hopkins University Press, 1993); Donald Rumbelow, *Jack the Ripper: The Complete Casebook*, introd. by Colin Wilson (New York: Contemporary Books, 1988); and Philip Sugden, *The Complete History of Jack the Ripper* (New York: Carroll & Graf Publishers, 1994). However, Jack the Ripper's title as the foundational serial killer, although erroneous, is almost universally taken for granted.

6. Richard Tithecott, *Of Men and Monsters: Jeffrey Dahmer and the Construction of the Serial Killer,* foreword by James R. Kincaid (Madison: University of Wisconsin Press, 1997), 5.

7. John Douglas with Mark Olshaker, *The Cases That Haunt Us* (New York: Scribner, 2000), 19–20. The London fog is a recurring theme in Sherlock Holmes v. Jack the Ripper fictions and in analyses of the Ripper murders. While fog is often invoked to create the properly creepy atmosphere, Joan Smith uses it effectively as a metaphor for a bungled investigatory process: "throughout the hunt for the Yorkshire Ripper, the police forces of several northern counties did little more than stumble about in a fog as dense as that used to invoke the atmosphere of Victorian London in many a film about Jack the Ripper. And, like the peasoupers which choked the lungs of the inhabitants of the metropolis right up until the 1950s, it was a fog very much of their own making" (166). Frayling even describes Jack the Ripper as an "absence in the fog" (214), in yet another juxtaposition of the ephemeral nature of the Ripper with the embodied presence of his victims, whose wounds Frayling describes in some detail.

8. John Douglas with Mark Olshaker, *Mindhunter: Inside the FBI's Elite Serial Crime Unit* (New York: Pocket Books, 1995), 18.

9. Deborah Cameron and Elizabeth Frazer, *The Lust to Kill: A Feminist Investigation of Serial Murder* (New York: New York University Press, 1987), 21. This gendered imbalance in discussions of Jack the Ripper and his de facto offspring has only lately begun to be redressed; see in particular Caputi and Cameron and Frazer, as well as some recent studies on female serial killers, especially Valerie Karno, "Between Victim and Offender: Aileen Wuornos and the Representation of Self-Defense," *Critical Matrix: The Princeton Journal of Women, Gender and Culture* 11, no. 2 (1999): 67–86.

10. One of the most persistent stories we tell of serial killers concerns their monstrousness. This characterization of the serial killer as monster can be gleaned with even a cursory glance at the titles of books of the true crime genre, as well as law enforcement memoirs such as Robert Ressler and Tom Shachtman's *Whoever Fights Monsters* and *I Have Lived in the Monster*. Academic treatments, such as Richard Tithecott's *Of Men and Monsters: Jeffrey Dahmer and the Construction of the Serial Killer* and Diana Fuss's "Monsters of Perversion: Jeffrey Dahmer and *The Silence of the Lambs*" (in *Media Spectacles*, ed. Marjorie Garber, Jann Matlock, and Rebecca L. Walkowitz [New York: Routledge, 1993]) have employed the description ironically for the most part. The notion of the monstrous draws on popular and enduring nineteenth-century Gothic and horror conventions and seeps into otherwise straightforward accounts of sexual murder, such as Cameron and Frazer's: "Because his identity was never established, 'Jack' has attained the status of a popular folk-devil, rather like Dracula or Frankenstein's monster. One imagines him stealing down foggy London streets, with a top hat and swirling black cloak, tapping his cane" (123). Frayling has divided the Ripper's identity into three main categories: decadent English Milord; mad doctor; and anarchist, socialist, or

philanthropist; all of these "identities" originated in the intense and often melodramatic news-paper coverage of the Whitechapel murders in the fall of 1888 and repeat the image of the Ripper as monstrous other.

11. For further discussion of the Ripper murders in the context of the socioeconomic con-ditions in Whitechapel at the time, see Robert F. Haggard, "Jack the Ripper as the Threat of Outcast London," *Essays in History* 35 (1993).

12. Arthur Conan Doyle, *The Memoirs of Sherlock Holmes* (Oxford: Oxford University Press, 1993), 252.

13. *Beyond the Pleasure Principle,* Standard Edition (New York: Norton, 1961), 13–15.

14. Havelock Ellis, *The Criminal,* 4th ed. (London: Blackwood, Scott & Company, 1910), 372.

15. Jack the Ripper has been the subject of fictionalizations without Sherlock Holmes and Sherlock Holmes has been the subject of "further adventures" by writers and filmmakers other than Arthur Conan Doyle, but here I am only concerned with the particular genre sub-set in which the two intersect. Four writers (at least) have used other characters from the Arthur Conan Doyle canon to solve the Ripper murders: in W. S. Baring-Gould's 1962 novel, *Sherlock Holmes of Baker Street,* Watson discovers that Inspector Athelney Jones of Scotland Yard was the Ripper; in John Gardner's *The Return of Moriarty,* the "Napoleon of crime," in an attempt to avoid being blamed for the murders himself, offers a large reward, "discovers" the identity of Jack the Ripper (Montague Druitt), and orders his henchmen to execute the suspect; Sherlock Holmes's brother Mycroft solves the Whitechapel murders in Ray Walsh's *The Mycroft Memorandum;* and, in M. J. Trow's *The Further Adventures of Inspector Lestrade,* Inspector Lestrade solves the Ripper case (amongst others—eleven murders total throughout the course of the novel), and thereby proves himself more savvy than his por-trayal in the Conan Doyle stories would lead the reader to believe. Both Baring-Gould and Trow are engaged in a recuperative process on behalf of their central characters by rescuing them from Doyle's dismissiveness.

Other Sherlock Holmes v. Jack the Ripper fictions include Carol Nelson Douglas, *Chapel Noir*; the 1985 Hugh Leonard play, *The Mask of Moriarty,* a comic parody in which Jack the Ripper appears; the 1970 Billy Wilder film, *The Private Life of Sherlock Holmes,* which "originally included . . . an epilogue in which Holmes, still shaken by recent events [the revelations of the film], turns down Scotland Yard's plea for help in the case of Jack the Ripper, thereby explaining Holmes's absence from this sensational historical episode" (Matthew E. Bunson, *Encyclopedia Sherlockiana* [New York: Macmillan, 1994], 200); Raymond Thor's *Bloodguilty*; Jô Soares's *A Samba for Sherlock*; and the Spanish short story "Jack El Destripador" (translated by Anthony Boucher).

16. See Kate Flint, "Plotting the Victorians: Narrative, Post-modernism, and Contemporary Fiction," in *Writing and Victorianism,* ed. J. B. Bullen (London: Addison Wesley Longman, 1997), on Dibdin and the Sherlock Holmes v. Jack the Ripper computer game, *Sherlock Holmes and the Case of the Serrated Scalpel,* which invites the player to step into Victorian London: "a foggy late November afternoon, hansom cabs splashing through the damp streets, familiar London landmarks rising through the gloom in the background, before a shadowy figure—soon to be identified as Jack the Ripper—strikes a young actress leaving the back door of a theatre" (286). Flint argues that by conflating Holmes and the Ripper and "By writing of fiction in terms of its capacity to be matched up against 'facts'—facts which themselves exist only in fiction—Dibdin is blurring the distinctions between real and represented world, reduc-ing both to a matter of language. He is also calling into question the conventional distinction between historical and fictional narratives" (288).

17. Besides Walkowitz and Cameron and Frazer, the most thorough work on the Yorkshire Ripper is Nicole Ward Jouve, *"The Streetcleaner": The Yorkshire Ripper Case on Trial* (London,

Marion Boyars Publishers, 1986). Also interesting is Gordon Burn, *Somebody's Husband, Somebody's Son: The Story of the Yorkshire Ripper* (London: Pan Books, 1974), written from a "true crime" standpoint.

18. Smith argues that the Yorkshire police's thought patterns—and by extension the assumptions of most law enforcement officials—indulged in pernicious kinds of faulty logic based on gender, race, and class stereotypes; however, the assumption of the familiarity of criminals, their similarity to the rest of the public and the police, often turns out to be grounded in experience in cases of "ordinary" murder. These assumptions can then even be read as originating, ironically, in a kind of feminist reality that emphasizes the danger for women *inside* the home: when a wife is murdered, look to her husband, that is, look first for obvious instead of esoteric motives and suspects. This banal reality of murder undercuts one of the premises of the mystery genre, which depends for its impetus on the obvious rarely being proven "true" and on criminals who do not follow expected patterns. Ironically, it is this adherence to *patterns* that makes the serial killer such a fruitful source of inspiration for detectives and detective fiction writers.

19. On the other hand, Walkowitz largely agrees with Smith's assessment of the Yorkshire police's gender politics, claiming that not much changed in the media's and the police's responses to the murders. She points out, however, that a strong feminist response to the murders prevented the Yorkshire Ripper murders being used to police female sexuality quite as strenuously as it was during the fall of 1888. Still, the Gothic imagery of male villainy was resurrected in the press and the by now established discourse of psychoanalysis allowed for Sutcliffe's mother and wife to be implicitly blamed for the murders (i.e., his female-dominated dysfunctional family caused him to be sexually confused and therefore understandably misogynist). Interestingly, 1970s feminists, according to Walkowitz, displayed a lack of interest in the subject of prostitution itself, unlike their Victorian predecessors, who saw the issue as integral to reform.

20. My definition of female corpse as abject derives from Julia Kristeva's *Powers of Horror: A Study in Abjection* (New York: Columbia University Press, 1982).

21. In *Mindhunter*, Douglas traces the practice of behavioral profiling to Sherlock Holmes and his predecessor, Edgar Allan Poe's C. August Dupin: "And though most of the books that dramatize and glorify what we [the FBI's Investigative Support Unit] do, such as Tom Harris's memorable *The Silence of the Lambs*, are somewhat fanciful and prone to dramatic license, our antecedents actually do go back to crime fiction more than crime fact. C. Auguste Dupin . . . may have been history's first behavioral profiler. This story ["The Murders on the Rue Morgue"] may also represent the first use of a proactive technique by the profiler to flush out an unknown subject and vindicate an innocent man imprisoned for the killings" (19–20). Ignoring entirely nearly two hundred years of scientific and forensic advances, Douglas prefers this version of his occupational ancestry.

Legal Uses of Victorian Fiction

Infant Felons to Juvenile Delinquents

CHRISTINE L. KRUEGER

Along with general anesthesia, limited liability, and test cricket, the concept of the "juvenile offender" is one of the Victorians' greatest inventions—if by greatest is meant broadly influential, if not necessarily beneficial. Thanks to the extraordinary success of this Victorian reconceptualization of the child, no matter how vociferously we protest our postmodern condition, we were all born into a post-Victorian state. The process by which the juvenile offender and juvenile delinquent were created was likewise peculiarly Victorian, and (like its products) remains a vital part of political discourse. Its constituent parts were not new: for example, "infant" as a category limiting agency and culpability had long been a part of common law; in criminal law, a child under seven years of age could not be convicted of a felony, and between the ages of seven and fourteen there was rebuttable presumption of his incapacity to distinguish good from evil. Therefore the courts and legislature were in fact congenial sites for realizing a new understanding of childhood, though they were—and are once again—more often cast as the enemies of children. Similarly, the belief that childhood constitutes a morally and psychologically unique period of human experience did not originate with the Victorians. Yet, an extraordinary public relations effort was required to convince a majority of Victorian decision makers that their ignorance of peculiarly childish motives, desires, and experiences hampered their ability to manage—or serve—this segment of society adequately. Juvenile delinquents had to be constituted as an epistemological problem in order to be dealt with as a social problem.

The methods by which this was achieved are my principal concern here. The history of Victorian juvenile penal reform methods elucidates with particular clarity the interconnected components of an emerging democratic epistemology in its relation to new social and political formations. And, because those methods are enjoying a revival in contemporary political philosophy and in the literature and law movement, their history deserves our attention. I will illustrate key features of juvenile penal reform arguments and the problems they raise by focusing on the career of Mary Carpenter, the period's foremost advocate of juvenile penal reform. Like other social reforms aimed at groups that were shown to deviate from the legal paradigm of the property-holding male, reform of penal policies regarding children appealed to the mix of rationalistic and sentimental arguments that various theorists have identified as typifying the legitimating strategies of the bourgeois state.[1] Drawing on sympathy and self-interest, storytelling and statistics, Carpenter addressed herself in articles, pamphlets, and books to the newly emerging authority of "public opinion," calling on this nebulous aggregate to change its corporate mind. This corporate mind, it seems, was changed by the same methods as the bourgeois individual's: through a combination of utilitarian calculation and spiritual conversion, which demanded a dialectic of empiricism and visionary insight, or imagination— a combination familiar to readers of nineteenth-century realistic fiction. However, as Carpenter's 1864 work entitled *Our Convicts* illustrates, that dialectic would become increasingly volatile as an emerging mass culture transformed public discourse and with it the means of authenticating truth claims. What is more, Carpenter's rise from schoolteacher to internationally recognized expert on juvenile delinquency tells us much about the gendering of method in English political history. Women's claims to rationality and powers of abstract reasoning had gone down with radical politics in the early decades of the century, to be replaced by conservatives' emphasis on women's sympathetic and nurturing powers. Not surprisingly, women would come to allege special expertise under the rubrics of sentimental moral theory and empirical observation, particularly when the subject involved children.[2]

Sentimental moral theory, empiricism, aesthetics, gender ideology, and mass culture remain salient features of present-day democratic processes. Indeed, critics who indict contemporary democratic institutions, notably the law, for their failure to recognize adequately the diverse experiences and needs of our multicultural populations often recur to specifically Victorian modes of representation and argument as ideal means by which decision makers can empathize with people whose circumstances differ from their own. Having diagnosed the antidemocratic outcomes of the law, for example, as resulting from failures of empathy, they turn to nineteenth-century literature for examples of the efficacy of what Wai-Chee Dimock has termed "literary reasoning."[3] Dickens is a particular favorite. Richard Rorty credits him with providing us "the details about kinds of suffering being endured by people to whom we [have] not previously attended," a reason that he considers the novel to be "among the principal vehicles of moral change and progress."[4] Interestingly, relatively little attention has been focused on children as one of those categories of people about whose suffering we need the kind of special, detailed knowledge literature is so adept at providing. Surely, anyone mining Victorian literature for examples of political uses of empathy could hardly miss Oliver Twist, Tiny Tim, Jo in *Bleak House,* or those epitomes of social ills—Ignorance and Want—harbored under the cloak of the Ghost of Christmas Present. To this list we could add the child laborers in Elizabeth Barrett Browning's "The Cry of the Children" and 'Liza in *Uncle Tom's Cabin,* or even Peter Pan and Lewis Carroll's Alice, as well as many others recalled, perhaps, only by Victorian literature scholars but nonetheless contributing to a bourgeois conception of sentimentalized and ideologically potent childhood. Victorian creators of child characters, in short, wrote the book on empathy.

It lies beyond the scope of this essay to speculate on why this important contribution by Victorian literature to a politics of empathy does not figure more prominently in current debates, except to note that it may reflect the success of the Victorians' goal of creating empathy with children and the failure of that empathy to effect better conditions for children. That is, we may believe that we thoroughly understand those alien others—children—at the same time that we are unwilling to enact the material changes that would bring them out of poverty or render them less vulnerable to abuse. Or, as the following discussion of Mary Carpenter's methods might suggest, appealing to Victorian literary advocacy on behalf of children would draw unwanted attention to its paternalistic elements, as well as its essentialist construction of gender, associated today with Carol Gilligan's feminine ethics of care. I wish to focus instead on a related problem, which similarly proceeds from the difficulties arising out of postmodernist appeals to Victorian literature shorn of its authors' regard for a distinction between fact and fiction. Mary Carpenter's career illustrates the powerful—and problematic—mix of fact, fiction, and gender ideology in the politics of empathy.

In our own culture, wherein "poster child" has become synonymous with a paradigmatic representative of a victimized class, we may need to recall what a remarkable feat of persuasion was required to convince decision makers that social status was in any meaningful way inflected by age. The most notable early success for Victorian child advocates was the Ten Hours Movement, and significantly, literary authors were rather behind the curve. Novels such as Frances Trollope's *Michael Armstrong, the Factory Boy* (1839) and Charlotte Elizabeth Tonna's *Helen Fleetwood* (1839–41) drew on the extensive data that had already been collected by Lord Ashley, leader of the Ten Hours movement in the House of Commons, and that had been published in Parliamentary Blue Books.[5] The Ten Hours Movement was the brainchild of parliamentarians and others of the decision-making elite whose knowledge of factory conditions, gleaned through their investigations over two decades into of the effects of previous Factory Acts, convinced them of the need for further reform. Whatever inspired these men to inquire into the lives of child laborers, it would be hard to argue that it was imaginative literature, strictly defined. As the sources of Trollope's and Tonna's novels make clear, legislators and social investigators had already turned storytellers. Their reports and expert testimonies were filled with anecdotal evidence, and their novelizers were often at their most powerful when quoting directly from empirical sources. So why were novelists engaged in this movement at all, and why were they considered effective?

As Joseph Kestner has argued, from the 1830s, the social narrative was increasingly produced by women and in the form of novels. These novels popularized the data and theories of factual sources in a period in which women were looking for engagement in the public sphere and the public sphere was increasingly defined by mass-circulation publications aimed at a broad reading public. Women such as Tonna and Elizabeth Gaskell were directly recruited by social reformers to novelize their agendas, as Hannah More had been in an earlier generation. And, as Hannah More had been, they were considered to be especially strategic advocates on behalf of children. That these writers substantially feminized the Victorian political agenda in ways male reformers had not anticipated is now widely recognized, as is the more deprecatory claim that these writers contributed to the project of bourgeois hegemony. Both are relevant to the career of Mary Carpenter as an advocate for juvenile penal reform—how she shaped public opinion and how it shaped her.

Among the many philanthropists and politicians who devoted their energies to creating the concept of the juvenile offender, Mary Carpenter (1807–1877) was the most famous in her own day and is the best remembered in ours. She evolved out of the philanthropic tradition of Unitarianism into an internationally recognized expert on juvenile delinquency, education, and prison reform. Carpenter began her public career in a manner at once peculiarly feminine and practical. At sixteen, she began teaching in the school run by her father, Lant Carpenter, a celebrated Unitarian preacher and reformer. In 1827, she went to work as a governess and returned home in 1829 when financial difficulties stemming from her father's illness required the Carpenter women to open a girls' school. In 1831, she undertook a Sunday School and, under the influence of Rammohun Roy and Joseph Tuckerman, began a visiting society in 1835. Her father died in 1840, and in her grief, Mary Carpenter proceeded not only to write a memoir of Lant Carpenter, which would issue in her first publication, *Morning and Evening Meditations,* but also to open a ragged school in the Bristol slum of Lewin's Mead.

Consistent with the reform tradition of her day, practical sympathy went hand in hand with rational analysis, and she set about to master the subject of juvenile delinquency. Like many philanthropists, Carpenter read Parliamentary Blue Books (first sold to the public in 1836) and prison returns, as well as the growing body of pamphlet literature and journalism arguing for legislative reform. Carpenter brought an active and sympathetic imagination to her reading, finding moving drama in the stories of children recorded in prison reports, but also identifying intensely with their authors. Years later she would confess in a letter to her friend Frances Power Cobbe that she always "devour[ed]" Prison Reports "as many people do the last new novel."[6] And she expressed to the same correspondent a profound sense of bonding with authors of juvenile reform literature, describing as kindred spirits even those writers whom she had never met. Though it may be difficult for us to appreciate the literary value of prison reports or Parliamentary Blue Books, for Carpenter, like many pious women of the period who dedicated themselves to social reform, nothing was more moving or a more reliable guide to their spiritual duty than what they took to be unadorned representations of the truth. As much as her direct experience with juvenile delinquents, then, Carpenter's reading habits are key to understanding her sense of vocation, a calling to do the "Heavenly Father's work," as she put it. Not surprisingly, that vocation would come to include a literary element, writing by which she could move others to action through sympathetic identification with her and her subject matter.

In 1835, the Duke of Richmond's Committee produced the first parliamentary report on transportation to distinguish between juvenile and adult offenders. Earlier, as in Peel's Gaol Acts of 1823 and 1824, there had been some effort to distinguish classes of prisoners, yet no mention had been made of juvenile offenders as a distinct class, and the Poor Law of 1834 had lumped all classes of criminals together. But the report of the Duke of Richmond's Committee was indicative of change, brought about, arguably, by the same mechanisms that had spurred Lord Ashley's Ten Hours Movement. The Acts of 1823 and 1824, though they made no provision for juvenile offenders, set in place an inspection system that brought the stories of juvenile offenders to the attention of Parliament. Often including allegedly verbatim interviews with juvenile offenders, these inspectors' reports did much to create the concept of juvenile offender as a distinct category. Nevertheless, they did not necessarily argue for lighter or distinct forms of treatment for children but merely for their segregation within existing prisons. Indeed, precisely because prison inspectors were aware of the "miserable circumstances that drove boys to crime,"[7] they warned that separate prisons for juveniles would be ineffective unless they were made too harsh to afford an attractive alternative to the conditions under which criminal children enjoyed freedom. The result was the Act of 1838 founding the Parkhurst Reformatory, an institution that Carpenter would attack for attempting to combine what she believed to be the incompatible goals of punishment and character reformation.

Carpenter made her first contribution to the literature on juvenile delinquency with an 1849 tract entitled "Ragged Schools," and, in 1851, her book *Reformatory Schools for the Perishing and Dangerous Classes* gained her immediate national recognition as an expert on the reform of child convicts. These works combined utilitarian arguments regarding the causes of childhood criminality and the most efficacious means of its prevention with graphic accounts of child convicts, taken both from personal experience and from the reports of prison inspectors who had solicited young convicts' stories. In 1849 and 1850, Richard Monkton Milnes, later Lord Houghton, had introduced Juvenile Offenders bills, which had failed. Carpenter put these failures down to public ignorance. In her preface to *Reformatory Schools,* she complained that

> The mass of society are better acquainted with the actual condition of remote savage nations, than with the real life and the springs of action of these children, whose true nature is less visible to the public eye when collected in a Ragged School, or swarming in the by-streets, than is the state of little heathen children as exhibited in the Reports of Missionaries.[8]

Her goal in writing *Reformatory Schools* was "to offer a full and clear picture of the actual condition of Juvenile Delinquents, to consider their various characteristics, to trace out their mode of life, to see their homes, and thence to learn their early influences" (iv).

Carpenter was instrumental in attracting public attention to her cause, in 1851 organizing with Matthew Davenport Hill the first Birmingham Conference on juvenile delinquency. Her role in that conference, along with the popularity of her book, led a Parliamentary Committee of inquiry on juvenile delinquency to call her to testify. She had not even addressed the Birmingham Conference, but she testified before the Select Committee with an authority and polemical conviction that in retrospect alarmed her. Nonetheless, she was well on her way to becoming the principal spokesperson for juvenile penal reform.

Carpenter opened another school at Kingswood in 1852, and in 1854 she founded the first reformatory school for girls, Red Lodge, which she superintended until her death in 1877. In 1853, she participated in the second Birmingham Conference on juvenile delinquency, attended by three thousand and chaired by Lord Shaftesbury. Yet parliamentary support was still slow in coming. Several measures were introduced in these years, only to be rejected. Carpenter and her colleagues had kept Parliament and the press focused on the need for reformatories for juvenile delinquents but had not managed to overcome the long-standing belief in the efficacy of the deterrence afforded by prison sentences. Indeed, at the same time segments of the press were joining Carpenter's cause, soliciting public sympathy for juvenile delinquents, they were also fueling public anxiety regarding the effect of the 1853 Penal Act, which allowed for the release of ticket-of-leave men into the community in lieu of transportation. Before this Act provoked a backlash against criminals, Parliament passed, in 1854, the Youthful Offenders Act, establishing reformatory schools. This act authorized the Home Secretary to issue certificates to private reformatory schools and to contribute to maintenance of convicted children. Magistrates were empowered to send any offender under sixteen to a reformatory school for not less than two nor more than five years, but their admission to reformatory school had to be preceded by imprisonment for a minimum of fourteen days. Carpenter was deeply dissatisfied with this bill, preserving as it did what she believed to be the wholly counterproductive element of a preliminary prison sentence. Her work was hardly at an end, but it would be carried out under significantly changed conditions of public discourse, including some of her own making.

The next decade saw the growth of two apparently unrelated phenomena: the reformatory school movement and the new journalism, the latter spurred by the repeal of the Stamp Tax in 1855. Carpenter's original goal of reformatory sentencing for juvenile convicts was expanded to include a preventative element: the creation of schools for children whose social circumstances made it likely that they would commit crimes if not removed from their irresponsible, criminal, or simply destitute families. Twenty-seven reformatory schools were established in the first three years of the Youthful Offenders Act. Further parliamentary action was spurred by the public attention focused on these schools, both by parliamentary reports and by the press. In 1857, Parliament passed the Industrial Schools Act as a supplement to the 1854 act aimed at an estimated fifty thousand vagrant children. Justices were empowered to send any vagrant child between the ages of seven and fourteen whose parents could not give sureties of his or her good behavior to a certified industrial school for as long as was thought necessary, but not beyond age fifteen. Carpenter complained in 1859 that of thirteen industrial schools reporting, only fourteen children had been committed by magistrates. In 1860, responsibility for industrial schools was transferred from the Education Committee of the Privy Council to the Home Office, and in the same year there were forty-eight certified reformatories, housing four thousand offenders. An 1861 amending act to the Industrial Schools Act widened the category of children to include any child under fourteen found begging or receiving alms, vagrant, or who "frequents the Company of reputed Thieves." Also, parents were allowed to commit children they could not control. The reformatory movement peaked in the 1860s. Still, there were never more than fifty-three reformatories; annual admissions peaked at 1,570 boys and girls. Facilities were concentrated in Yorkshire, Lancashire, Middlesex, Surrey, and Warwickshire—a fact that depended on the chance efforts of private benevolence rather than systematic social policy. The acceptance of industrial schools was slow. Nevertheless, it would seem that Carpenter had won an extraordinary public relations victory in little more than a decade. Yet, those gains would soon be embedded in the dialectic of public sympathy manufactured by means problematically similar to those Carpenter had herself exploited.[9]

Reforms in juvenile penal policy paralleled the transformation of the concept of public opinion under the conditions of mass-circulation journalism. The repeal of the Stamp Act in 1855 led to a revolution in mass-circulation publication. Historians of the new journalism have thoroughly documented the effect on editorial policies, driven now by profit motive rather than the desire for political influence.[10] Crime reporting was the undisputed key to sales. The very Blue Books and inspectors' reports that had fueled legislation now became fodder for exposés, and the perennial favorites of crime fiction, like Jack Sheppard and Dick Turpin, were overshadowed by the real-life criminals newspaper writers culled from police reports. The underworld of child criminals that had been so dramatically— and lucratively—represented by, for example, Charles Dickens in *Oliver Twist* and in *Household Words* articles, could also provide a rich source for sensationalizing journalism. Indeed, as these new material conditions foregrounded, the line between empathy and sensationalism in forming public opinion was never clear.

The first crime panic of the newspapers' making came in the year following the repeal of the Stamp Act, and three years after the 1853 Penal Act. Major papers, like the *Times*, helped to create a myth of the ticket-of-leave men as the perpetrators of a garroting epidemic. Crime statistics of the period are for various reasons difficult to interpret, but legislators undeniably responded to the newspapers as newly powerful organs of public opinion with amazing alacrity, passing the Penal Servitude Act of 1857, tightening up the provisions and administration of the 1853 Act. The papers turned their attention elsewhere. But in 1862, the papers once again raised the cry against crime after Mr. Pilkington, the M.P. for Blackburn, was attacked by a garroter. This was the incident that served as Trollope's model for the attack on Mr. Kennedy in *Phineas Finn*. The newspapers turned it into a full-fledged moral panic, provoking a legislative backlash against the penal reform movement. Public outrage against ticket-of-leave men is credited with securing royal assent to the Security from Violence Act, which reintroduced flogging for robbery with violence. And in 1864, the Penal Servitude Act marked a fundamental change of public opinion away from reform of criminals to punishment. Minimum sentences were increased from three years to five, and the 1865 Prisons Act reestablished harsh prison regimes aimed at punishing rather than reforming criminals.[11]

It was in this climate that Mary Carpenter produced her final major work on prison reform, *Our Convicts,* published in 1864. She began that work by acknowledging the panic: "The events of the last two years have filled every one with consternation and fear for personal safety," she wrote.[12] Yet, as it had been throughout her career, empathetic identification was the only principled and practical response to crime. "'Our Convicts!'" she exclaimed in the book's first paragraph.

> They are part of our society! They belong to ourselves! They are not only subjects with us of the same great British Empire on which the sun never sets, but they belong to the same British Isles, the same small centre of civilization, the same heart of all the world's life, the same Island, small in geographical extent, infinitely great in its influence on the nations,—whence must go forth laws, principles, examples, which will guide for better or for worse the whole world! (1:1)

Furthermore, addressing adult crime was impossible without attending to the very issue to which Carpenter had devoted her life—juvenile delinquency. So, in one last great effort to secure the goals of a lifetime, to turn the tide of public opinion yet again, Carpenter asked her readers to look to the children.

Much of Carpenter's book *Our Convicts* deals, then, with children. Carpenter drew evidence not only from her own experience as a teacher in ragged schools but on the extensive literature that had been produced by the newly created reformatory school and prison inspection system. These bureaucratic documents provided her with a wealth of stories of children raised up in crime by their parents, abandoned and forced to steal food, or co-opted into criminal gangs by older children. Again and again she stressed the folly of sending such children to prison, where they would become hardened criminals, and urged her plan for extensive industrial schools for all children at risk.

But in addition to such sources, Carpenter now drew on the very newspapers that had helped to cause the panic and, most problematically, two works that impugn the method by which she had established her own expertise and influenced public policy: *Female Life in Prison* (1862) and *The Memoir of Jane Cameron, Female Convict* (1864), both written ostensibly by a prison matron.[13] The former is a series of character sketches of female prisoners generally illustrating the sentiment that "to see some of these women hour by hour, and listen to them in their mad defiance, rage and blasphemy, is almost to believe that they are creatures of another mould and race, born with no idea of God's truth, and destined to die in their own benighted ignorance . . . one is almost skeptical of believing that there was ever an innocent childhood or a better life belonging to them." (1:45–46). Mad infanticides, unrepentant thieves, and hardened juvenile convicts are sketched by the prison matron, who characteristically checks her expressions of sympathy with a worldly-wise fatalism regarding these women's reform. In *Jane Cameron,* for example, the prison matron records the life story of a prisoner raised up in crime by her own mother, brought to repentance by the prison matron's sympathy and moral influence only to fall into bad company after her release and finally to commit a transportable offense.

These books were great popular sensations, offering, as they claimed to do, the intimate details of female prisoners' lives such as would be uniquely available to a prison matron. As Carpenter's biographer Jo Manton describes them, "Books catering so delectably to feelings of prurient curiosity and moral superiority at the same time were sure of a sale; the second [*Jane Cameron*] ran through three editions in a year."[14] There is evidence in *Our Convicts* of Carpenter's concern to authenticate the prison matron's testimony, though she does not directly question the identity of its author. After all, anonymous publication by women was conventional, a sign of the writer's sense of decorum. Indeed, Carpenter herself was suspected of having been the author. But Carpenter was also concerned that the prison matron had revealed facts about female convicts' degeneracy that threatened to put them beyond the pale of reclamation, feeding the growing public sentiment to lock criminals up and throw away the key. Still, she could not deny the value of testimony that appeared perfectly to satisfy the very epistemological criteria she had urged as fundamental to sound penal policy. The prison matron was the ideal investigator of female convicts' lives: not only did her position give her access to these women, but her superior feminine sympathies drew prisoners out, softened their hearts, and encouraged them to speak not only of their criminal exploits but of their childhoods and of their own children. These were precisely the kinds of stories Carpenter had always claimed would enable the higher classes to empathize with convicts so as better to understand that proper treatment of child criminals—and potential child criminals—was the key to preventing crime. As she wrote in *Our Convicts,*

The condition in which the young of our country are growing up, or as it has been truly expressed, are dragged up, to take the place of the present generation in the ranks of crime and pauperism, should especially engage the attention of society, and enlist extensive voluntary effort. It is not known to the bulk of the middle and upper classes of society;—it cannot be known, for no word can give an adequate idea of it to those who have not *personally* [my emphasis] witnessed it. (2:378–79)

Mary Carpenter herself had witnessed these conditions, and so, too, she believed had the prison matron and the charges whose stories she told. "The Prison Matron's narrative has been so extensively read," wrote Carpenter,

that acquaintance with it may here be assumed. It presents a true picture of what the unfortunate women who are the subject of it actually are when in a Convict Gaol. Peculiarities of character, which are familiar to all who have had the care of female Reformatories and Prisons, are there excited to a frightful intensity, which is constantly increasing until they become a settled habit. Yet it does not appear that the women there depicted, who seem like monsters when in that unnatural condition, are different in their natures from other women who may be met with at large in the world. (1:2)

In *Our Convicts,* there were to be simple differences of expert opinion between Carpenter and the prison matron regarding the potential for reform. The prison matron, though Carpenter had no personal knowledge of her, appeared to be a kindred soul.

Defending the prison matron's narratives as evidence superior to that of official reports, Carpenter wrote in *Our Convicts:*

Such is the only insight which we can obtain into the general working of the Female Convict Prisons from official sources. Vague rumours, of course, from time to time, give some insight in the "secrets of the prison house;" the volumes of the Prison Matron give a vivid picture of their internal working. Respecting the reliable nature of this work we cannot entertain any doubt, as it is referred to by the Royal Commissioners in their interrogations of the Chief Director, and no doubt is expressed by them or him of the truth of the statements it contains; no suspicion appears to be entertained in it of serious faults in the system, and the greatest deference and respect is every-

where shown to the Directors, to one of whom the book is dedicated. (2:228)

Viewed cynically—or, merely with hindsight—the prison matron's "deference and respect" to the prison directors, indeed, the book's dedication to
a director, appear to be self-authenticating devices, designed to forestall
skepticism. They worked. Why did these authenticating strategies persuade
Mary Carpenter, of all people? Mary Carpenter, who two years later would
write in an article entitled "On the Non-Imprisonment of Children," "the
present mode of treatment of women in our convict prisons is a complete
failure. . . . The system adopted must be completely wrong, and can never
do what is intended, *reform* female convicts."[15] What seemed not to occur
to Carpenter was that she was reading a fictionalized version of the very
information that she and other reformers, and now the newspapers, had
popularized, a fiction that exploited the thrilling sensation of identifying
with the criminal class. Carpenter's own account in *Our Convicts* of the
typical prisoner's course through life could have served as the template for
the prison matron's narratives:

> This is one of the most usual ways in which our Convicts are raised.
> They begin as wild and neglected children; they have no true home
> influence; they learn in the streets all that ought to be far removed
> from the knowledge of the young; they are sent to prison; they come
> out more daring and qualified, by their having thus graduated in
> crime, to become the companions of more precocious thieves; one
> short imprisonment follows after another with the poor boy, until
> the character given of him at his trial obtains for him the final stamp
> of a Convict. Can we wonder at the hardened reckless bearing of a
> youth so trained? Could the early histories of the inmates of our
> Convict Prisons be ascertained, it would probably be found that a
> very large proportion had so begun their career in early youth. (1:58)

The prison matron was pleased to oblige Carpenter's desire for histories of
childhood, and conformed to her teachings in many other respects as well.
For example, based on her experiences at Red Lodge, Carpenter had to
concur with the prison matron that girls were more difficult to reform than
boys. Regarding the perversion of women's affections, she cited the prison
matron for corroborating evidence: "when perverted, as we saw them in
JANE CAMERON, they may be and are frequently made an instrument of
much evil"(2:211). What is more, *Jane Cameron* and official reports could

be used to confirm one another. Speaking of reports on juvenile crime gangs, Carpenter wrote, "we might hope that these are isolated cases, and that the painful and vivid descriptions of the den of thieves in Glasgow, by the author of JANE CAMERON, are either highly coloured or peculiar to that city; but we cannot" (1:68). She then turned to corroborating evidence taken from the "Reports Made of Notorious Harbours for Juveniles of Both Sexes," made in Liverpool in 1856.

Clearly, if the prison matron's narratives simply reproduced official reports already rich in narratives of the lives of convicts, including those of juvenile convicts, it is unlikely that Carpenter would have relied on them so extensively, despite their popularity. The prison matron's narratives also provide the kind of information that could only be known—or created—by a novelist. Carpenter would have encountered many scenes in *Female Convicts* and *Jane Cameron* in which characters' states of mind were represented, or unwitnessed events narrated, and she often cited such scenes. One is particularly notable both for its melodrama and its use of omniscient narration. Speaking of outbreaks of disruptive behavior at female prisons, Carpenter remarked, "though the official testimony already given, fully proves in general terms the violence of the outbreaks, yet as it is well to realize the kind of evil involved in them, and the difficulties the officials have to contend with, we copy the following scene from 'Jane Cameron.' It is evidently sketched from life" (2:233). In that scene, we are given Jane's thoughts as she sits alone in her cell, the memories and regrets that drive her to madness. Then follows a series of observable events: Jane tears her blanket, leaps on the table, batters at the window with her cup, and screams. Other prisoners respond in kind, and Jane continues screaming and singing the whole night, "with satisfaction," the prison matron tells us. Carpenter knowingly comments on this scene, "These fits of uncontrolled and desperate passion sometimes end in insanity; attempts, either real or feigned, at self-destruction are not uncommon" (2:234).

This incident gets to the heart of Mary Carpenter's need for the prison matron's narratives. Carpenter had won success as an advocate for juvenile delinquents because she had established the legitimacy of a peculiar form of expertise that depended on the unique powers of women's empathy, and these narratives provided the logical end point of that expertise: the omniscience we know is enjoyed only by creators of fiction. And that is precisely what the prison matron's narratives turned out to be. They had been written by Frederick William Robinson, the author of scores of pulp novels, none of which ever achieved the popularity or sales of the prison matron's narratives.

Should it matter that the kind of evidence deemed foundational to juvenile delinquents' reform by the foremost Victorian expert on the subject was not merely fictional, rather than factual, but the product of a man writing for commercial motives rather than a woman offering her empathetic experiences out of the kindness of her heart? We cannot know how Mary Carpenter herself would have answered this question, since the identity of the prison matron was not revealed in Carpenter's lifetime. In one respect she might have welcomed the news, since she had sought to counteract the prison matron's grimly fatalistic view of prisoners, raised up to be criminals since infancy, hardened by their teens, and hopelessly corrupt as adults. This was the very process of human development in which Carpenter believed society was obliged to intervene with the measures she had devoted her life to realizing. Two years after writing *Our Convicts*, Carpenter wrote to Frances Power Cobbe not only defending her own work on the grounds "that it was necessary for *me* to write 'Our Convicts' two years ago, because I saw that the public *ought* to know certain things . . . which those who *could* tell them would not," but also urging her friend to produce a similar book on behalf of Work House reform. "Your philosophic mind & literary talents combined with your womanly and loving nature," Carpenter wrote, "would enable you to do an infinitely greater good to the country . . . by writing. If you devote yourself to produce for the paupers system such a book, only better, as 'Our Convicts,' this system will be doomed, for the public will understand it. . . . Do think of this; no one *can* do it as you could."[16]

Yet, the success of the prison matron's narratives—both as a commercial venture and as a literary fraud—does, I believe, significantly impugn Carpenter's own methods. She had attacked the penal system for basing policy on abstract notions of human nature, on deterrence and retributive theories of punishment, policy that she found both inhumane and counterproductive. Only firsthand experience of individual juvenile delinquents provided by the sympathetic reformers who worked with them could offer the foundation for effective penal policy. And, as we have seen, that was an argument Carpenter believed had to be addressed not only to legislators but to the hearts of the people, for it was their moral duty as well as their self-interest that must compel them to own their convicts.

They took an interest all right, but not in ways that Carpenter and her supporters could control. Indeed, their interest became a desire, like any other, that might be better satisfied by a fiction mimicking her own stories without troubling readers with claims on their benevolence.[17] We do know that Carpenter was hostile to fictions that inflamed and corrupted the imaginations of the poor. At several points in *Our Convicts* she recounted the stories of juvenile prisoners who blamed popular novels like *Jack Sheppard* for leading them astray. She turned this evidence on novelists, writing,

> We trust this avowal may be taken to heart by those who pander to the vitiated tastes of our depraved classes. Surely the bad influence to which youths are exposed in the wretched haunts among which our sin-bred populace first draw breath, need no aggravation from the pens of men of intellect and imagination. May our popular novelists learn a lesson from this occurrence, and if they deal in criminal subjects at all, state facts as they are, with the veracious accompaniments of the criminal's habitual, trembling, apprehensive dread of discovery, his frequent subjection to poverty, hunger, cold and fatigue, ending in the privation of personal liberty and severe discipline, or still more severe monotony of prison life. No more suggestive lesson than this can be needed by the philanthropist. (1:75)

It is sadly ironic that this exhortation should exist cheek by jowl with Carpenter's citations of texts that followed her own formula for "proper" crime writing in order to pander to the vitiated tastes of the middle class. Carpenter's method of legitimating her authority had helped to create this taste and contributed to the success of those who would exploit it. Like many Victorian reformers who, in appealing to public sentiment, engendered a newly powerful political force, Carpenter found herself competing with narratives far more influential over volatile public opinion than her own.

It is undeniable that Carpenter's methods were influential. The legislative changes predicated on a new conception of juvenile delinquency, which I have reviewed in this essay, were no doubt achieved thanks in part to the stories of individual children Carpenter brought to light. Harriet Martineau, reviewing *Our Convicts,* applauded her friend for apprehending juvenile delinquents—especially girls—where all others had failed. "No one understands them," Martineau exclaimed, "neither judge nor jury, chaplain nor matron, neither doctor nor warder, can enter into the mind and feeling of a being who seems to be made up of the idiot and the intriguer, the infant and the devil, the ferocious animal and the idolater."[18] Yet we know that even Mary Carpenter believed that Frederick William Robinson—the prison matron—had done so, and that his creation had lent power to Carpenter's own representation.

Today we are witnessing another attack on abstract, rule-based reasoning in the law, only this time the target includes not only the principles of dis-embodied rationality that incensed Mary Carpenter but also the social sci-entific practices that arose to check the effects of Victorian appeals to public sentiment. As Carpenter did with juvenile delinquents, many contemporary legal theorists use particularistic narrative evidence to create new categories of subjectivity with unique claims on public sympathy. These groups—women, racial minorities, the poor, gays and lesbians—are represented as silenced in normative legal discourse and in the scientific discourses on which the law relies for evidence. Only stories, it is argued, be they fiction or auto-biography, afford evidence of the alternative realities these people experi-ence.[19] The susceptibility to commodification of such stories, which cultural history records, should make us cautious of these claims.[20] Judith R. Walkowitz's assessment of the effect of representations of the working class in bourgeois literature is relevant in this case as well: "Thanks to these liter-ary outpourings, the middle-class reading public became emotionally in-vested in a set of representations about the poor that cast poor Londoners as central characters in narratives that divested them of any agency or ability to extricate themselves from their situation" (30). And, as Regenia Gagnier has demonstrated, such representations positively impeded the ability of working-class writers to represent themselves. I would suggest that exam-ples from cultural history, such as I have recounted here, should teach us that in recommending the value of literary reasoning we ought not lose sight of the value of the sorts of rule-based reasoning and empirical investigation with which it should remain in dialectic—as it did for Carpenter. For even the most unsympathetic of juvenile delinquents—or unappealing individuals in any class—should be understood to have rights that are not dependent on commercialized public sentiment.[21]

Notes

1. See, e.g., Terry Eagleton, *The Ideology of the Aesthetic* (Oxford: Basil Blackwell, 1990), David Simpson, *Romanticism, Nationalism, and the Revolt against Theory* (Chicago: University of Chicago Press, 1993), and Dror Wahrman, "Public Opinion, Violence and the Limits of Constitutional Politics," in *Re-Reading the Constitution: New Narratives in the Political History of England's Long Nineteenth Century*, ed. James Vernon (Cambridge: Cambridge University Press, 1996).

2. See Simpson, chapter 5.

3. Wai-Chee Dimock, "Cognition as a Category of Literary Analysis," *American Literature* 67, no. 4 (Dec. 1995): 830.

4. Richard Rorty, *Contingency, Irony, and Solidarity* (Cambridge: Cambridge University Press, 1989), xvi.

5. For a discussion of the use of Parliamentary Blue Books by female social problem novelists, see Joseph A. Kestner, *Protest and Reform: The British Social Narrative by Women, 1827–1867* (Madison: University of Wisconsin Press, 1985), 52.

6. Letter, Mary Carpenter to Frances Power Cobbe, July 9, 1859, Frances Power Cobbe Correspondence, Huntington Library, San Marino, Calif.

7. Leon Radzinowicz, *A History of English Criminal Law and Its Administration from 1750* (London: Stevens and Sons, 1986), 5:148–49.

8. Mary Carpenter, *Reformatory Schools for the Children of the Perishing and Dangerous Classes and for Juvenile Offenders* (1851; rpt., London: Woburn Press, 1968), v.

9. Radzinowicz summarizes Carpenter's place in Victorian penal reform, 5:178–81.

10. See Aled Jones, *Powers of the Press: Newspapers, Power, and the Public in Nineteenth-Century England* (Aldershot: Scolar Press, 1996); James Vernon, *Politics and the People: A Study in English Political Culture, c. 1815–1867* (Cambridge: Cambridge University Press, 1993); Rob Sindall, *Street Violence in the Nineteenth Century: Media Panic or Real Danger?* (Leicester: Leicester University Press, 1990); and Martin J. Wiener, *Reconstructing the Criminal: Culture, Law, and Policy in England, 1830–1914* (Cambridge: Cambridge University Press, 1990).

11. The connections among crime reporting, public sentiment, and penal policy are discussed by Sindall, 51, 89, 137–40.

12. Mary Carpenter, *Our Convicts* (1864; rpt., Montclair, N.J.: Patterson, Smith, 1969), 1:4.

13. Frederick William Robinson, *Female Life in Prison, by a Prison Matron*, 2 vols. (London, 1862), and *Memoirs of Jane Cameron; Female Convict*, 2 vols. (London, 1864).

14. Jo Manton, *Mary Carpenter and the Children of the Streets* (London: Heinemann Educational, 1976), 180.

15. *Reformatory and Refuge Journal*, Nov. and Dec. 1864, qtd. in Manton, 18.

16. Letter, Mary Carpenter to Frances Power Cobbe, Jan. 22, 1865, Frances Power Cobbe Correspondence, Huntington Library, San Marino, Calif.

17. Peter Brooks connects narrative desire with capitalist consumerism in *Reading for the Plot: Design and Intention in Narrative* (New York : Knopf, 1984). Ann Cvetkovich addresses the difficulties in which the commodification of female sentiment involves contemporary feminist critics of Victorian sensation fiction in *Mixed Feelings: Feminism, Mass Culture, and Victorian Sensationalism* (New Brunswick, N.J.: Rutgers University Press, 1992), 24–25.

18. *Edinburgh Review*, Oct. 1865, qtd. in Manton, 189.

19. See, for example, Kathryn Abrams, "Hearing the Call of Stories," *California Law Review* 79, no. 4 (July 1991): 971–1052; Derrick Bell, *Faces at the Bottom of the Well: The Permanence of Racism* (New York: Basic Books, 1992); Richard Delgado, "Storytelling for Oppositionists and Others: A Plea for Narrative," *Michigan Law Review* 87 (Aug. 1989): 2412–41; Rorty; Robin West, *Narrative, Authority, and Law* (Ann Arbor: University of Michigan Press, 1993); and Patricia J. Williams, *The Alchemy of Race and Rights* (Cambridge: Harvard University Press, 1991). For the growing skepticism concerning the emancipatory powers of narrative, see Richard Delgado and Jean Stefancic, *Failed Revolutions: Social Reform and the Limits of the Legal Imagination* (Boulder: Westview Press, 1994).

20. For a discussion of this phenomenon regarding Victorian representations of the working class, see Regenia Gagnier, *Subjectivities: A History of Self-Representation in Britain, 1832–1920* (Oxford: Oxford University Press, 1991), 38–170, and Judith R. Walkowitz, *City of Dreadful Delight: Narratives of Sexual Danger in Late-Victorian London* (Chicago: University of Chicago Press, 1992), 30.

21. For a discussion of the continuing need for a normative discourse of rights, see Cynthia V. Ward, "A Kinder, Gentler Liberalism? Visions of Empathy in Feminist and Communitarian Literature," *University of Chicago Law Review* 61 (1994): 954.

PART 5

Future Reading: Recovery, Dissemination, Pedagogy

"Nurs'd up amongst the scenes
I have describ'd"

*Political Resonances in the Poetry of
Working-Class Women*

FLORENCE BOOS

How should we read poems by nineteenth-century working-class women in early-twenty-first-century political contexts? Many critics alert to the implications of class bias have nonetheless slighted the work of wives, mothers, and sisters of male Chartist poets.[1] Were these writings too meager, too rudimentary, or too sentimental to address significant political issues? Do they merit serious critical attention?[2] If we answer "no" to these questions, do we commit the theoretical error of "presentist recuperation"?

It will not be novel to observe that these women's works seldom invoked "high" literary or historical archetypes. More surprising, I believe, is the extent to which they drew on complex regional and demotic contexts—contexts that were as resonant, in their ways, as Matthew Arnold's public-school Greek and subsequent "classical" education were in theirs.

Most of these working-class women did not have the problems of their nineteenth-century middle-class sisters, who struggled throughout the century to gain access to universities, the professions, and of course the vote. Generally excluded from "working-men's" projects and organizations, working-class women were also not very likely to be found among Chartist and socialist "aristocrats of labor." These women did, however, attend to their own reformist and sometimes "radical" muses. They defended separate sensibilities grounded in songs and spiritual traditions; in their experiences of (multiple) motherhood; and, most starkly, in the pain and endurance of prematurely severed family ties.

The social vulnerability and precarious survival of these Victorian women's writings strongly suggest that class-based idealizations have also ill-charted the "other country" of the past, and their wide poetic range points to something parochial about traditionally credentialed interpretations of the British cultural past. If certain entitlements to define what we call "culture" have indeed been begged, broader interpretive schemata might do better justice to hybrid forms of poetic expression and deepen our hermeneutic understanding of Victorian subjectivity and complex anarchic aspects of culture itself.

Finally, such lines of inquiry and conjecture also seem to open up an unusually concrete historical *Neuland,* in that few feminist scholars had guessed that so many working-class women poets had written so much. My particular efforts to canvass extant texts in twenty or more Scottish and English repositories led me to poetry by more than sixty women scattered in forty books and several score periodicals.[3] But despite this broad originary base, I sometimes held what appeared to be sole surviving copies in my hand.

Prompted by all these normative as well as theoretical incentives, I have tried to set out here four interrelated ways in which one might read politically as well as aesthetically the poems of ten of these Victorian "humble rhymers"—self-taught and self-acknowledged proletarian nursemaids, embroiderers, factory workers, farm laborers, midwives, itinerant poets, and ballad writers. More precisely, I will try to draw together aspects of their work under four rubrics: (1) explicitly political works; (2) "personal" forms of assertion, defiance, and solidarity; (3) "deeply embedded" political verse; and (4) poems of oral protest.

Explicitly Political Works (Often Sarcastic or Satirical in Tone)

Victorian working-class women began to publish poems in greater numbers in the 1860s, a full generation after their Chartist brothers. Most took for granted the absence of the franchise that few Chartists had sought for them[4] and decried the penury and industrial squalor that sometimes closed over them. They hungered for education and responded deeply and often bitterly to the obliteration of their regional languages and cultures, especially in Scotland. They often attacked slavery, as perhaps a limiting case of forms of de facto indenturement they well knew; espoused independence movements in Hungary, Poland, Italy, and Spain; and mourned the dead—Britons and others—in the Crimean War.

Janet Hamilton

Consider, first, the work of Janet Thomson Hamilton, born in 1795, married to the shoemaker John Hamilton at thirteen, mother of ten children, and once one of the best-known working-class poets in Victorian Scotland.[5] Janet Thomson never attended school, but her mother taught her to read (but not write), and she read avidly throughout her life. She began her work at the tambour-loom at nine, began to compose verses in her head in her teens, taught herself to write a semi-cursive script in middle age, was partly blind by sixty, and was completely blind at seventy-one. A mixture of high intelligence and agraphia may have sharpened her memory, for there is an oral quality to her work, and she knew a wide range of poems by heart. Quick dialogue, mercurial humor, and a sense of repartee sharpened her satiric gifts, and she eventually published four volumes of essays and poems in her lifetime (a unique achievement), aided in her last years by one of her sons.[6]

Hamilton's first published works were poems in standard English and temperance essays, but she turned later to prose memoirs of early-nineteenth-century village life and poetic tributes to women's insights in her beloved "Doric," and she dedicated her third book "lovingly and respectfully . . . to her Brothers, the Men of the Working Class." Her birthplace, Langloan (now a part of Coatbridge, a city ten miles east of Glasgow), evolved during her lifetime from a rural village into one of the most polluted areas in all of Britain, and some of her most bitter verse condemned the savage human costs of these changes.

In parts of "A Wheen Aul' Memories," for example, coal dust and clamor in nearby Gartsherrie became a pounding, four-beat balladic chant:

> Noo the bodies are gane an' their dwallin's awa',
> And the place whaur they stood I scarce ken noo ava,

For there's roarin' o' steam, an' there's reengin o' wheels,
Men workin', and sweatin', and swearin' like deils.

And the flame-tappit furnaces staun' in a raw,
A'bleezin', and blawin', and' smeekin' awa,
Their eerie licht brichtein' the laigh hingin' cluds,
Gleamin' far ower the loch an' the mirk lanely wuds.

In "A Lay of the Tambour Frame," her speaker vigorously denounced male opponents of better pay for women:

> Selfish, unfeeling men!
>   Have ye not had your will?
> High pay, short hours; yet your cry, like the leech,
>   Is, Give us, give us still.
> She who tambours—tambours
>   For fifteen hours a day—
> Would have shoes on her feet, and dress for church,
>   Had she a third of your pay.

Ellen Johnston

Ellen Johnston, a self-described "Factory Girl," was abandoned by her father when she was two, and began work in a factory at eleven.[7] Her stepfather abused her in her teens, and she bore a daughter at seventeen. She began to publish verses in local periodicals in her early twenties, and she later earned the support of Alexander Campbell, editor of the regional *Penny Post* and an old socialist, who energetically encouraged readers to subscribe to two editions of her *Autobiography, Poems and Songs*. She drafted fourteen of her poems in her native Lallands, the rest of them in standard English.

A few patterns in her work have no obvious link to class. Every woman slighted because she appears "slight," for example, will recognize her response to people who

> At first . . . my name exalt,
> And with my works find little fault;
> But when upon myself they gaze,
> They say some other claims the praise. . . .
> But those who see me in this dress,
> So small and thin I must confess, . . .

Well may they ask, dare I profess
The talent of an authoress?

("An Address to Nature on Its Cruelty," 141)

In "The Last Sark," Johnston's best-known work, an enervated Scottish mother cries out in rage to her husband:

Gude guide me, are ye hame again, and hae ye got nae
  wark?
We've naething noo tae pit awa, unless your auld blue sark.
My heid is rinnin roond aboot, far lichter nor a flee:
What care some gentry if they're weel though a' the puir
  wad dee?

It is the puir man's hard-won cash that fills the rich man's
  purse;
I'm sure his gowden coffers they are hit wi mony a curse.
Were it no for the working man what wad the rich man be?
What care some gentry if they're weel though a' the puir
  wad dee?

(pp. 100–101)

Mary Smith

Mary Smith was a poor but intellectually ambitious daughter of "nonconformists" in Oxford.[8] She spent most of her adult life in Carlisle, where she worked as a servant and school aide, and eventually opened a small primary school. She organized free classes for poor women, campaigned for women's suffrage and kindred causes, and published—with great effort—*Poems* (1860), *Progress, and Other Poems; The Latter Including Poems on the Social Affections and Poems on Life and Labour* (1863), and *The Autobiography of Mary Smith, Schoolmistress and Nonconformist: A Fragment of a Life* (posthumously, in 1892). As a poet, she indited her ideals in ardent periodic octameters:

"Women's Rights" are not hers only, they are all the world's
  beside,
And the whole world faints and suffers, while these are
  scorn'd, denied.
Childhood, with its mighty questions, Manhood with its restless heart,

Life in all its varied phrases, standing class from class apart,
Need the voice, the thought of woman, woman wise as she
    shall be,
When at last the erring ages shall in all things make her Free.

(*Progress*, "Women's Claims," 156–57)

Jessie Russell

Jessie Russell's parents were lower middle class, but she was orphaned, left
school at twelve, became a carpenter's wife, and mothered three children.
In *The Blinkin' o' the Fire* (1877), she denounced the sufferings of

. . . slaves whom we dream not of, and many a drudge to be
    found
In our city gentlemen's houses, in those kitchens under-
    ground. . . .

but also of less obviously abused women, who were

. . . called by the name of wife,
. . . a life for a life, and the murderer's hung, and we think
    not the law inhuman,
Then why not the lash for the man who . . . strikes a
    defenseless woman?

("Woman's Rights *versus* Woman's Wrongs," 30)

Like several of her sisters, Russell wrote temperance poetry, in which she
focused on the forms of *violence* working-class women suffered without
escape or other recourse.[9]

"Personal" Forms of Assertion, Defiance, and Solidarity

Idealistic verse-tributes to the dignity of labor and expressions of pride in
their poetic artistry appeared again and again in the work of women whose
defiance helped them endure what they could not escape or overcome.

"Marie"

"Marie" (no last name known), for example, was a dye worker from

Chorley. She apparently published her work for the first time in William and Mary Howitt's *The People's and Howitt's Journal* in 1847 and placed other poems in assorted journals for several years thereafter (*The People's Journal, Eliza Cook's Journal, Cassell's Family Magazine*).[10] Flashes of persuasive wit appeared in her cadenced expressions of ardent faith in her poetic vocation[11] and the dignity of all "Labour":

> Thou who toilest, bless thy toiling!
>   Not all nature sings
> Nobler anthem, than the music
>   When thy hammer rings! . . . .
> Stroke by stroke, glad time [man] keepeth
>   To his leaping heart;
> Who shall, scorning, call him *poor* man
>   Having this rich part?
> He can boldly look existence
>   In the very eye;
> Nor needs tremble when night whispers
>   'Neath the starlit sky—
>
>   . . . .
>   "Labour is the truest worship
>   Any soul can bring."
>
> ("Labour," 62)

Epictetus might have admired her lyric variant of stoic self-abnegation:

> Though ignored our lowly lot,
> Scornful glances harm us not;
> We accept our homely fate:
> And a beauteous life create;—
> From earth's bosom, brown and bare,
> Flowerets draw their colours rare;
> And, though we are seeming stinted,
> All our days are rainbow-tinted
>   By our noble will!
>
> ("The Indomitable Will," 63)

Marie opposed "earnest hope" to the specter of death in "To Liberty" (1852), and her simple name or pseudonym disappeared from print in 1854.

Ellen Johnston

Ellen Johnston's own "earnest hope" was that an enduring audience of working-class readers would rescue her from oblivion, or at least remember her. She never escaped the grinding millwork a doctor had warned her would kill her, and she seems to have implicitly addressed a farewell in "The Factory Girl's Last Lay"—the last poem in fact that I have been able to trace—to her kindly radical patron, Alexander Campbell:

> Stay; I will leave my fame's crown in thy keeping,
>   Its gems may cheer thee at some future day;
> Adieu, my lov'd one, when I'm calmly sleeping,
>   Sing to the world—"The Factory Girl's Last Lay."

She died in a poorhouse hospital four years later.

Mary Smith

Mary Smith, the reforming teacher, expressed her most ardent meliorist ideals in "Progress," a 116-page memorial to "spirits of dead centuries" (71) who "had no great name on the earth" but have made "things not so ill for you and me as they might have been" (in Eliot's words). Among the deepest ideals of her faith was a Carlylean/Morrisian belief that unremembered toilers—herself among them—formed a kind of community of secular saints. Indeed, this receding ideal seems to have become the animating radical-democratic ideal of her strenuous and self-sacrificing life:

> Ye have no name nor place in all our lore,
>   Forgot by e'en tradition's garrulous tongue,
> But ye—oh could we know you!—evermore
>   War with us against evil foes of wrong;
> Your breath is still upon us, still we feel
> Faint whispers of your glories through us steal;
> Faint whispers of your thinkings; your great heart
> With time still blending, still its noblest part.
>
> And when our hearts, unresting, seek pure peace;
>   When the tide overflows them of pure thought;
> When the world's noisy tongues that hold us cease,
>   And all the troubled soul to rest is wrought:
> 'Tis then your spirit, greater than our own,

Which thrills us with a sense of things unknown,
Which folds us in a glory, that makes bright
Our fleeting moments, with Eternal Light.

(72–73)

Janet Hamilton

Janet Hamilton offered her most resonant homages to cultural integrity and working-class pride in her native Scots. In her "Plea for the Doric," her speaker apologized for previous "Parnassian" efforts "to busk oot my sang wi' the prood Southron tongue" and dismissed a long line of Scottish journalistic émigrés who went south:

I'm wae for Auld Reekie; her big men o' print
To Lunnon ha'e gane, to be nearer the mint;
But the coinage o' brain looks no a'e haet better,
Though Doric is banish'd frae sang, tale, and letter.

I would like to believe that Hamilton's blunt defense of the vernacular helped encourage other Scottish working-class poets—Russell, Johnston, John Young, Joseph Wright—in their efforts to exploit the satiric and metaphorical possibilities of their native tongue.

"Deeply Embedded" Political Verse

Many of the women I have studied wrote verse that *embodied* some of the psychological and institutional constraints under which they "labored": in expressions of solidarity with refugees and outcasts, for example (slaves, prisoners, soldiers, "travellers," and even animals), and in their stark accounts of frequent and brutal early deaths.

Some of these humble verse allegories were literally broken, and others might be dismissed as "bad" or "incoherent." But the most moving cried out for contextual interpretation and a heedful audience. Among the latter were Fanny Forrester's fragmented narratives, Jane Stevenson's free-verse meditations, and Elizabeth Campbell's paper-covered pamphlets of angry and grieving verse.

Fanny Forrester

Fanny Forrester, a Lancashire dye worker, published sixty-odd poems in

Ben Brierley's Journal in Manchester between 1870 and 1876. Brierley himself published a well-intended but rather generic description of her on January 23, 1875:

> Born in Manchester of poor parents, and parents whom misfortune seems to have marked for its own, the cradle of her muse has been in the nursery of toil and vicissitude, as may have been gathered by an observer who has noted the sombre tints in which most of her pictures of life are painted, and the deep sympathy with suffering humanity that breathes through every note of her music. (37)

Forrester's "sombre tints" seem to have contrasted rather sharply with Brierley's general tone of optimistic self-promotion, but he published tributes to Forrester by her fellow poets John Lawton Owen, Martha Harriet Smith, and Anna E. Fennell—analogues, perhaps, of the epistolary responses to Ellen Johnston that Alexander Campbell had published in the *Penny Post*.

Forrester's diction was "elevated," but her work embraced painful flashbacks and a few curious gender-ambiguities and quasi-homoerotic interludes, and her poetic personae included poor orphans, handicapped children, dying soldiers, elderly parents, struggling Irish immigrants, "fallen" or abandoned women, and unwed mothers. Many seem exhausted, and most have suffered wrenching dislocations—from country to city, Ireland to the midland slums, hopeful youth to exhausted middle age, and life to death.

In "Toiling in the City," for example, an Irish immigrant factory worker

> . . . is weary, oh, so weary! of the engine's deafening sound;
> Though her head is dazed and aching, still the mighty wheels
>   go round.
> "Will they never cease their grinding?" oft the wondering
>   maiden cries,
> As the straps go whirling round her, then go whizzing past her
>   eyes. . . .

In "Saturday Night" (one of several "Lancashire Pictures"):

> . . . many a woman, cold and stern, forgets her loveless life—
> Its barren paths, so bleak so drear—its never-ending strife;
> The ruined, lone, forsaken shrine within her empty heart—
> The wound that bleeds for evermore—the pang that won't
>   depart.
>
>   (October 1873)

Introspective and brooding reveries punctuated by abrupt changes of register were staples of "high" poetry, of course—compare Robert Browning's "Porphyria's Lover" or Gerard Manley Hopkins's "The Wreck of the Deutschland." But Forrester's narrative voices also resonated with complex passions of cruel exhaustion and irretrievable loss.

Jane Stevenson

Jane Stevenson also wrote sympathetically about uprooted lives—those of poor emigrants, ploughmen, itinerant prophets, newly evicted Highlanders, and a stray dog among them—but she cast many of her *Homely Musings by a Rustic Maiden* in rather plain free verse. Of her girlhood "songs"—composed in defiance of her family's derision—she remarked that "I suppose it is not prose, and I am not such a judge of poetry as to know whether it may be called poetry or not, or some kind of a mixture of both" (5). We do learn that Stevenson began work tending cows in early girlhood, and that she and her six brothers and two sisters lost their small farm when her parents died. She later made a long foot journey to the site, and mourned the family's dispersal in "The Homes of My Fathers" and lines "Written on the Death of My Father, and the Prospect of Then Leaving My Birthplace."

Anticipating the judgment of a "cold critic" in another poem, Stevenson sought to probe the finality of her loss:[12]

> . . . should this paper chance
> To fall into the hands of some cold critic,
> They may laugh and wonder why a girl
> (Surely an enthusiast) should thus descant
> Upon a spot wherein they saw no loveliness;
>
> . . . .
>
> I may be prejudic'd, this is my birthplace,
> Spot where I have spent my life from earliest infancy;
> Nurs'd up amongst the scenes I have describ'd,
>
> . . . .
>
> A wild and solitary thing have thus contract
> A love for things inanimate;
> Or like the Swiss or Laplanders who love their country
> And their native hills, though wild and bleak,
> And whether transplant[ed] to climes more warm and sunny,
> Fairer far to other eyes than theirs,

Will sigh, and pine, and sometimes die
Of broken heart.

("Home," 29–30)

In her accompanying prose description of her journey, she remarked that she had lost contact with her brothers and sisters and did not expect to retrace her journey "home" again.

Empathy with other sentient beings also led her to find common cause with a lonely "Wandering Dog":

Poor dog, I pity thee,
A wanderer thou art;
And all may pity thee
Whoe'er have felt that loneliness of heart—
Will creep o'er those who once have had a home,
Where peace and plenty was;
And then are forced to roam.

. . . .

Nor ever meet a face, but faces that are strange,
And find this world is but a place
Of never ceasing change.

(40–42)

Stevenson's gentle assonant cadences enhanced her "simple" style, and her volume's fate recapitulated the loss and dispersion she described. I have found no other allusions to her or to her "musings" on the beauty of ordinary landscapes, the irrevocability of loss, and the mystical interstices of ordinary life.

Elizabeth Campbell

Elizabeth Duncan (Campbell) was a ploughman's daughter, the sixth of eight surviving children. When a midwife's error led to her mother's early death, the three-year-old and her sisters "wandered like forlorn crows from morn to night" (*Songs of My Pilgrimage* [Edinburgh: Andrew Elliot, 1875], ix, xi), and she began work as a cowtender and whingatherer at seven, after a single quarter-session of school.

More than sixty-five years later, she remembered clearly "how miserable I felt in that strange ugly hovel—me that had such a strange love for the beautiful" (xii), and the solace she found in natural beauty, animals of all sorts (including insects), and her "strange" love of learning. By contrast, she had little desire in old age "to tell about my after life; it would take far too long" (xvi).

Her "after life" was dominated in fact by toil, poverty, many moves, and early deaths of most of the people she loved. She was twenty-nine when she married William Campbell,[13] a flaxdresser, and had already worked as a cow- and sheepherder, handloom weaver, farm servant, house servant, and cook. She moved with him to Brechin, where she worked "fill[ing] pirns to four weavers" (xvi), then to Arbroath, where she tried to bring in tiny bits of money from the sale of four verse-pamphlets. She eventually bore four daughters and four sons, but her husband's life was blighted by a long, debilitating illness, and all four of her sons died young, two in infancy and two in workplace accidents. In her preface to her poems she wrote that "my life has been full of toil and sorrows so many and so deep that I never could tell them" (xvii).

She was seventy-two when she managed to publish *Songs of My Pilgrimage* (1875), introduced and edited by George Gilfillan, who excised out of "her" book—in a small paradigm of the pattern of middle-class-patronage-cum-bowdlerization—much of the best work in Campbell's pamphlets: poems of anguish and social commentary, for example, denunciations of American slavery and the Crimean War, and criticisms of governmental ministers and the Queen.[14]

She had much to "tell" in her pamphlets, which included many poems about the agony and injustice of war.[15] She was especially hostile to Britain's incursion into the Crimea—her son Willie had entered Sebastopol with the first British contingent—and she also went out of her way to express pointed sympathy with Russian soldiers and British deserters ("Bill Arden"). In other poems, she asked whether "[British commanders'] titles and proceedings [will] cover their sin" "[w]hen their hour comes to die," and "ranted" rhythmically against *all* the "murd'rous inventions" of war:

> I think it's a pity that kings go to war,
>
> . . . .
>
> I weep for those that's the victims of kings.
> I weep for the coward, I weep for the brave,
> I weep for the monarch, I weep for the slave,
> I weep for all those that in battle are slain;
> I've a tear and a prayer for the souls of all men.
>
> (*Poems*, 4th Series, "The Crimean War")

The pamphlets also included ardent abolitionist verses ("Kidnapped Slaves," Francis the Slave"), a denunciation of unjust imprisonment ("A Prison Cell"), and a vigorous response to a local minister who had tried to interdict her tiny effort at self-publication.

As an old woman, Campbell too made a lonely pilgrimage to her rural childhood home:

> There all I could see was an old ash tree,
>   'Twas hallowed, 'twas gloriously green;
> Still as death as it stood, and no breath stirred the wood,
>   As the setting sun brilliant did sheen.
>
> I stepped very slow, with a heart full of woe,
>   From wounds that death can but heal;
> I wept like the cloud, and praised God aloud,
>   Who else would have cared for my tale?
>
> I passed a brow that shut the scene from my view,
>   And the glory that over it shone;
> Lit up every tree, and flower on the lea,
>   All so calm, all so still, but my moan.
>
>   ("A Summer Night")

Forrester's, Stevenson's, and Campbell's evocations of personal loss bore witness to the reflective dignity of "ordinary" people in a period of economic injustice and cataclysmic social change.

Poems of Oral Protest

Isabella Chisholm

A stray trace of a lost oral culture appeared in the gypsy curse recorded by Alexander Carmichael, a late-nineteenth-century folklorist and collector of Gaelic songs. His informant, the traveling tinker Isabella Chisholm, was "still tall and straight, fine-featured, and fresh-complexioned," and had "the gipsy language, variously called 'Cant,' 'Shelta,' 'Romany,' [and] rich fluent Gaelic and English . . . [along with] many curious spells, runes, and hymns, that would have enriched Gaelic literature."[16]

The itinerant British Rom roamed or were driven from place to place and apparently focused anger at their enemies and attackers in "performative" maledictions such as the one Chisholm recited, a "curse" against "The Wicked Who Would Do Me Harm":

> May he take the [throat disease,] . . .
> Be it harder than the stone,
> Be it blacker than the coal, . . .
> Be it fiercer, fiercer, sharper, harsher, more malignant,
> Than the hard, wound-quivering holly, . . .
> Seven seven times.
>
> A dysentery of blood from heart, . . . from bones,
>   . . . .
> And a searching of veins, of throat, and of kidneys,
> To my contemners and traducers.[17]

Chisholm herself may have had concrete "contemners and traducers" in mind, but she may simply have intoned her rather inscrutable imprecations as a general protective charm. One can say little now about such chants' genesis, significance, or authorial intentions.

Mary Macpherson

Oral declamation in clear-text appeared in the work of Mairi Nic a'Phearsain (Mary Macpherson)—"Big Mary of the Songs"—a vigorous middle-aged Gaelic protest singer of the Highland Clearances. "Big Mary" could read English and Gaelic, but her "songs" were oral, and a sympathetic Skye landowner paid a transcriber to write them down.[18] Only a few of her poems have been translated, but some were influential "curses" in their way: they helped elect Land Law Reform Association members of Parliament she supported. These in turn helped pass the 1886 Crofters' Holdings Act, which brought a gradual end to the notorious Highland Clearances.

Mary Macdonald was born in Skeabost on Skye in 1821, and never attended school, but Alexander MacBain, her editor, told his readers that she had "ample experience in the management of cattle and all that pertains to the conduct of a house in the olden days, from cooking to cloth making, and further, in storing her mind with the lays and lyrics of her native isles" (xi). She married Isaac Macpherson, an Inverness shoemaker, in 1848, and moved to Glasgow to support herself and her four surviving children after he died in 1871.

At *fifty,* she then began a five-year course of study in the Royal Infirmary—a rigorous undertaking that would seem to belie claims that she could not write—and earned diplomas there in nursing and obstetrics. She worked thereafter as a midwife in Glasgow and Greenock until 1882, when Lachlan Macdonald, the patron who paid for the transcription of her verse, offered her rent-free use of Woodside Cottage in Skeabost, where she lived until her death in 1898. An 1891 frontispiece photograph showed her as a stout elderly woman in a feathered cap and long fur stole, and she appeared elsewhere in the volume carding, spinning, and "warping the Highland tartan."

When anger at "certain miscarriages of justice" (xiii) roused her to denounce her people's oppressors in 1872, Macpherson's Gaelic songs supported the land reformer Fraser-Mackintosh in 1874, and helped elect Land Law Reform Association candidates throughout the Highlands in 1884. Lachlan Macdonald paid the Gaelic scholar John Whyte to transcribe more than eight thousand lines of her verse during the 1880s. In his introduction, MacBain remarked that she could recite "at least half as much more of her own," and eight or nine thousand more lines of verse by other poets from Skye and the other Western Islands.

In "Incitement of the Gaels," her best-known verse-condemnation, Macpherson memorialized the "Battle of the Braes," an early incident in the "Crofters' War" (1882–86). In this "battle," local men and women had fought sheriff's men sent to evict them, and the ensuing casualties included seven women of the Braes and twelve of their better-armed opponents. Macpherson also composed more traditional elegies, and at least one more poem of introspective return, "Farewell to the New Christmas." This narrated the reactions of the poet, back for a time in Skye from Glasgow. She marked the enclosures and forced evictions that left "where once the honest people lived, / only the great sheep and their lambs" and

> . . . reached the well of Iain Ban
> That my beloved father named,
> The stones whereon he laid his hands,
>   are left a legacy to me.
> I stood a while above it there,
> The tears came raining from my eyes,
> As I recalled the dear-loved folk,
>   earthed now in their eternal sleep.

Then all my senses ebbed away,
Death's pallor came upon my cheek;
But there I cupped my hand and drank,
    and felt my being made anew.

(Watson, 491)

Afterwards, her "dearest people gathered, / [and] made for me warm welcome," and she watched impromptu play with a meal-bag ball, admired "orchis flowers," raised "a bumper lipping to the brim" (no temperance advocate she), and heard a voice "behind her" call "her people" to return, for

We would know again the fields,
The cornstacks standing in the yard,
If but the spirit of the folk
Could rise again in hand and heart.

All these images—healing wells, flowers, cups of liquor, and voices from the dead—were politically resonant as well as concretely evocative. They also evoked a crofter's counterpart of Blake's "Jerusalem," and foreshadowed the populist faith of William Morris's "spirit of the folk" and of Lewis Grassic Gibbon's *Scots Quair*.

Another Return

The houses of Victorian working-class women's poetry did *not*, it is true, have "many mansions." But they *did* offer a variety of side rooms, cottages, and tenements, seldom visited by their more fortunate brothers. Most Victorian working-class women poets had little direct access to the Chartist movement and its cultural institutions, of course, and most were poorer and more rural than the male writers studied in Owen Ashton and Stephen Roberts's *The Victorian Working Class Writer*.[19] The latter struggled to write and support themselves but could hope to become newspaper journalists, even editors (as did Thomas Cooper, John Bedford Leno, Ben Brierley, and Thomas Miller).[20] They could even hope to publish several books, an attainment beyond almost all of the poets I have discussed. (Smith and Hamilton were rare exceptions among the scores of working-class women poets I have found.)

The works I have discovered also seem to me to belie critical assumptions that Victorian women's preoccupations with religion vitiated their verse.

The women whose lives and published works I have sketched clearly sought to solace the ravages of their grief and sustain their needs for minimal self-respect, but few wasted time or poetic breath on ritual, doctrine, or pious institutions. Confronted by their transience and insignificance, "Marie," Mary Smith, Jessie Russell, Ellen Johnston, Janet Hamilton, Jane Stevenson, Fanny Forrester, Elizabeth Campbell, Isabella Chisholm, Mary Macpherson, and their sisters found consolation instead in numinous Blakean-Wordsworthian visions and millenarian hopes. And only *some* of these hopes were conventionally religious.

These women's struggles to realize their hopes also bore immediate witness—in many of the "return" poems, for example—to the devastating effects of industrial exploitation on individual lives and families, and the successes they achieved sustained poetry's role as a preserver of an individual and collective inner life. Janet Hamilton's "Oor Location," Ellen Johnston's "The Last Sark," and Mary Macpherson's Gaelic "Farewell to the New Christmas" also recorded distinctive linguistic voices, inner lives, and outer milieus, in effect, of another country.

My "recuperative" aim in this overview has therefore been to offer some textual fragments and convey something of the mystery and fragility of these poets' lives and work. We cannot "know again the fields" from which we are separated by six generations and continental divides of hindsight and privilege. But we can suspend dismissive assumptions that the work of these "democratic subjects" was "nostalgic," "sentimental," and "conventional." For we have much to learn and understand from the ways in which these "simple" nineteenth-century women poets brought pain, humor, loss, reflection, political insight, and vision to their verses and lives.

Notes

1. Relevant anthologies from the 1970s and '80s included Peter Scheckner, ed., *An Anthology of Chartist Poetry: Poetry of the British Working Class, 1830s–1850s* (Rutherford, N.J.: Fairleigh Dickinson University Press; London and Toronto: Associated University Press, 1989); Brian Maidment, ed., *Poorhouse Fugitives: Self-Taught Poets and Poetry in Victorian Britain* (Manchester: Manchester University Press, 1987); and Brian Hollingworth, ed., *Songs of the People: Lancashire Dialect Poetry of the Industrial Revolution* (Manchester: Manchester University Press, 1977). Scheckner omitted all women poets; Hollingworth included selections by Mary Thomason, whose work appeared in print in the 1930s, and Maidment included selections by Marie, Ellen Johnston, and Janet Hamilton.

Among more recent anthologies, Catherine Kerrigan, ed., *An Anthology of Scottish Women Poets* (Edinburgh: Edinburgh University Press, 1991), reprints poems by Hamilton,

Johnston, and Mary MacPherson; Tom Leonard, ed., *Radical Renfrew: Poetry from the French Revolution to the First World War* (Edinburgh: Polygon, 1990), reprints poems by Marion Bernstein and Jessie Russell; Angela Leighton and Margaret Reynolds, eds., *Victorian Women Poets: An Anthology* (Oxford: Blackwell, 1995), reprints poems by Ellen Johnston; and Isobel Armstrong, Cath Sharrock, and Joseph Bristow, eds., *Nineteenth-Century Women Poets* (Oxford: Clarendon, 1996), reprints poems by Ruth Wills, Ellen Johnston, "A Factory Girl," and Isa Craig-Knox.

2. General discussions of working-class writings have included Martha Vicinus, *The Industrial Muse: A Study of Nineteenth-Century British Working-Class Literature* (New York: Barnes and Noble; London: Croom Helm, 1974); Patrick Joyce, *Democratic Subjects: The Self and the Social in Nineteenth-Century England* (Cambridge: Cambridge University Press, 1994); Julia Swindells, *Victorian Writing and Working Women: The Other Side of Silence* (Minneapolis: University of Minnesota Press, 1985); Anne Janowitz, *Lyric and Labour in the Romantic Tradition* (New York: Cambridge University Press, 1998); Susan Zlotnick, *Women, Writing, and the Industrial Revolution* (Baltimore: Johns Hopkins University Press, 1997); and Jonathan Rose, *The Intellectual Life of the British Working Classes* (New Haven: Yale University Press, 2001). Only Swindells and Zlotnick examine the writings of working-class women in detail.

3. These included the British Library, the London University Library, the Working-Class Movements Library (Manchester), the Mitchell Library (Glasgow), the National Library of Scotland, the Edinburgh University Library, the Houghton Library, the Beinecke Library, the public libraries of Edinburgh, Manchester, Paisley, Airdre, Coatbridge, Motherwell, Springburn, Inverness, Aberdeen, and Dundee, the Kohler Collection of the University of California at Davis, and the University of Iowa.

4. Barbara Taylor, *Eve and the New Jerusalem* (London: Virago, 1983).

5. Of her ten children, seven reached adulthood. Discussions of Hamilton appear in Edwin Morgan, *Crossing the Border: Essays in Scottish Literature* (Manchester: Carcanet, 1990); Florence Boos, "Cauld Engle-Cheek: Working-Class Poets in Victorian Scotland," *Victorian Poetry* 33, no. 1 (1995): 53–74; Boos, "'Oor Location': Victorian Women Poets and the Transition from Rural to Urban Scottish Culture," in *Victorian Urban Settings,* ed. Debra Mancoff and Dale Trela (New York: Garland, 1996); Boos, "Janet Hamilton," in *Victorian Women Poets, Dictionary of Literary Biography,* ed. William Thesing (Columbia, S.C.: Bruccoli and Clark, 1998), 149–58; "Working-Class Women Poets and the Periodical Press: 'Marie,' Janet Hamilton, and Fanny Forrester," *Victorian Poetry* 39, no. 2 (2001): 255–87; and Boos, "Janet Hamilton," in *Dictionary of National Biography,* ed. Colin Mathews (Oxford: Oxford University Press, forthcoming).

6. Janet Hamilton's books are *Poems and Essays of a Miscellaneous Character on Subjects of General Interest* (Glasgow: Thomas Murray; Edinburgh: Paton and Ritchie; London: Arthur Hall, 1863); *Poems of Purpose and Sketches in Prose of Scottish Peasant Life and Character in Auld Langsyne, Sketches of Local Scenes and Characters, with a Glossary* (Glasgow: Thomas Murray; Edinburgh: William Ritchie; London: James Nisbet, 1865); *Poems and Ballads* (Glasgow: James Maclehose, 1868); *Poems Essays and Sketches. A Selection from the First Two Volumes, "Poems and Essays" and "Poems and Sketches," with Several New Pieces* (Glasgow: James Maclehose, 1870), enlarged as *Poems, Essays, and Sketches: Comprising the Principal Pieces from Her Complete Works,* ed. James Hamilton (Glasgow: James Maclehose, 1880), and republished as *Poems, Sketches, and Essays* (Glasgow: James Maclehose, 1885).

7. Johnston's work is studied in Susan Zlotnick, "'A Thousand Times I'd Rather Be a Factory Girl': Dialect, Domesticity, and Working-Class Women's Poetry in Victorian Britain," *Victorian Studies* 35, no. 1 (1991): 7–27; Zlotnick, *Women, Writing, and the Industrial*

Revolution; Boos, "Cauld Engle-Cheek"; Boos, "Ellen Johnston," in *Nineteenth-Century British Women Writers,* ed. Abigail Burnham Bloom (Westport, Conn.: Greenwood Press, 2000), 231–34; Susan Alves, "A Thousand Times I'd Rather Be a Factory Girl: The Politics of Reading American and British Female Factory Workers' Poetry, 1840–1914," Ph.D. diss., Northeastern University, 1996; H. Gustav Klaus, *Ellen Johnston and Working-Class Poetry in Victorian Scotland* (Peter Lang, 1997); and Judith Rosen, "Class and Poetic Communities in the Works of Ellen Johnston, 'The Factory Girl,'" *Victorian Poetry* 39, no. 2 (2001): 207–29.

8. Smith does not identify their denomination, but they were probably Congregationalists.

9. Only Janet Hamilton wrote explicitly for the temperance press, but other working-class women—Johnston, Russell, Smith, Jane Goldie, Agnes Mabon, Elizabeth Davidson, Elizabeth Campbell, and others—addressed cognate problems in their verse.

10. A more extended study of the work of "Marie," Forrester, and Hamilton appears in Boos, "Working-Class Women Poets and the Periodical Press: 'Marie,' Janet Hamilton and Fanny Forrester," *Victorian Poetry* 39, no. 2 (2001): 255–86.

11. For example, in "A Cuckoo," "Poet! Why Sing," and "Sweet Poetry" (all 1849), and "Sibyl, The Far-Seer" (1850).

12. Other poems on this theme are "Garnock Water" and "My Birthplace."

13. The register for Forfar/Brechin (vol. 275/8, p. 21, frame 2115) records a license granted to William Campbell and Elizabeth Duncan on January 5, 1833.

14. A few lyrics of grief and distress remained, among them poems on "The Graves of My Sons," "The Death of Willie, My Second Son," and "My Infant Day and My Hair Grown Gray."

15. These included "The Absent Soldier," "A Dream," "The Mother's Lament," "The Windmill of Sebastopol," "Bill Arden," "The Crimean War," "The Attack on the Great Redan, and Fall of the Malkhoff," "The Amber Cloud," and "Spring."

16. *Charms of the Gaels: Hymns and Incantations, with Illustrative Notes on Words, Rites and Customs, Dying and Obsolete; Orally Collected in the Highlands and Islands of Scotland by Alexander Carmichael,* ed. D. J. Moore, intro. John McInnis (Edinburgh: Floris Books, 1994).

17. The curse appears in *Carmina Gadelica: Hymns and Incantations,* ed. Alexander Carmichael (Edinburgh: Scottish Academic Press, 1972), 2:155–57.

18. Mairi Nic'A'Phearsoin, *Dain Agus Oran: Ghaidhlig,* ed. Alastair Mac-Bheathain, intro. by Alexander MacBain (Inverness: A. Agus U. Mac'Coinnich, 1891). Translations appear in Kerrigan and in Roderick Watson, ed., *The Poetry of Scotland: Gaelic, Scots, and English* (Edinburgh: Edinburgh University Press, 1995).

19. Owen Ashton and Stephen Roberts, *The Victorian Working-Class Writer* (London and New York: Cassell, 1999).

20. Only Eliza Cook edited a journal. The poems of "Marie," Fanny Forrester, and the anonymous gypsy never appeared in volume form.

10

Revisiting the Serial Format of Dickens's Novels; or, *Little Dorrit* Goes a Long Way

DAVID BARNDOLLAR AND SUSAN SCHORN

Almost invariably when introducing a Dickens novel to modern audiences, a professor or editor makes mention of the phenomenon of serialization. Dickens's Victorian audience, we affirm, experienced his novels more intimately, poring over each few chapters for an extended period of time, and also more socially, sharing the narrative journey with many fellow-travelers. But rarely does anyone attempt to gauge how different an experience it is to read, say, *Our Mutual Friend* today as a fat trade paperback, knowing you can skip ahead to the end, hurry over some sections to pick up the thread of a confusing plot line, or put the book down and walk away from it for months, confident that friends and family are unlikely to spoil the ending by discussing it in your hearing. Although Dickens's novels eventually ap-peared in Victorian home libraries as impressive, weighty volumes, the initial physical experience of a Dickens novel was far different. *Little Dorrit,* for example, as it was first read, discussed, and celebrated, was a set of twenty unassuming blue paper-bound leaflets, crammed with advertisements for burial sites and outfitters offering gear to new officers bound for the Crimean War. Some of Dickens's most famous works, such as *Great Expectations,* became famous three chapters at a time, sandwiched between poems and essays in Dickens's newspapers, *Household Words* and *All the Year Round.* They were the same stories we read today, yet the difference in readerly experience of the two forms is not as insignificant as we often assume. What was the novel-reading experience like for the reader more fully under Dickens's authorial control? How did it feel to have to wait an entire month to find out if Little Nell or Paul Dombey had died? And what could the difference between the two reading experiences illuminate for Dickens fans and scholars?

These questions gave birth to two projects organized by the authors and conducted at the University of Texas at Austin from 1996 to 1999. Participants in Dickens by Inches read and met to discuss one number of *Little Dorrit* each month for roughly two years (skipping some summer months), while Dickens by Pixels allowed participants to read a weekly number of *A Tale of Two Cities* entirely on the web (or in print, if they so desired) and discuss it in an online forum. Our experience suggests that reading Dickens in serial format is a challenging task for modern audiences. The schedule did allow readers to focus on aspects of Dickens's writing that might be lost with a less fragmented approach, but participants expressed discomfort (for one author, at least, acute discomfort) with the serial approach. It was not merely a question of the inconvenience of attending the meetings and of remembering when and what to read; the discomfort arose in surrendering to the author so much control over the pace and length of the reading, factors we modern readers like to determine for ourselves. This discomfort may in part explain why Dickens's work appears now in almost every conceivable form—trade publication novels, comic books, stage productions, movies, television shows—*except* its original serial print format.

Electronic reading of Dickens was especially difficult to promote, and though the authors will be the first to admit that promotional failure may have contributed to this difficulty, the recent history of Stephen King's serial on-line novel *The Plant* indicates that the maintenance of any serial readership is hampered by one or more aspects of Internet culture or, more broadly, contemporary culture.

Dickens and Serialization

Grahame Smith, in his essay "Dickens and Critical Theory," says of the serially written novel that "its state of being as a literary text is of a quite different order to the static being of a Victorian three-decker novel, the writing of

which was completed before it saw the light of day in the hands of a reader."
He notes such works' "interactive relationship with the public, the possibilities of change and modification in the light of changing patterns of sales and of audience response." Dickens's own comments make it clear that his attitude toward serial publication was ambivalent; the demands of the schedule always haunted him, but the rewards of an "interactive relationship" with his audience captivated him. Of course, the considerable monetary rewards of serial publication also held Dickens enthralled. Robert L. Patten's *Charles Dickens and His Publishers* points out that even though the majority of Victorian novels were not serialized, "serial publication opened up a new reading and buying public that subsequent publishers and formats did then exploit in a variety of ways."[1] Dickens's own description of his vexed position is characteristic, when he regretfully informed his readers he was abandoning the weekly *Master Humphrey's Clock* in October 1841:

> I should not regard the anxiety, the close confinement, or the constant attention, inseparable from the weekly form of publication (for to commune with you in any form, is to me a labour of love), if I had found it advantageous to the conduct of my stories, the elucidation of my meaning, or the gradual development of my characters. But I have not done so. I have often felt cramped and confined in a very irksome and harassing degree, by the space in which I have been constrained to move.

The words "commune" and "love" have special resonance because, while many modern readers profess to love Dickens, communion with him on any plane but the spiritual is now manifestly impossible—a state of affairs that the Victorian reader of Dickens's serial work did not have to contend with. That is, though as readers we may feel that Dickens speaks to us, do we not usually feel he is speaking to us from the past? We read his works in part to admire his portraits of a time gone by (at least in the detail, even if we feel his portraits of human types are timeless), not to achieve communion with him in our own temporal reality. But Dickens the man, as a real physical presence in the world, was central to Victorian experience of his works. Dickens could, and did, adapt the plots of ongoing novels to account for readers' responses, giving them a stake in the creative act. The simple fact of the author's death is therefore the foremost area of difference in serial reading of Dickens now as opposed to during Dickens's lifetime.

During Dickens's lifetime, serial publication and reading were tremendously popular. Because of careful marketing strategy, publication in numbers even seems to have encouraged the demand for the same novels "in covers." E. D. H. Johnson (writing as Edward D. Johnson), in *Charles Dickens: An Introduction to His Novels,* reports:

> After *Pickwick Papers* took hold, the sales of monthly installments rarely fell below 25,000, and averaged between 30,000 and 40,000. While *The Old Curiosity Shop* was running, the weekly circulation of *Master Humphrey's Clock* rose to 100,000; and *Great Expectations* pushed the circulation of *All the Year Round* well above that of the London *Times.* These figures, of course, do not take into account the novels in book form, whether in the original editions or in cheaper reprints. A fourth printing of *Great Expectations,* for example, was called for within a few weeks of its publication in covers; and more than four million copies of the novels were sold in the twelve years following the author's death. It has been estimated that during his lifetime Dickens addressed an audience of a million and a half, or approximately one out of ten readers in Great Britain.[2]

Communion with a million and a half souls is quite an achievement. Clearly, Dickens and his readers were on to something. The question was whether we as readers at the end of the twentieth century could catch on to it as well. Could we, too, "feel the love" of Boz's labor?

Dickens by Inches: Group Reading of *Little Dorrit*

To explore some of these issues, one of the authors, Susan Schorn, organized the Dickens by Inches reading group at the University of Texas at Austin in the spring of 1996. The group would meet once monthly, commencing in September of that year, to discuss one number of *Little Dorrit,* which the members had read in the intervening month.[3] Originally, organizers intended to include presentations at each monthly meeting, covering such topics as current events taking place during the month of each number's publication, critical response to the novel, and biographical background on Dickens. Unfortunately, the founding member's subsequent pregnancy resulted in a somewhat sporadic schedule of presentations. Nevertheless many felt that reading a Dickens novel over the course of a full-term pregnancy added great legitimacy to the project's stated aim of entwining *Little Dorrit* with participants' daily lives.[4]

Both projects met with initial skepticism from the academic community.

One respected (and extremely generous) colleague pointed out that first-hand investigation of serial reading was almost necessarily a Dickens-centered endeavor. "Can you imagine anyone trying this with, say, a Henry James novel?" he asked, a comment that elicited some (really rather mean-spirited) laughter from his students. (Most of these students, it should be noted, were Americanists.) Point taken—perhaps it is Dickens's charisma that leads to projects like this, and perhaps their overall critical value may therefore be suspect in some way, but the fact remains that we as academics often cite serialization as central to Dickens's success, his writing style, and his audience's response to his works. There could hardly be a more obvious, easy, and cheap means of experiencing the effect of serial format firsthand than reading a Dickens novel slowly.

Attendance at the meetings began with a healthy dozen or so partici-pants and dwindled, as one might perhaps expect (we certainly did), to five or six hardy souls. A wider circle could probably have been attracted by advertising outside the Department of English, but no systematic effort to do this was ever made. In retrospect, casting a wider net for participants at the project's beginning would have been a good idea, as it was especially difficult to draft new readers midway through the novel.

Though all participants in the group expressed pleasure in having com-pleted the project, the journey was in some cases a difficult one. For a few readers, the short monthly installments focused attention on Dickens's osten-tatiously descriptive prose to the point where the plot became difficult to follow. In fact, reading *Little Dorrit* as it was originally published can become a gruesome Brobdingnagian experience—every pit, pore, and pock-mark in the complexion of Dickens's prose is made huge, magnified by the expansion of reading time and resultant deepening of reader inspection.[5] Moreover, for academics and Dickens fans—who are almost by definition avid readers—measured doses of Dickens can be frustrating simply because they thwart our usual reading habits: one thing we almost never do with a Dickens book is close it voluntarily. Thus Dickens's masterful stance as storyteller can become a kind of tyranny when humor, description, moraliz-ing, and action are parceled out in measured amounts as if by an omnipotent being. We readers who are used to forging ahead soon began to feel like Oliver Twist, wanting to ask the Great Man, "Please Sir, may I have some more?" and simultaneously resenting Dickens for making us ask.

Dickens was fully aware of his status as both guide and creator, Virgil and Almighty. In his postscript to *Our Mutual Friend,* he even reassures readers that the difference in discernment between God (himself) and Man (the audience) is completely reasonable and nothing they should worry about. If they wish to comprehend the Universe in its entirety, they should buy the bound volume of the novel:

> for, it would be very unreasonable to expect that many readers, pursuing a story in portions from month to month through nineteen months will, until they have it before them complete, perceive the relations of its finer threads to the whole pattern which is always before the eyes of the story-weaver at his loom.[6]

On the other hand, Dickens is an extremely involved, hands-on God. Johnson notes, "In contrast to such novelists as Samuel Richardson or Jane Austen or George Eliot or Henry James, [Dickens] never seeks even in his most mature work to create the impression that his plots evolve by their own impetus out of an inner logic of events. Form and meaning do not organically coalesce; rather they are related through a process of deliberate and overt manipulation."[7] Serial reading of a novel such as *Little Dorrit* makes this deliberate manipulation abundantly clear. For some, it is a disheartening revelation. And yet it reveals much about Dickens's skill and his working methods as an author. Whatever we think of his descriptions of writing as a "labour of love," we cannot fail to be impressed by the sheer workload that writing in this manner imposed. (A potential project for some other willing academic guinea pigs would be to attempt to *write* a serial novel of the same length, and on the same schedule, as a Dickens novel.) Moreover, annoying as the slow pace of serial reading may prove for some readers, such a focus can prove invaluable to our understanding of Dickens's narrative technique and characterization. Not that these usually receive short shrift in our attention to his work, but in reading his work with the plot suspended, so to speak, over our heads, rather than feeling it firmly under our feet, we gain a keener understanding of why Dickens is celebrated for his characterization and narrative flow rather than for his plot construction.

Dickens by Pixels: Online Group Reading of
A Tale of Two Cities

In the fall of 1998, the second project attempted to take up where Dickens by Inches left off, and to see whether a different medium of conversation might address some of the problems encountered in the previous two years of serial reading. Since one frequent complaint of the *Little Dorrit* group was the difficulty of coordinating schedules to meet in person once per month, one author thought that a serial reading group could be facilitated by the resources afforded by the World Wide Web. Classic texts such as Dickens's were readily available online, and the authors had access to quite powerful, easy-to-use, and free tools for creating interactive web pages such as bulletin boards and forums. Many literature instructors at Texas used these tools in teaching their own classes; why not try them with a serial reading group? The discussions would take place entirely online, meaning that participants could contribute on their own schedules. Email reminders would prompt members about the "availability" of the next installment, with links to the electronic version (although paper versions were certainly encouraged—participation was the thing) as well as to the website itself. We selected *A Tale of Two Cities* so that we could attract a wider audience (including high school classes), and we advertised on national email discussion lists and Dickens websites as well as on local walls. The site was created (and has been archived) at <http://www.cwrl.utexas.edu/dickens>.

For a time the group had fairly lively participation, as measured by the activity on the main discussion forum. What was especially encouraging was the appearance of several readers from outside our campus. But as the year wore on, contributions to the forum lagged, until finally very few were posted at all. The discussion was transferred to an email discussion list in an attempt to make the discussion more immediate for readers, but the move had little effect. In April, that cruelest month, at the end of the scheduled readings, the forum and discussion list closed without even a whimper.

What happened? We will never know for sure whether the project failed in its mission of getting the readers to experience Dickens in serial format; for all we know, everyone who started the novel finished it according to the published installment schedule. What we do know is that, by the end, few people wanted to share their experiences, so even if the attrition rate was not high, the interest level certainly was low.

One possible explanation for this apparently (and likely actually) high dropout rate is, paradoxically, the medium of the discussions. Barring the possibility that the postings themselves grew less interesting over time and drove participants to spend their time in other ways, we conclude that the medium itself contributed to the demise of the discussion. Without having to encounter people face-to-face, most participants apparently found it difficult to hold themselves to the task of reading a weekly installment and posting something about it or responding to someone else's posting. What was originally designed to increase participation by allowing flexibility turned out to undermine the sense of shared enterprise. Reading a novel slowly over the course of a year requires effort and support, regular engagement and frequent accountability—in short, a community of readers. Asynchronous chat forums (that is, bulletin boards with threads that need not appear in strictly chronological order) tend *not* to encourage this kind of interactive community of support. Instead, they facilitate a kind of "help desk" mentality: post a question, check back for an answer. Case in point: during the last half of the project, two separate postings appeared from far-flung students who, in the course of their research on a Dickens paper, found our forum and requested help with their work. Aside from a response from the site webmaster, these "intrusions" went entirely unremarked by the group. And why not? The off-topic postings were no different *in spirit* from the rest, most of which were seemingly flung into the void, lucky to find a response and even luckier if it were timely (the average response time for a posting grew from 1–2 weeks during the fall to 1–2 months during the spring).

The trajectory of Dickens by Pixels shows that electronic discussion groups cannot function without a clear sense of community right from the start; the medium inhibits one from developing where it does not already exist. While Dickens aficionados exist worldwide and even get together with surprising frequency, for the most part they do not meet for the purposes of discussing serial reading. And for the reasons discovered by the Dickens by Inches group, reading serially causes problems for contemporary readers, problems that are not overcome even by creating a support group in a completely contemporary venue. One possible reason could be the disjunction between the Victorian and the hypermodern to the sensibilities of a present-day admirer of Dickens. Perhaps reading, or even just discussing, Dickens electronically seems inappropriate to Dickensians?

Maybe so, but contemporary serial publications have tended to fare no better in their readership trajectories.[8] The most famous example is that of Stephen King's *The Plant*, an entirely electronic serial novel. In July 2000, King placed the first installment of the novel on his website, <stephenking.com>. In the first week, more than 150,000 people downloaded the document, and slightly over 76 percent of them complied with the author's honor system by sending payment of one dollar.[9] King stipulated he would continue providing installments as long as the pay rate remained above 75 percent.[10] One of the few living novelists whose popularity can compare with Dickens's, King had enjoyed previous success with the serial format. *The Green Mile,* published in six monthly numbers, sold well and was later made into an Academy Award-nominated film. And King had also enjoyed great success with an online "eBook," *Riding the Bullet,* which readers downloaded and paid for, much as they did *The Plant. The Plant's* serial *and* electronic format was intended as an experimental testing of the waters of Internet publishing. But in November 2000, after uploading six installments, King announced that he was putting *The Plant* "on hiatus"[11] until further notice.[12]

The *New York Times* attributed *The Plant's* problems to King's writing style:

> This experiment was based on a false premise. When the first install-ment of "The Plant" was published, analogies were drawn to Vic-torian serial publication, to Dickens and the impatient wait on American shores for arrival of the ship bearing the latest installment of his most recent novel. But one reads Stephen King novels in a single gulp. Their chief effect is suspense of a kind that cannot be drawn out over months. It is far better consumed in a single sitting, like a bag of hot popcorn or a bowl of cold cereal. "The Plant" with-ered mainly because its author misunderstood the nature of his read-ership.[13]

King responded by pointing out that he *had* published serially with great success. "Contrary to what the Times editorial department may think," he chided in a letter that the *Times* declined to print, "tales of suspense almost cry out for serialization. They don't call them 'cliffhangers' for nothing."[14] Instead, King argued, there were three problems with *The Plant,* none of them related to content or style:

> One is that most Internet users seem to have the attention span of grasshoppers. Another is that Internet users have gotten used to the idea that most of what's available to them on the Net is either free or should be. The third—and biggest—is that book-readers don't regard electronic books as real books.

Setting aside the question of the accuracy of these conclusions, they are notable for their assumption that if the text is not to blame for not being popular (and with a Stephen King novel, this assumption is fair), the prob-lem must lie with the readers, either through their being warped by Internet use or jaded by their devotion to old-fashioned delivery formats. Further-more, we are surrounded by evidence that makes such assumptions tempting:

in a culture of practically unlimited mass media (of which the web is but a part), we have been conditioned not to wait for installments of anything. Even episodic narratives such as soap operas, comic books, and situation comedies are available collected in either volumes or longer videotapes or in marathons on various cable networks. Why wait when you can have all of what you want right now?

The problem with assuming the fault lies solely with readers is that modern readers don't consider novels to be episodic narratives at all; therefore, readers resist treating a web document, which by necessity must appear fragmented if not entirely in episodes, as a novel. It's not that they don't consider it a "real book," whatever that is; rather, "novels," whatever they are, don't work well in a medium designed for entirely different forms of communication. An electronic serial novel's lack of physical presence works against it for most people: out of sight, out of mind. The half-finished book-form novel sitting on the nightstand serves as a reminder to the reader to pick it up, to continue if the reader has decided it's worth continuing. But readers must seek out electronically published serials. Even if email reminders appear in their in-boxes, readers must still visit the site, take the time to download the text, and pay for it. As simple as these steps may sound, online serial reading is an investment of time (and money, in King's case) that must be repeated, whereas buying a book is a one-time endeavor, and reading it an activity to be enjoyed anywhere at leisure, not just at the computer. Consider how many novels we would read if every time we closed the book it went back to the library. When the experience becomes work, there must be an appropriate payoff to justify it. Absent the structures of, say, formal class requirements, readers apparently don't find the electronic format of a serial book convenient enough to replace their traditional paper books, nor do they find the serial approach to an electronic book (or discussion group), with its low level of community spirit, rewarding enough to maintain the discipline it requires. Maybe readers have changed since the Victorian period, maybe not. More certain is that the kinds of reading communities that Dickens enjoyed for his works are irretrievably lost when (1) Dickens is dead, and (2) his novels appear in a medium ill-suited to their length. Without such a community, the reading simply doesn't happen; thus serial reading has not found fertile soil in which to develop as a contemporary approach to most traditional print literature (even if distributed electronically).

Conclusion: A Cost-Benefit Analysis of Serialized Reading

Whatever the drawbacks to reading novels in serial form and to creating a venue for discussing them, there are benefits to such reading and discussion. By and large, however, the group most likely to profit from them consists of specialists—that is, scholars and students of literature and culture, Victorian in particular. Such people comprise the most obvious already-existing communities in which a serial reading approach could have some appeal. As we have claimed, without such a community already in place, readers are unlikely to maintain the artificial strictures on their own reading.[15]

Serial reading has clear advantages to advanced scholars in English. As noted earlier, it provides an experience more like that of the original readership in the nineteenth century, and such an experience can illuminate many aspects of the work that might otherwise go unnoticed. These insights make up the groundwork of scholarship and of pedagogy, and we should seek to encourage both. Thus our understanding of Victorian literature, Victorian culture, narrative theory, and creative writing might all be enriched by serial reading.

But the serial approach might be put to even better use in introductory collegiate and even high school courses. Many survey courses, including the traditional "great books" courses, tend to include at most one novel of any length in their syllabi. The burdens of coverage make it difficult to give enough time on the syllabus to a single text demanding at least two weeks of study. Furthermore, instructors find that putting long works in such courses invites students simply to skip that part of the reading, whether because reading a Big Novel is more work all at once than they are prepared to handle (many college students have never read an entire canonical novel before) or are willing to perform (it's easy to find published notes on almost anything one might teach). Including a novel to be read serially over the entire semester (or year) can address these problems. By breaking the text into smaller chunks, students find it less intimidating; and instructors need not even invent the break points if the text was originally published in serial form. Instructors can include works much longer than they would otherwise consider because a weekly number takes relatively little time away from other components of the syllabus. Serial reading schedules provide an automatic structure to the course that might complement other units if desired. And in large lecture courses with weekly discussion groups, or in classes that meet daily, the recurrence of a weekly number provides a domain for teaching assistants and a routine that particularly helps younger students. Depending on the discussion format—in small groups or in electronic forums, according to the desired intensity of focus—instructors have a relatively easy means of monitoring student progress as well.

If serial reading schedules were perfect, though, we'd already have them as a regular part of our courses. They have drawbacks and costs worth considering also. In terms of equipment and infrastructure, an electronic venue for discussion has significant costs, and even though many people have access to web resources, such access is not universal, nor is it necessarily cheap. As technology becomes even more pervasive in our culture, this concern will become less salient, but for now it is a major consideration. But even without including an electronic component, serial reading has costs of time and energy. Everyone in the process must devote regular time to the text for an extended period; in doing so, instructors and especially students will rapidly tire of the process unless the work is well worth that extended time. For instance, although a graduate class on narratology reading *Little Dorrit* in conjunction with Bakhtin's discussion of it in "Discourse in the Novel" might profit from the extended view of the dialogics at work therein, most readers will probably simply grow to loathe *Little Dorrit* and wonder, as we did, why Bakhtin chose *that* novel to discuss out of all the better ones he might have chosen. Classes without such contexts will find the already difficult process of serial reading even more burdensome, and thus run the risk of losing students who fall behind early in the process. Such students might attempt to cram the entire novel in before exams, which of course defeats the entire purpose of the exercise; more likely, they simply would never catch up, a lamentable outcome. And instructors will need to revise their approaches to their courses, some of which have been developed over several years. Including a text that spans an entire academic term necessitates breaking some divisions in the syllabus: chronological, formal/generic, cultural/national, authorial. While such border breaking might illustrate the arbitrary nature of such divisions, it does involve significant rethinking of the texts and the course.[16]

Do the benefits of serial reading outweigh these costs? While each instructor will have to make that decision individually, we firmly believe that they do, especially in survey courses like the ones required to fulfill college distribution requirements. Serial reading serves so many purposes of those courses in ways fundamentally compatible with their structures and goals, whether they are seminars or lecture courses, that it is an approach that begs to be utilized. At minimum, simply devising a reasonable schedule of weekly readings and devoting a little attention to the novel each week will suffice to work it into the fabric of the course.

And that's the main benefit we see: discovering that the term "text" really does relate to its root, "weaving." By working a serial novel into the entire semester, students might begin to see its relationship to other serial texts in their lives (news stories and scandals, ongoing reality TV shows, and so on) and to other texts in the course, setting up discussions of *contexts* of various kinds. The resistance of readers to the serial format can serve to emphasize both the relationship between Victorian serial novels and contemporary serial texts that literature instructors are best equipped to exploit in their teaching, as well as their relationship to other kinds of texts in the students' routine experiences. And if the study of literature can illustrate relationships between text and context, and possibly even teach students how to recognize them for themselves, that would be a great service.

After all, in his postscript to *Our Mutual Friend,* Dickens calls himself a story-weaver whose tales should be regarded as threads in a pattern on his loom. What better way to illustrate this view than to create a situation where the textual threads are exposed and the workings of the narrative loom laid open to examination? We may not always like what we see, but the development of critical judgment in these matters thrives upon such cognitive dissonance. Whether our discussion communities take advantage of the World Wide Web to push the idea of weaving even further, or whether they take place in the far more complex human web of face-to-face interaction, teasing out the minute strands of a Victorian novel through serial reading—precisely *because* of reader resistance—offers tremendous opportunities for all their participants.

Notes

1. Robert L. Patten, *Charles Dickens and His Publishers* (Oxford: Clarendon Press, 1978), 46.

2. Edward D. (E. D. H.) Johnson, *Charles Dickens: An Introduction to His Novels* (New York: Random House, 1969), 62, in The Victorian Web, ed. George P. Landow, Mar. 16, 2001 <http://landow.stg.brown.edu/victorian/dickens/edh/contents.html>.

3. *Little Dorrit* was chosen because it was originally published in monthly numbers and because the initiators of the project had never read it. While some members of the group had read it before, they were requested not to reveal any upcoming plot points and were remarkably successful in complying.

4. Happily, the fears of a few members of the group regarding prenatal exposure to Dickens proved unfounded. Dr. Schorn's son David made his first postnatal appearance at the reading circle in January 1997 and attended most of the subsequent meetings with no lasting effect on his health.

5. This perception was not shared by all members of the group, though most expressed some fellow feeling. Whatever the reason, there is one indisputable result of one author's serial approach to *Little Dorrit:* she remembers less about it, and remembers it less fondly, than any other Dickens novel.

6. Charles Dickens, *Our Mutual Friend,* ed. Adrian Poole (London: Penguin, 1997), 798.

7. Johnson, 84, in The Victorian Web (see note 2).

8. One serial publication worth noting here is *The League of Extraordinary Gentlemen* by Alan Moore and Kevin O'Neill (illustrator). This graphic narrative (a series of six comic books)

casts several characters from fantastic Victorian fiction (Captain Nemo, the Invisible Man, Dr. Jekyll/Mr. Hyde, et al.) in a new tale of adventure set in the late Victorian era. This series attracted a strong cult following, although its publication schedule was somewhat erratic, and it has remained a steady player in the marketplace (the collected bound version of the series was ranked 9,891 at Amazon.com on March 22, 2001, two years after its first publication in comic book form). Its adherents are generally well versed in Victorian/Edwardian literature, including Dickens; surely there still exists a potential audience for Victorian (or at least Victorian-flavor) serial narratives. Of course, graphic-novel readers may already constitute a tightly formed reading community of their own, and comic books are far shorter than Dickens or King novels.

9. "Update: Stephen King's Plant Flourishes." Atnewyork.com: Silicon Alley News. Feb. 3, 2001 <http://www.stephenking.com/sk_120400.html>.

10. The pay rate subsequently fell to below 50 percent by the fourth installment (Stephen King, "Author's Note," The Official Stephen King Web Presence, Feb. 3, 2001 <http:// www.stephenking.com/sk_100900.html>). The attention King and his readership have paid to economic factors surrounding the novel is interesting. Installments of *The Plant* were not priced identically—the first three cost one dollar, the next five two dollars each, and the remainder were to be free—and King was at pains to explain the rationale behind this price structure. "In other words," King explained to his readers, "you[r] complete financial liability for the first 8 installments of this story will be $13 or about the cost of a trade paperback or a hardcover novel offered at 40% discount in a chain bookstore. Any parts beyond 8—which would be the balance of the story, would be posted free" ("The Plant: Frequently Asked Questions," The Official Stephen King Web Presence, Feb. 3, 2001 <http://www.stephenking.com/plant_FAQ.html>). Additionally, a summary of *The Plant*'s earnings to date is available online, part of King's attempt to show the financial viability of the project ("The Plant: Income/Expense Report Through 12/31/00," The Official Stephen King Web Presence, Feb. 3, 2001 <http:// www.stephenking.com/PlantNumbers_010101.html>).

11. Stephen King, "Stephen's Comments," The Official Stephen King Web Presence, Feb. 3, 2001 <http://www.stephenking.com/sk_120400.html>.

12. Ironically, King said this move was necessary to free up his time for work on a book titled *Black House* (Stephen King, "Author's Note," The Official Stephen King Web Presence, Feb. 3, 2001 <http://www.stephenking.com/sk_100900.html>).

13. "King Closure," reprinted from The New York Times Opinions and Editorials for 12/01/00, The Official Stephen King Web Presence, Feb. 3, 2001 <http://www.stephenking.com/ nyt_oped_120100.html>.

14. Stephen King, "The Plant: Getting a Little Goofy," Stephen's Comments for 12/04/00, The Official Stephen King Web Presence, Feb. 3, 2001 <http://www.stephenking.com /sk_120400_2.html>.

15. Projects such as "One Book, One Chicago," in which residents of a city are encouraged to read and discuss a single book, thus have two advantages over the Dickens by . . . projects: they call upon a preexisting (and large) community, and they do not read in serial format.

16. The only way to avoid this would be to read the entire syllabus serially and eliminate the arbitrary divisions, in which case the effort shifts to remembering all the characters and plots.

Disseminating Victorian Culture in the Postmillennial Classroom

SUE LONOFF

Writers in our discipline rarely reveal how they came to compose their essays.[1] If they do, the disclosure occurs in a space apart: an afterword or preface, a biography or interview, letters to colleagues, excuses to an editor. I deviate here because the process of composing this one bears directly on its arguments.

When Christine Krueger invited me to join an MLA Victorian Division panel, I had no idea what I wanted to say, beyond investigating future problems in the teaching of Victorian literature and culture. The project was still unformed when titles fell due, although by then I was planning to include the results of a survey of younger teachers' outlooks. But I could estimate the kind of heading that audience members would respect. It could never be as simple as "The Issues We Face in the New Century." No, to signal my status as a member of the tribe, it would have to be polysyllabic, polysemic, and beyond the comprehension of the *barbaroi*. I therefore concocted a list of the most outrageous titles I could think of and asked Christine to choose her favorite. I also sketched an outline of prospective topics, which I tucked into a "future projects" folder.

In mid-December, with the MLA looming, I returned from a three-month stay in Paris. Confronted with the title

I had foolishly submitted, not to mention a deadline eleven days ahead, I decided there was just one way to get the paper written: by reducing the title to its elements. After that, the paper more or less flowed, although it threatened to outrun its allotted time span and left a heavy residue of questions. Happily, they could be addressed in this volume. But how to fit the new part to the old? Without a massive overhaul, they wouldn't coalesce with the seamlessness that marks the traditional essay. There was, however, an alternative format: pastiche/postmodernist disunity. One could set the original paper in the center, flank it with commentary fore and aft, and hope that the assemblage would function.

Now I will reproduce the speech as delivered, with minor adaptations to written discourse and a warning that might have come straight from Wilkie Collins: dear reader, don't forget what I've just said. You will need this information as we near the denouement.

Speaking at the MLA Convention

In the following pages, I want to raise questions that we can investigate during the discussion that follows. I'll start by picking apart the words of my title—and note that I do not say "deconstruct," an altogether premillennial term:

First word: *Disseminating* (literally, scattering the seed): How will the pedagogy of dissemination change in the twenty-first century? In the middle and later twentieth century, teaching methods included the lecture (professor predominant), the seminar (student participation primary), and courses combining lecture with student input and, increasingly, audiovisuals. Will professors withdraw from center stage as postmillennial technology eradicates their platform, enabling anyone to enter the discourse via web-based discussion groups and email? Or will they become more dominant as courses are offered via distance learning and students plug into the prof?[2]

Almost certainly, the use of film clips, graphics, and drawings will spread, since most students are far more sophisticated readers of visual data than they are of printed texts. But will texts continue to be printed? We may yet see the day when every reading on the syllabus fits into an object the size of a palm pilot that beams words directly to the brain. More immediately, many out-of-print documents are now accessible or will become available online. Instructor aids have also been steadily increasing. We now have the Norton Critical editions, the Bedford Case Studies in Contemporary Criticism, the Broadview Press series for period contexts, the MLA Approaches to Teaching series, the Victorian Web and other websites, as well as intelligent guides to their use, and threaded discussions on Victoria. However, these new vectors of dissemination also impose new burdens; consider the sheer volume of resources that a conscientious teacher should examine.

A further factor in dissemination is the BBC-ing of Victorian fiction, the fact that students are now more likely to have seen some film or video version of *Tess* or *Bleak House* than they are to have read the book. How will these twentieth-century renditions of nineteenth-century novels be perceived as the twenty-first century advances? Will they help future teachers to historicize a period ever more remote from students, or will they necessitate continuing corrections about what is, and isn't, Victorian?

And what about that second word: *Victorian?* Will the boundaries continue to hold? Already, the market has triggered the breakdown of traditional categories. In my pre-premillennial college experience, the English department had a specialist apiece in Victorian fiction, poetry, and prose, and then finally a feminist to take up the cudgels. I won't ask how many current departments would hire even one purebred Victorianist, as opposed to an —ist who can also do theory, postcolonialism, cultural studies, the romantics, and her colleagues' websites.

But beyond these market-driven forces of change, there are pressures from within to alter categories. Some of us now teach the nineteenth-century novel, which may or may not be limited to England, and others do not teach the novel or prose per se but rather a course in cultural history, or one that abolishes the old genre boundaries, moving from prose to art to fiction. Perhaps, as Isobel Armstrong has suggested, the period itself will be redefined so that its time line extends from the romantics to World War I.[3] In any case, the need for establishing contexts, for defining the questions and issues of the era, can only increase as it recedes into the past.

Which brings me to the third word: *Culture.* And here I'll need to subdivide or trifurcate into (a) the culture we purport to study, (b) the divergent cultures of our students, and (c) our department cultures.

In the very informal survey I've conducted—I sent emails to a number of young professors, combed through pedagogy discussions on Victoria, and read through a few dozen posted syllabi—one clear message was the need for giving students a sense of the issues that Victorian literature manifests and, indeed, develops. This message is far from new, but in the latter decades of the twentieth century, it has gained support from the ascendancy of "Cultural Studies," a term that has increasingly become a legitimating label. For example, a chair who would reject a proposal to teach *In Memoriam* to non-English majors might point with pride to that new course offering, "Cross-cultural Studies of Death and Survival." Eventually, the label "Cultural Studies" may become as dated as New Criticism now appears to be. Nonetheless, the demand for contextualization will grow as the new century progresses. We may also find that current annotations, even in the most student-friendly editions, will fall far short of what our students require to comprehend the sense of a George Eliot sentence or the tropes in a passage by Tennyson.

Another problem that my survey corroborates is the growing gap between our best and worst students. The problem does not lie in multiculturalism (the diversity of ethnic and economic backgrounds), nor can it be completely linked to the status of the institution. As Phoebe Wray, who teaches in "an expensive private arts college with high performance standards," writes on Victoria: "It's as if these middle-class, rather privileged kids . . . are from the mines of the 19th century. They do not read. Some of them do not know how to read. They have not a clue about HOW to read in a close way."[4] Why not? Because, unlike the Victorians we study, we live in a culture that increasingly denigrates sustained, reflective reading, and students, who are very savvy consumers, will rarely make efforts that yield minimal payoffs. In a handful of selective universities, the prevailing student culture encourages the kind of liberal education that Newman so powerfully defended. Far more often, however, our dedicated students have chosen to fight against the current. But even they must struggle with reading loads that are incommensurate with their reading abilities, a problem that will grow even more acute as the century advances. To what extent should we, or our successors, cut back on the amounts of reading we require? And where do we leave graduate education, if the most gifted of our undergraduates read only four or five Victorian novels, and consider assignments of three hundred pages per week inhumanly tough?[5]

Department and institutional cultures reflect and, more damagingly, promulgate the gap between intellectual riches and poverty. So at one end, Nick Dames writes in an email (Dec. 19, 2000), "The most passionate responses [of my students] . . . have always come from *Culture and Anarchy;* perhaps that's because of Columbia's Core program, so that they all know the canon intimately and have strong opinions about its value." And at the other, Ellen Moody writes to Victoria, "the college I teach at recently abolished the Survey courses, the first and second halves of British and the first and second halves of American literature."[6] Will the marginalization of what we do continue, and, if so, how are we to halt it?

In the last third of the twentieth century, rifts in English departments arose between the traditionalists and the theory-heads, who also warred against each other. The latest Victorianist split is emerging between those who do based-in-England studies and those who work in postcolonial areas. What implications will this division have for our teaching? And here, I'm not just thinking of the contents of our syllabi, but more hard-headedly, about the numbers and the kinds of students we'll attract. In discussion threads where teachers commiserate with each other, an additional message comes through very clearly: if you want your students to care about their learning, "focus on the pleasures of the text." But which texts should we offer for their pleasure? We have witnessed massive revisions of the canon, and further revisions are sure to come, whether they are driven by forces now operant or those we do not even suspect.

How will twenty-first-century pleasures differ from those we discovered in the twentieth century, or those we have in common with Victorian readers? In choosing to include *Postmillennial* in my title, I consciously employed a premillennial strategy: using a word that announces to initiates, "this is contemporary discourse." Will it be the discourse of the future? We have post-ed our way past structuralism, modernism, colonialism, and others of their ilk. Will we ourselves now become a post-generation, as new waves of students gleefully abandon the theories that seduced their elders?

My title ends with the old-fashioned word *Classroom,* a space whose boundaries grow increasingly porous, as more and more teachers design web-based assignments and take advantage of online opportunities for research and communication. In the later decades of the twentieth century, classroom practices and methods of pedagogy changed in many disciplines to include more forms of "interactive" learning: having students work in peer groups in and out of class, assigning collaborative research and writing, asking for frequent feedback on the course, and, in general, converting the professor from a sage to a guide. These changes have been slow to reach most English departments, where the lecture and the thesis-driven student paper remain curricular staples. But new technology often impels changes in method, and as more of us experiment with it, we will have to reconsider how our students learn and how we can best facilitate their learning. For example, Jonathan Smith writes,

> The use of hypertext . . . really does offer the potential to expose students to a wider range of possibilities in the study of literature, to develop their disciplinary reading skills, to enhance their engagement

with the material and with each other, and to develop course materials that can be used and expanded by future classes.

Smith adds, however, that

the more it is used, the more it exposes student weaknesses in
reading—especially the inability to read non-linearly and to link
text with context, specific detail with general theme, or one facet of
the text with another. And since most students have been trained to
be passive readers rather than active, independent, and subversive
ones, such exposure tends to increase their anxieties, at least initially.[7]

I would add that it may also increase ours. Nonetheless, he concludes that
this anxiety is probably "a necessary step" and that if hypertext compels
instructors "to revise not just their individual class sessions and writing
assignments but the very conception of how they teach, [t]he rewards . . .
are worth the effort."[8]

Whether or not we embrace the new technologies—or have them thrust
upon us as the century advances—it seems clear that classroom and beyond-
the-classroom practices have entered an era of transition. Whatever those
transitions may entail for our students, and for the future of Victorian studies, they attest to the vitality and vigor of our enterprise, despite the many
challenges it faces.

On this optimistic note the talk ended, though its closure was only
rhetorical. In fact, as its many questions imply, our problems far outnum-
ber our solutions. Subsequent reflection suggests two major issues on
which all the others converge.

The Future of Reading

In "The Fate of Reading," Geoffrey Hartman claims that "the romance of
reading has not faded entirely," although what now exists in an etiolated
form was burgeoning in the nineteenth century when, with the growth of universal education, culture became the rallying point for the forces that com-
bated anarchy. No longer elitist, the "world of arts and letters" functioned
as a "*commonwealth*" accessible to all who were literate.[9] To use another
trope, there was an upward spiral: ordinary middle-class people read
avidly, hungry for what the printed word could offer. The act of reading
trained them to become sharper readers and nurtured an appetite for future

texts of commensurate or greater complexity. It also nurtured an appetite for length, at least until the death of the three-decker.

Today, the momentum is downward. Because most people read less or read primarily as scanners, they are less equipped to comprehend subtlety and nuance; therefore they quickly become impatient with texts that seem too much of a stretch. Impatience and boredom reduce the attention span, further diminishing the possibility of long-term gratification. Serious, sustained engagement in reading thus becomes elitist or escapist—the province of stubborn individuals, of coteries (book clubs are undergoing a resurgence), and of the literature classroom.

Half an hour after writing the paragraph above, I came across an article by David Brooks on a new generation of elite college students, "leaders-in-training" who work nonstop toward the high positions they expect to win. At first, Brooks's interviews seemed to hold out hope that this subgroup of sophisticated, dedicated students would reverse the trend away from close reading. But absent from his article is any reference to the humanities or literature. Indeed, the *New York Times* proved too heavy for one student, who confessed that she had abandoned her subscription because the newspapers "just piled up unread."[10] Reading, one infers, is not intrinsically rewarding; rather, it is part of an information apparatus geared toward the reaching of goals.

If reading in general gets short shrift in our culture, Victorianists are in a particular bind because of the length of what they teach. Furthermore, the prose of most Victorian writers—its vocabulary, sentence length, and even punctuation—poses problems for students used to slogans and sound bites. The size of the computer screen further accustoms them to processing only small quantities of prose, and to seeing passages of print broken up by illustrations, lavish graphics, and ads. But since these are the realities confronting us as teachers, we need to learn how to respond to them effectively, that is, if we choose to keep our jobs. And the primary step is to reenvision the ways in which our teaching can enable student learning—or, better, can motivate students to take charge of a process that provides its own rewards.

Our discipline lags behind others in developing innovative pedagogies. Composition and foreign language teachers pay far more attention to method than we do, in part because the outcomes of those methods—fluency, clarity, defensible theses—can be so much more readily assessed. Traditionally too we have made the assumption that teaching can be learned by osmosis or experience rather than by well-planned modes of training. Our snobbery toward formalized instruction is paralleled by snobbery within our own ranks. As George Levine writes in his aptly titled essay, "The Two Nations,"

> for as long as I have been in the profession, there has been an obviously internal division, often even in the work of individual faculty, between dedication to teaching (which may in some instances impede professional success) and dedication to research and criticism (which is the preliminary condition for stardom). The effect has been to produce something like an intraprofessional class war.[11]

We face battles enough in the twenty-first century against administrators who are driven by the bottom line[12] and widespread student indifference. Simply to hold ground, we may have to join forces, examine the techniques that have worked in other disciplines, share what we discover, promote methods that work, and develop ways of gauging their effectiveness.

In my speech, I touched briefly on a few of the strategies already in practice:

- Using cultural materials to supplement the reading of the (ever-fewer) novels on the list.
- Running comparisons with media versions.
- Designing interactive Web materials—much as people who teach language courses do—that will motivate students to improve their skills and knowledge, and give them immediate feedback.
- Keeping current with the latest resources and with reports on their effectiveness.

Two others may be even more essential in the fight against attrition:

- Assigning more frequent writing projects. These need not be extensive or exhaustively critiqued.[13] Their purpose is to maintain frequent checkpoints and encourage students both to keep up and to track their own progress as analysts.
- Devoting more class time to the techniques of analytic reading.

I am well aware that, for many readers, these suggestions align me with the forces of evil. Why debase Victorian studies further by turning ourselves into kiddie-camp counselors? Why add to the burdens the academy imposes by increasing our workload as teachers? My response will entail consideration of the other major issue that the talk brought into focus.

The Hegemony of the Hierophants

In the last three decades of the twentieth century, in virtually all English and literature programs, theory became de rigueur. Deconstructionists, Foucauldians, queer theorists, and feminists might challenge each other in battles for turf, but on one front, at least, they were united: that literary studies were no province for the amateur, no gentleman's club in which the simple love of reading could qualify the bearer for membership. The nineteenth-century ideal of a cultural commonwealth sank before the image of a prison-house of language, a construct from which there could be no escape, although initiates might seek to lower the bars by interrogating its assumptions. The key word was, of course "initiate." The department that wanted to attract the best and brightest, the professor who intended to prolong his viability, the student who aspired to the professoriat had, sooner or later, to immerse themselves in theory and so implicitly sanction the ascendancy of experts in the arcane.

When Carlyle exhorted his readers, "close thy *Byron,* open thy *Goethe,*" he too was endorsing a source of power that emanated from the Continent.[14] But unlike our current pluralists, he acknowledged the win-lose terms of his mandate. His ideal readers could not simultaneously function as Byronists and Goetheists. They would have to turn from the English romantics to the higher mode of thinking that the Germans represented; gain entailed necessary loss.

In an era when students read far less than they did when Carlyle thundered, we demand much more. We would like them to become familiar with the canon (or with whatever version of the canon is current), to read noncanonical culture-centered texts, and to steep themselves in the critical and metacritical writings of a host of luminaries. If this agenda proves too massive, cuts are made in the opposite order: canonical texts are set aside so that critical thinking may be promoted through the study of cutting-edge theory.[15]

What most Americans fail to consider is that those grand innovators from the Continent received a rigorous traditional education before they were set loose to theorize. The French system is famous, or notorious, for its imposition of a standardized curriculum. Whether students attend a lycée in Poitiers (like Foucault), or in Algeria (like Derrida and Cixous), or in Bulgaria (like Kristeva), they are drilled in fundamentals before they are allowed, much less encouraged, to become original. They memorize large chunks of the classics. They transcribe dictations in which every misplaced accent counts as an error. They learn the rules for writing at least three kinds of summary (the *résumé*, the *compte rendu*, the *synthèse*), and all deviations incur penalties. When they read a novel or poem, they are taught precisely how to approach it. Their futures quite literally depend on their compliance, since the examinations that determine whether and where they will go to university assess their ability to analyze texts according to pre-scribed methodologies. When the best of these students reach graduate level, they are more than ready to play in the double sense—to mock the old systemic rigidities and to do so with a thorough preparation. As for more typical or mediocre students, they may be less inventive when they graduate than many of their American counterparts, but they will also know far more about their nation's literature, history, and culture; and they are far more likely to sustain their engagement in the years that follow.

This is not to deny that some American students enter our classrooms superbly prepared and eager to launch into theory. But even in the top-ranked research institutions and the most competitive of liberal arts col-leges, will there be enough of them to keep our departments functioning in the new century? To put the issue another way: Is our mission to clone ourselves? Should we focus on preparing candidates for fields that show little sign of expanding? Or should we consider the other uses to which students might put an Eng-lit education and adjust our curricula accord-ingly?

The night before delivering my own MLA speech, I attended the special session, "Alternative Histories of Cultural Studies." The respondent was Mary E. Murrell, an editor at Princeton University Press. Presumably, she had been invited to react to the papers in this trendsetting area; instead, she chose to make a plea that I will try to paraphrase. She reminded the audience that publishers are steadily reducing their commitment to the books that scholars in the field prefer to write, because the market for them just isn't there. She hinted that the esoteric nature of those books was making them increasingly difficult to sell. Then she said, "You people do one thing superbly, which no other discipline does: you are *readers*. You know how to analyze texts, and you know how to train students to read analytically. Your services are urgently needed" (and publishers, she hinted, would pay for them). Why, she asked, did we deprecate this asset?

To that market of educable readers, Victorianists bear a unique respon-sibility, not only because the works they teach assume that one should be morally accountable but also because the culture they disseminate priori-tized the reader's role in the reception and construction of texts. Dickens initiated the characteristically Victorian relationship between the writer and his public, a "communion" described by Thackeray as "something continual, confidential, something like personal affection."[16] It survived the death of both authors, but Edwardian mockery drove it out of fashion, and modernism banished it from serious fiction, although, in a transition across media, it thrives in the relations between soaps and their fans, and celebrities and theirs.

Given the debasement of the impulse toward communion and the power accorded to the high priests of theory, it's hardly surprising that many teachers shun the newer, student-centered pedagogies. The term "student-centered" alone raises hackles, as if it necessitated dumbing down one's courses in order to gratify the ignorant. I do not know how teachers in the twenty-first century will balance what they think their students must learn with practical responses to the crisis in enrollments and, in many cases, preparedness. But the future of our discipline depends on our ability to visualize complex issues clearly and develop appropriate strategies. We can also persuade students to share our commitment by practicing that typically Victorian ploy of treating them as allies in an enterprise in process. In effect, those of us who use email and the Web are already dismantling traditional hierarchies. Students who send their teachers letters at midnight, often in the same batch as letters to their friends, are far less likely to conceive of professors as remote authority figures.

I suggest that it is in our interest, and theirs, to encourage the belief that we are human. If we want to teach them about agency, we can explain that our syllabi, requirements, and methods have not been instituted by divine fiat and could benefit from ongoing feedback. If we want to teach them about context, we can make the conditions of production explicit by letting them know how we structure our classes and how we deal with the constraints. In letting you know how I designed this essay and how it has evolved in the act of writing, I am using the tactics it advocates. Whether they will be disseminated further is anybody's guess.

Notes

1. In contrast, writers in the field of composition, most notably Peter Elbow ("High Stakes and Low Stakes in Assigning and Responding to Writing," in *Everyone Can Write* [New York: Oxford University Press, 2000], 351–59), frequently refer to their own methods of composing, and authors of books on creative writing frequently urge teachers to share examples of their practice with their students.

2. As Glenn Everett points out, online methodology "necessitates converting every

interaction with students into written text, and thereby negates the improvisational mode" as well as face-to-face exchanges. The danger, as he says, is "course delivery" (presentation, "Victorian Breakdowns," Northeast Victorian Studies Association Conference, Apr. 15, 2000).

3. Isobel Armstrong, "Let's Get Rid of the Victorians," Seminar on Victorian Literature and Culture, Humanities Center, Harvard University, Mar. 1999.

4. Phoebe Wray, posting: "What to Do about Unprepared and Uninterested Students." Victoria, <http://listserve.indiana.edu/archives/victoria.html>, <Zozie@aol.com>. Mar. 10, 1999.

5. In an admittedly sketchy look at texts assigned in courses posted on Indiana University's "Teaching Resources: Syllabi" (Victorian Research Web, Dec. 2000 *<http://www.indiana.edu/~victoria.teaching.html>*), I discovered only one course that assigned thirteen novels. Other courses in nineteenth-century or Victorian literature assigned anywhere from three to nine novels, long and short; the average was six. In literature surveys that included poetry, prose, and occasionally art, the average was closer to two. In those latter courses, the preferred Dickens novel was the relatively short *Hard Times*.

6. Ellen Moody, posting: "What to Do About Unprepared and Uninterested Students." Victoria, <http://listserve.indiana.edu/archives/victoria.html>, <emoody@moon.jic.com>. Mar. 9, 1999.

7. Jonathan Smith, "Is There a Hypertext in This Class? Teaching Victorian Literature in the Electronic Age" (1997), available at "Teaching Resources: Syllabi," Victorian Research Web <http://www.indiana.edu/~victoria.teaching.html> or <http://www.personal.umd.umich.edu/~jonsmith/tlwcart.html#abstract>.

8. See also George P. Landow, *Hypertext: The Convergence of Contemporary Critical Theory and Technology* (Baltimore: Johns Hopkins University Press, 1992).

9. Geoffrey H. Hartman, *The Fate of Reading and Other Essays* (Chicago: University of Chicago Press, 1975), 248–49.

10. David Brooks, "The Organization Kid," *Atlantic*, Apr. 2001, 40.

11. George Levine, "The Two Nations," *Pedagogy* 1 (Winter 2001): 19.

12. On the decline of economic support for the humanities, see John Guillory, *Cultural Capital: The Problem of Literary Canon Formation* (Chicago: University of Chicago Press, 1993), x, 44–55, et al. The *MLA Newsletter* is a continuing source of articles and discussions on this topic.

13. On the uses of this kind of writing, see Elbow, 351–59.

14. Ch. 9, "The Everlasting Yea," *Sartor Resartus*.

15. On this subject, see Emily Eakin, "More Ado (Yawn) about Great Books," *New York Times*, Education Life Section 4A (Apr. 8, 2001): 24–25, 40–41. See also Patrick Brantlinger's forthcoming book, *Who Killed Shakespeare? What's Happened to English since the Radical 60's*.

16. "A Box of Novels," *Fraser's Magazine*, Feb. 1844, 167. The entire sentence has been lifted from Lonoff, *Wilkie Collins and His Victorian Readers* (New York: AMS, 1982), 5.

Contributors

MIRIAM BAILIN is associate professor of English at Washington University in St. Louis. She is the author of *The Sickroom in Victorian Fiction: The Art of Being Ill* and is currently working on a book on status mobility in British fiction from 1850 to 1914.

DAVID BARNDOLLAR is a doctoral candidate in English literature at the University of Texas at Austin. He is also the program coordinator of UT's Computer Writing and Research Lab in the Division of Rhetoric and Composition. Besides Victorian fiction, his research interests include Victorian and twentieth-century poetry as well as interdisciplinary approaches to literature, particularly through music, computing, and social systems theory.

FLORENCE S. BOOS is professor of English at the University of Iowa and the author of *The Poetry of Dante Gabriel Rossetti* (1976) and *The Design of William Morris's "The Earthly Paradise"* (1991). She has also edited Morris's *Socialist Diary* (1982) and *The Earthly Paradise* (2001), and most recently, a special issue of *Victorian Poetry* (39, no. 2, 2001) devoted to the "poetics of the working class." She is currently preparing a book on working-class women poets of Victorian Scotland.

SIMON JOYCE teaches nineteenth- and twentieth-century literature at the College of William and Mary. He recently completed *Capital Offenses: Geographies of Class and Crime in Victorian London* and has published essays on cultural studies, crime fiction, and late-Victorian social policy. "The Victorians in the Rearview Mirror" is drawn from a larger work with the same title, which assesses how the legacy of the Victorians has been viewed, distorted, used, and abused by twentieth-century thinkers.

CHRISTINE L. KRUEGER is associate professor of English at Marquette University. She is the author of *The Reader's Repentance: Women Preachers, Women Writers, and Nineteenth-Century Social Discourse* and essays on gender, literature and law, and Victorian fiction. She is writing a book entitled *Reading for the Law: Narrative Legal Theory and the Uses of British Literary History* and a biography of the Victorian historian Mary Anne Everett Green.

SUE LONOFF is senior associate of the Derek Bok Center for Teaching and Learning at Harvard; she teaches courses in Victorian and early twentieth-century literature at Harvard's Extension School. She has published books on Wilkie Collins and the Brontës, edited an anthology for writing courses, and continues to write on pedagogy as well as Victorian fiction. She is currently coediting *Approaches to Teaching Emily Brontë's Wuthering Heights* for the Modern Language Association.

KATE LONSDALE recently completed her Ph.D. in nineteenth-century British literature at the University of Southern California. She is writing a book on bodily and figurative dismemberment in Victorian culture that includes a study of Jack the Ripper.

JESSE MATZ is assistant professor of English at Kenyon College. He is author of *Literary Impressionism and Modernist Aesthetics* and *The Modern Novel: A Short Introduction* (forthcoming).

ELLEN BAYUK ROSENMAN is associate professor of English at the University of Kentucky. She has published on George Eliot, Charlotte Brontë, Elizabeth Gaskell, and G. W. M. Reynolds and has just completed a book-length manuscript entitled "Unauthorized Pleasures: Frontiers of Victorian Sexuality."

SUSAN SCHORN is the coordinator of writing resources at the University of Texas at Austin. Her previous work has examined the effect of historical context on reader reception of nineteenth-century fiction. She has written on echoes of the Irish famine in the work of Charlotte Brontë, and on the cultural memory of actresses invoked in the works of Austen, Brontë, and Edgeworth.

RONALD R. THOMAS is professor of English at Trinity College in Hartford, Connecticut, where he has served as acting president, vice president and chief of staff, and English department chairman. Thomas has also taught at Harvard University as a Mellon Faculty Fellow in the Humanities and at the University of Chicago as an assistant professor of English. He has written two books on nineteenth-century fiction—*Dreams of Authority* and *Detective Fiction and the Rise of Forensic Science*. In addition to publishing numerous articles on the novel, photography, and film, he has coedited a book with Helena Michie entitled *Nineteenth-Century Geographies: The Transformation of Space from the Victorian Age to the American Century* (forthcoming).

SHARON ARONOFSKY WELTMAN, associate professor of English at Louisiana State University, has written extensively on Ruskin, including her book *Ruskin's Mythic Queen: Gender Subversion in Victorian Culture*. She has also published on John Keats, Thomas Carlyle, Christina Rossetti, Robert Frost, and Jane Ellen Harrison. Currently she is working on two major projects: first, a new book on Ruskin and science, theater, and girls' education; second, *Victorians on Broadway*, a study of the cultural work accomplished by late-twentieth-century musical adaptations of Victorian materials.

Index

values, Victorian, xiii, xiv, 4. *See also* aesthetic value
Venice, 24
Victoria, Queen, xi, xiii, xv, 7–8, 9–10, 24, 85, 91, 149
Victoria Magazine, 38, 43, 44, 46 n. 24
Victorian Home, The, 39
Victorian Homes, 38
Victorian self-definition, 10, 13
Victorian Society, 46 n. 23
Victorian Web, 173
Victoriana, 39, 40, 46 n. 20
Victorianism, 14
Victorianists, 4, 12, 15, 167, 173, 175, 177, 181; and professional culture, 179. *See also* New Victorians
violence, 102, 142. *See also* women: violence against
vulgar, vulgarity, 39, 50

Waite, Supreme Court Justice Morrison Remnick, 69
Walcott, Derek, 43
Wales, 31
Walkowitz, Judith, 100, 101, 102, 104, 109, 114 n. 19, 131
Warner, Michael, 72
Washington, D.C., 22
Waugh, Evelyn, 11, 16–17 n. 26
websites, xv, xix, 30, 38, 46 n. 24, 163, 164; Victorian Web, 173
Wells, H. G., 9, 10, 38, 39
Weltman, Sharon Aronofsky, xvii–xviii
Whistler, James, 85, 93 n. 16

Whitechapel murders. *See* Jack the Ripper
Wilde, Oscar, xvi, xvii, 11, 13, 14, 66, 69, 70, 72, 76, 80, 89, 90; trials of, 65, 66, 70–71, 72–73, 76, 79
Williams, Raymond, xii, 10–11, 16 n. 26
Wings and Roses, 38
woman's picture, 56–57
women: as consumers, 48–49; as criminals, 125, 126, 127; idealized, 87, 88; intellectual, 58–59; as murder victims, 99, 103–4, 105, 106, 108, 114n. 18; novelists, 118–19; poets, 137–54; violence against, 102, 142; working-class, xix, 137–54
Woolf, Virginia, 9–10, 16 n. 24; *A Room of One's Own,* 57
working class, xix, 101, 106, 108, 138, 153. *See also* Chartists; women: working-class
World War I, 9
World Wide Web. *See* Internet
World's Fair, 27
Wray, Phoebe, 174
Wright, Frank Lloyd, 80
Wright, Joseph, 145

Yorkshire Ripper, xviii, 104, 106–10, 114n. 19
Young, John, 145

Zambella, Francesca, 85